Roman Conquests: Italy

Roman Conquests:
Italy

Ross H. Cowan

Pen & Sword
MILITARY

First published in Great Britain in 2009 by
PEN & SWORD MILITARY
An imprint of
Pen & Sword Books Ltd
47 Church Street
Barnsley
South Yorkshire
S70 2AS

ISBN 978-1-84415-937-6

A CIP catalogue record for this book is
available from the British Library

Typeset by Concept, Huddersfield, West Yorkshire
Printed and bound in England by the MPG Books Group in the UK

Pen & Sword Books Ltd incorporates the Imprints of Pen & Sword Aviation,
Pen & Sword Maritime, Pen & Sword Military, Wharncliffe Local History,
Pen & Sword Select, Pen & Sword Military Classics, Leo Cooper, Remember When,
Seaforth Publishing and Frontline Publishing

For a complete list of Pen & Sword titles please contact
PEN & SWORD BOOKS LIMITED
47 Church Street, Barnsley, South Yorkshire, S70 2AS, England
E-mail: enquiries@pen-and-sword.co.uk
Website: www.pen-and-sword.co.uk

Pen & Sword IUK
October 2009

Contents

List of Plates

Acknowledgements

The author would like to thank the Cowan family, Dr Duncan B. Campbell, Prof. Lawrence Keppie, Thomas McGrory, Philip Sidnell, Graham Sumner, Dr Jean MacIntosh Turfa and Dr Krista M. Ubbels for their assistance.

Maps 3 and 6 after E. T. Salmon, *Samnium and the Samnites* (1967).

Translations from the ancient sources are adapted from the Loeb Classical Library.

Maps

List of Maps

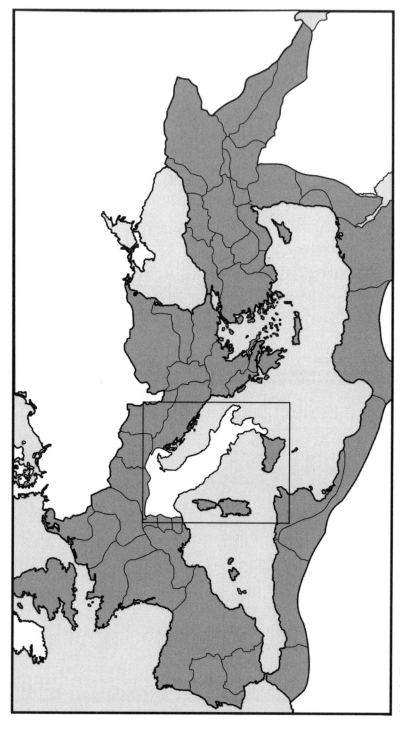

Map 1. The Roman Empire at its greatest extent with the area covered by this volume highlighted. (© Ian Hughes)

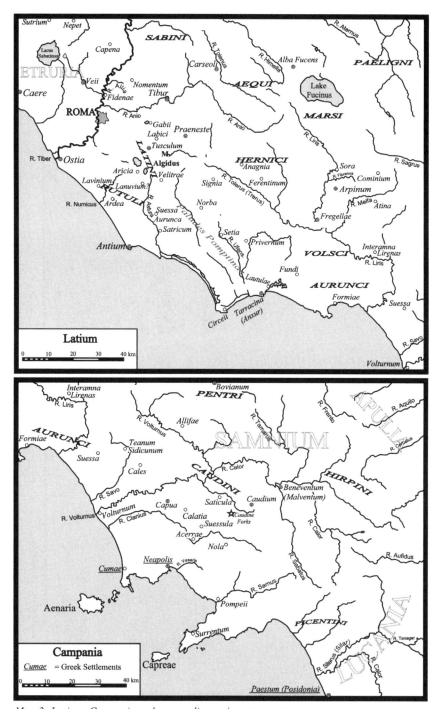

Map 2. Latium, Campania and surrounding regions. (© Ian Hughes)

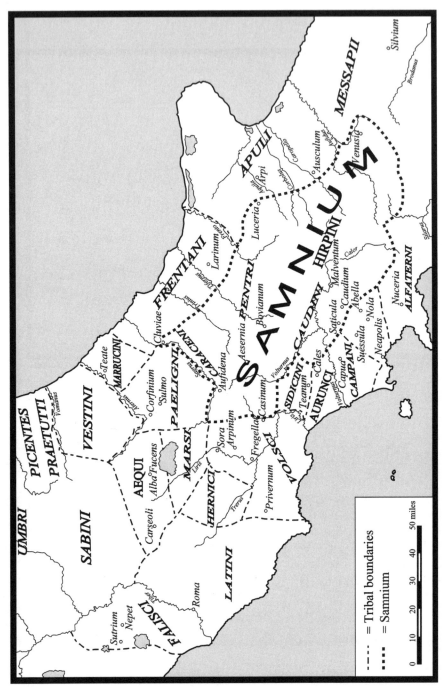

Map 3. Central and Southern Italian peoples, c. 350 BC. (© Ian Hughes)

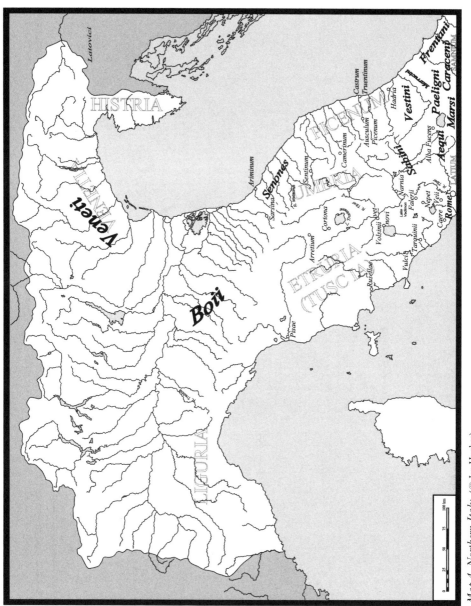

Map 4. Northern Italy. (© Ian Hughes)

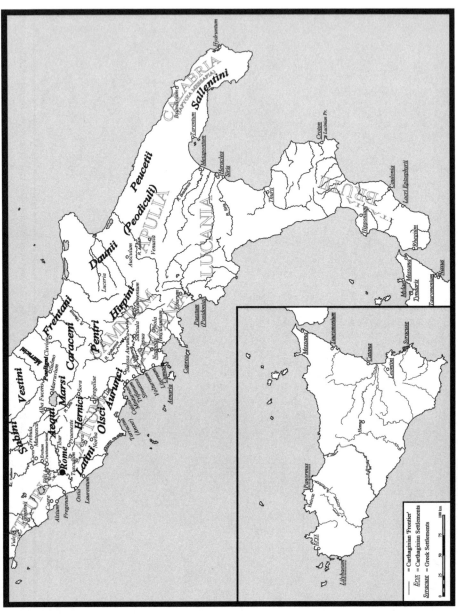

Map 5. Southern Italy and Sicily. (© Ian Hughes)

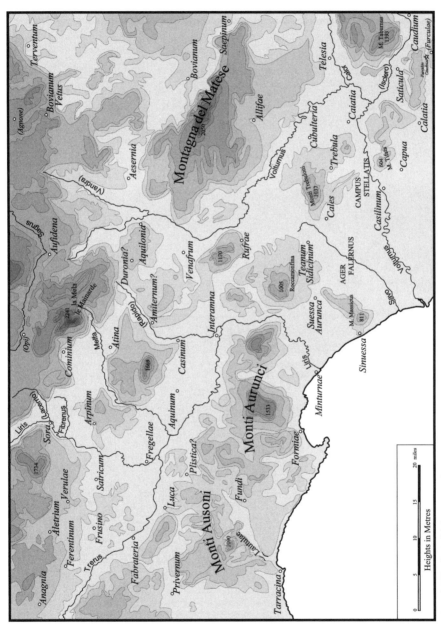

Map 6. The Liris-Volturnus region. (© Ian Hughes)

Introduction

The Enduring Empire

In 323 BC Alexander the Great, king of Macedonia, charismatic madman and unrivalled conqueror, died of fever at Babylon. His enormous empire, stretching from the Balkans to the Hindu Kush and conquered in a mere decade, fragmented almost immediately as his generals sought to establish their own kingdoms. In the same year, another empire was being forged. It was very small, miniscule in comparison to the vast domains of the Macedonian. The empire of Rome then occupied little more than west central Italy. It had taken the Romans almost two centuries to win their modest possessions in Latium, northern Campania and southern Etruria, and they had to battle hard to defend them from Etruscans, Gauls, Sabellians and the other warlike nations of Italy. In 323 BC the Romans were campaigning in Samnium and Apulia in southern Italy, but those regions would resist for decades. It was not until 265 BC that Rome had conquered all of peninsular Italy, but the conquests of the city-state thereafter were as stunning as they were enduring. In the mid-second century BC, Polybius of Megalopolis, a political hostage in Rome, declared

> For who is so worthless or indolent as not to wish to know by what means and under what system of polity the Romans in less than fifty-three years [from 220–167 BC] have succeeded in subjecting nearly the whole inhabited world to their sole government – a thing unique in history? . . . The Romans have subjected to their rule not portions, but nearly the whole of the world and possess an empire which is not only immeasurably greater than any which preceded it, but need not fear rivalry in the future.[1]

Polybius, a military man himself, recognised that the long and often grim process of conquest in Italy had forged the Romans into warriors without equal, and that the next logical steps were the conquest of the nations around the Mediterranean basin and then the rest of the known world.

Ultimately, the Roman Empire would extend from the foothills of the Scottish Highlands in the north to the fringes of the Sahara in the south, and from Cape Roca in the extreme west of Europe to the great rivers Euphrates and Tigris in the Middle East. The Empire was at its height in the early third century AD, the era of the Severan emperors. Its decline and gradual reduction began in the middle of that century, but the process was slow and punctuated by remarkable Roman revivals, such as the great re-conquests of Italy, and parts of Spain and North Africa overseen by the emperor Justinian in the sixth century AD, or the destruction of the Bulgars' Balkan empire by Basil II ('the Bulgar Slayer') in the early eleventh century. It was not until AD 1453, when the Ottoman Turks captured Constantinople – the New Rome – and Constantine XI, last of the emperors, fell in battle, that the remaining fragment of the original Roman Empire finally succumbed. But even that was not the end of the epic story. On Christmas Day in AD 800, Charles the Great, king of the Franks, was crowned emperor in Rome by Pope Leo III. Charles' Germanic kingdom, which incorporated old Roman provinces and German regions unconquered by Rome, was recast as the new Roman Empire in the West. By AD 962 it had evolved into the Holy Roman Empire and dominated central Europe into the early modern era. It was only in AD 1806 that it was finally dissolved by Napoleon, the conqueror of a huge but ephemeral empire.

The Road to World Domination
The Romans' conquest of peninsular Italy was the first stage in their long domination of much of, what was to them, at least, the known world. It is a matter of immense historical importance, but it is obscured by their later and more famous conquests, such as that of Gaul, and especially by the personalities who conducted those wars – Scipio Africanus and Aemilianus, Pompey Magnus, Octavian-Augustus, Trajan, Septimius Severus, Constantine the Great and, above all, Julius Caesar. This book, therefore, seeks to re-emphasise the earliest and most crucial stage in the conquest of the Roman Empire. The famous Caesar would have accomplished nothing if the groundwork in Italy and the creation of a solid base for overseas expansion had not been achieved by the likes of the lesser-known Torquatus, Corvus, Cursor, Rullianus and Dentatus in the fourth and third centuries BC.

Ancient Italy was an incredibly violent and chaotic land. Warfare was endemic because it was viewed as a profitable enterprise (in terms of booty, slaves and land that could be captured), as well as being immensely glorious – if successful, of course. In the Italian city-states and tribal societies only men who had proved themselves in war could advance to high political rank and lead their peoples. Rome was hardly unique in her aggressive war making; indeed her territory was often the target of violent raids, especially by the Volsci and Aequi, and the city was even captured and occupied by Etruscan and Gallic armies. Yet Rome possessed a unique resilience; her citizens, both rich patricians and poor plebeians, were driven to prove themselves in battle, to acquire plunder and, above all, make and maintain reputations for courage and glory. The Roman state and Roman society were pervaded by militarism, centred on a belief that Romulus, the legendary founder of Rome, was the son of the war god Mars: the Roman children of the war god came to believe they were destined to conquer the world. Ancient Sparta springs to mind as a society geared for war, but the Spartans pale in comparison to the Romans in their love of combat, inability to admit defeat and for the relentless and implacable manner in which they carried out their wars.

Rome's conquest of peninsular Italy took so long because her legions were battled every inch of the way by the ferocious warrior nations of Italy, above all the Sabellian Samnites. The German tribal groups and mercenaries that brought down the western provinces, including the ancient *patria* ('fatherland') of Italy, during the course of the fifth century AD are usually cited as Rome's most dangerous opponents, but that crown really belongs to the Samnites. If the Samnites – who also claimed descent from Mars – had won their epic duel with the Romans for the domination of Italy, which lasted until 269 BC, there simply would not have been a Roman Empire and the course of European and World history would have been very different.[2]

Chapter 1

War Bands

The Conquered City

In c. 390 BC a powerful Gallic war band descended on central Italy. Composed mainly of warriors from the Senones tribe and led by their king, Brennus, its objectives were plunder and pay. It acted first as a mercenary force in a factional war at Clusium in Etruria, and then advanced south down the Chiana and Tiber river valleys, heading for the wealthy cities of Latium. On 18 July the war band found its way barred by the army of Rome, the pre-eminent Latin city. The Romans, and perhaps some of their Latin allies, had formed up at the point where the little River Allia flows into the Tiber, but they broke and fled as soon as the Gallic warriors attacked. The bulk of the fugitives attempted to escape across the Tiber; those who evaded the pursuit and did not drown in the river holed up in the fortified Etruscan city of Veii. Located on a rocky plateau some 10 miles to the north of Rome, it had been conquered by the Romans in 396 BC following a long and bitter siege. Now Roman legionaries sought shelter behind its strong walls because their own city was inadequately defended by an incomplete system of ditches and earthen ramparts. It is not surprising that the *dies Alliensis*, the anniversary of the battle, was henceforth reckoned as an inauspicious day.

The Gauls tarried for a few days before embarking on the short march down the Via Salaria ('Salt Road') to Rome. They were occupied with decapitating the Roman dead; heads were highly prized as trophies in Gallic warrior society. It was not until the third day after the battle that they stormed into Rome and ransacked the city for valuables. However, they did not, as Roman historians would claim centuries later, burn it to the ground. This belief was based on the assumption that the disorderly streets of the oldest parts of the city were the result of hasty rebuilding following the Gallic sack, but modern archaeologists have demonstrated that there was no widespread destruction or rebuilding at this time. The ramshackle city was the product of centuries of unplanned development and rebuilding. If the city had been destroyed, the Romans would probably have rebuilt it to an orderly plan in the same manner as they built their uniform colonies.

Those Romans who had not already fled (priests and priestesses had been evacuated to the friendly Etruscan city of Caere) took refuge on the fortified

Capitoline Hill, on which stood the temple of Jupiter. Brennus was content to blockade the Capitol while using Rome as a base from which to raid Latium and probably also southern Etruria. After seven months the Gauls were restive and a deal was negotiated with the garrison of the Capitol: the war band left the city for a ransom of 1,000 pounds (Roman) of gold. The amount may well be exaggerated. The tale that the Roman general Marcus Furius Camillus, the conqueror of Veii, returned from exile in the nick of time to prevent payment of the ransom and proceeded to defeat the Gauls in battle is a later face-saving fabrication.

Some of the Gauls were keen to return north at the news that the Veneti had invaded their lands in the Po Valley and Adriatic coast. The Veneti were the only Italic people to successfully resist the Gallic expansion in the north. The remainder of the war band headed south, seeking service with Dionysius I of Syracuse, the well-known employer of mercenaries and who was then campaigning in the toe of Italy. Brennus, famous for sarcastically uttering '*Vae victis*' ('Woe to the vanquished!') when the Romans complained about the accuracy of the scales he used to weigh the ransom, disappears from history. It is unclear if he went north or south.

Dionysius of Syracuse was glad to employ these proven warriors and it was probably through his general and court historian, Philistus, that the capture of Rome became known to the wider Greek world. Thus, later in the fourth century, the historian Theopompus and the philosopher Aristotle would refer to the sack of a civilized city-state (albeit a non-Greek city) by barbarians as an event of some import.

A few years later, the war band was again in central Italy, perhaps returning home but maybe still under contract to Dionysius I. In 384 BC Dionysius sent a fleet of sixty warships to raid and plunder the Etruscan coast; he needed to raise funds to finance his war against Carthage. Pyrgi, the port of Caere, was sacked, its sanctuary stripped of votive treasures and its inhabitants seized and sold as slaves. The net haul to Dionysius amounted to 1,500 talents of silver, a very considerable sum. Now, while the traditional Varronian chronology used by the Romans assigned the Gallic sack to 390 BC, Greek historians such as Polybius believed that the event occurred in 387 or 386 BC. Polybius' date is most probably accurate but the Varronian system is retained here for convenience. (The great Roman historian Livy, who had to contend with the discrepancies, exaggerations and inventions that he found in the writings of his predecessors, also bemoaned the problems of accurately reconstructing the chronology of the early Republic.) It is probable that the Gauls were operating in conjunction with the fleet, distracting Etruscan forces and diverting them inland and so leaving the coast vulnerable. So, as the Gauls camped one night at the place called the Trausian Plain, the army of Caere attacked and slaughtered them. The Gauls were rich with their mercenary pay and the portable plunder they had taken from Rome. Caere returned the latter to the grateful Romans, and they in turn granted the Caeretans honorary citizenship. This episode provided the source material for the fiction that Camillus returned from exile and prevented the ransom from being paid. In fact, he was probably involved in the debacle at the Allia. But not all Romans accepted the Camillus story as fact. For example, the aristocratic Livii Drusi clan later celebrated the exploit of one their heroic ancestors who won the *cognomen* (nickname) Drusus when he killed the Gallic chief Drausus in single combat and recovered part of the ransom extorted by Brennus (probably in the later 220s BC), thus indicating the alternative, and more believable, tradition in which the Gauls got away with their loot. One element of the Camillus myth, that he spent his exile in the Latin city of Ardea and from there mounted his rescue mission, may be another deliberate twisting of the facts by later Roman historians who were keen to lessen the disgrace of Rome's capture. It is possible that Ardea and other Latin cities sent forces to aid the Romans and this was another factor that encouraged the withdrawal of Brennus' army.

The Gauls' capture of Rome was actually the second time that the city had fallen into enemy hands. Some enterprising Roman historians contrived yet more face-saving myths to deny Rome's conquest by Lars Porsenna, the king of Clusium, in c. 508/7 BC. In their version Porsenna was so in awe of Roman courage and tenacity that he abandoned his siege. However, other Roman historians and antiquarians were prepared to admit that he too inflicted a disgraceful defeat on the city.

Having presumably defeated the Roman army in the strip of the *ager Romanus* (Roman territory) that extended along the north bank of the Tiber, perhaps at the semi-legendary Battle of Silva Arsia (Arsian Forest), which later Romans regarded as a draw, Porsenna occupied the Janiculum Hill just across the Tiber from Rome. Horatius the One-Eyed (Cocles) may well have heroically defended the far end of the Sublician Bridge, holding back Porsenna's warriors while the bridge was demolished behind him, but they did find a way to cross the river. They are recorded as occupying the Capitol, and Porsenna issued an edict banning the Romans from carrying iron weapons.

It was at this time that Tarquinius Superbus, the last of the Roman kings, fell from power (he traditionally reigned from 534 to 509 BC), and it may be that he was actually deposed by Porsenna rather than by discontented Roman aristocrats prior to the Etruscan king's attack. It is a distinct possibility that Porsenna was the real founder of the Roman Republic, instituting the annual office of consul as a means of controlling the city through puppet magistrates.

Unlike the Gallic attack, Porsenna's campaign against Rome aimed at a prize greater than plunder. Rome was wealthy as a direct result of her geographical position. The city dominated the main crossing point of the Tiber between Latium and Etruria. There were other crossings further up stream at Fidenae and Crustumerium, but Rome was nearest to the coast, and the famous seven hills on which the city was built provided excellent points from which to guard the crossing and filter traffic. The city was therefore the main hub of trade and communications in west-central Italy. She was also agriculturally rich. The *ager Romanus* and the Latin plain comprised some of the most fertile land in the peninsula and thus supported a large population. During the rule of Tarquinius Superbus, Rome had become the dominant power in Latium. This is made clear by a treaty Rome made with Carthage, the great North African maritime power, at the close of the sixth century BC. A number of Latin cities, including Circeii and Taracina in the far south of *Latium Adiectum* are described as Rome's subjects, and safe from Carthaginian raids. The Carthaginians also acknowledged Rome's power and intentions over those Latin states not yet her subjects, by agreeing not to raid or establish forts in their territories. Even in 495 BC, by which time Rome's Latin dominions had been reduced, she still occupied one third of *Latium Vetus* (see below for *Vetus* and *Adiectum*).

Porsenna's descent on Rome demonstrates that he had extended Clusian power down into the Tiber valley and his conquest of Rome was clearly motivated by desire to usurp her hegemony over the Latins and establish a central Italian empire. The Latin city-states, however, were clearly discontented with Roman overlordship and had no intention of meekly submitting to an Etruscan ruler. In 504 BC Porsenna entrusted his army (now probably including the Roman *legio* – 'levy') to his son Arruns, but the prince met with a catastrophic defeat at Aricia, where he was caught in a pincer movement between the Latin forces and their allies from the Greek city of Cumae in Campania. The destruction of the bulk of his army forced Porsenna to abandon Rome. The unpopular Roman monarchy was not reinstated; the aristocracy took over the consulship and over time evolved a hierarchy of other elected annual magistracies. The Senate, previously an advisory body to the kings, now constituted a governing assembly.

The senators looked hungrily at what Rome had lost in Latium, while the Latins girded themselves to finish what they had started at Aricia. Tusculum assumed leadership of the Latin cities, but they were narrowly defeated by the Romans at the Battle of Lake Regillus (499 or 496 BC). On the point of victory, the Roman commander, Aulus Postumius Albus (*albus* = white), called on the aid of the cavalry gods, Castor and Pollux, to ensure the triumph and vowed them a temple (eventually completed and dedicated in 484 BC). Such vows were a regular feature of the early and middle Republican periods; the perceived aid of the most powerful and bellicose gods inspiring the devout and superstitious Romans to victory.

The victory at Lake Regillus was hardly decisive, but in 493 BC (though a date immediately after the battle may be more appropriate) the Romans and Latins came to terms. In the treaty known as the *foedus Cassianum* (Cassian treaty) after its Roman negotiator, Spurius Cassius Vecellinus, Rome and the Latin League – a convenient term for the allied cities – were acknowledged as equal partners. A copy of this treaty, inscribed in archaic Latin on a bronze column, was still on display in the Roman Forum in the first century BC. Dionysius of Halicarnassus, a historian of the late first century BC, gives a summary of its contents:

> Let there be peace between the Romans and all the Latin cities as long as the heavens and the earth shall remain where they are. Let them neither make war upon another themselves nor bring in foreign enemies nor grant a safe passage to those who shall make war upon either. Let them assist one another, when warred upon, with all their forces, and let each have an equal share of the spoils and booty taken in their common wars. Let suits relating to private contracts be determined within ten days, and in the nation where the contract was made. And let it not be permitted to add anything to, or take anything away from these treaties except by the consent both of the Romans and of all the Latins.[3]

What brought about this rapprochement? In the decade or so that the Etruscans, Romans and Latins struggled for control of Latium, two Italic peoples, the Volsci and Aequi took advantage of their preoccupations and overran eastern and southern Latium. Rome and most of the Latin city-states were located in *Latium Vetus* (Old Latium), the area bounded approximately to the north by the rivers Tiber and Anio, to the east by spurs of the Appenines, and to the south by the Monti Lepini and the marshy Pomptine plain. *Latium Adiectum* (Greater Latium) extended south to the border with Campania and east to the valley of the Liris. The Volsci and Aequi quickly established themselves in these areas and turned their attention to the conquest of Old Latium. The *foedus Cassianum* was thus concerned with mutual defence and the hope that the combined resources of Rome and the League could reconquer Greater Latium.

The terms, as summarized by Dionysius, suggest that the Latin League would match Rome's contribution to any army. That Rome would supply half of the troops in any army is a good indication of her power. It is also notable that the treaty stressed the equal distribution of spoils and plunder – all portable goods, foodstuffs, livestock, slaves and land distributed in the form of agricultural plots in the territories of the military colonies. The alliance was stimulated by the need to combat the Volsci and Aequi, but warfare was viewed as a profitable endeavour in ancient Italy. Economic incentives to fight went hand-in-hand with patriotism for Roman and Latin citizens, especially in a period of acute class divisions, chronic debt and land-hunger.

Men of the Marsh, Plain and Rocks

Who were the Volsci and the Aequi? They were Osco-Umbrian speaking peoples who originated in the central Apennines. Despite fertile pockets of land suitable for agriculture and good pastures on the lower slopes, the mountains could only support so many inhabitants. As was common with the Italic mountain tribes, the ancestors of the Volsci and Aequi dealt with the problem of overpopulation by sending out bands of young warriors to conquer and occupy new lands. These bands were dedicated to Mamers (Mars to the Romans and Latins) the great god of agriculture and war, and the process of conquest was carried out through the ritual of the *ver sacrum* ('Sacred Spring'). The warrior bands followed path-finder animals sacred to Mamers such as the wolf, bull and woodpecker, usually to more fertile and prosperous lowland regions. While tribes such as the Picentes (the 'Woodpeckers', from *picus*) or the Samnite Hirpini (the 'Wolf-Men', from Oscan *hirpus*) took their names from path-finders, the names of the Volsci and Aequi appear to derive from the marshy and level regions around the Fucine Lake to which they had first descended from the mountains.

From the Fucine Lake they advanced down the valley of the Liris and then westwards into Greater Latium. The Volsci found the passage to Old Latium through the Trerus Valley barred by the Hernici. This tough people spoke Latin but their name is Osco-Umbrian and means 'Men of the Rocks' and indicates their origin as a much earlier wave of invaders from the mountains. Bands of Volsci therefore continued westwards, occupying the Monti Lepini and the Pomptine Plain. During the first decade of the fifth century BC they captured Pometia, Cora and the recently-established Latin military colony of Velitrae. (Such colonies were joint endeavours between Rome and the Latin League, serving the dual purposes of defence and of providing plots of land to poor citizens, but the colonies were organized as independent Latin city-states and the Romans who accepted allotments had to give up their Roman citizenship.) The Volsci also dominated the coast, taking the important ports of Antium, Circeii and Tarracina (renamed Anxur) at the southern tip of Latium.

The Aequi stormed westwards into the Monti Prenestini, occupying strategically vital Praeneste and Tusculum, and commanding the Praeneste Gap and the Pass of Algidus and the route to the Latin plain. Thus, by c. 490 BC the Volsci and Aequi had occupied most of Greater Latium and half of Old Latium. In c. 491/88 the Volsci attempted to link up with the Aequi and isolate the Hernici in the Trerus valley from the Latins. Led by the aristocratic

Roman renegade Gnaeus Marcius Coriolanus, the Volsci advanced northwards from Velitrae to seize Labici and Pedum, and even raided the area around Rome. The *cognomen* Coriolanus may derive from c. 493 BC when, still loyal to Rome, Gnaeus and his 'gentilical' war band (effectively a private army of Marcii clan – *gens* – members, clients and sworn comrades known as *sodales*) recaptured the little town of Corioli from the invaders. His defection to the Volsci is paralleled by the move of the Sabine warlord Attus Clausus who, when hard pressed by other Sabine chiefs, brought his gentilical war band to Rome in 504 BC. Welcomed by the Senate, he went on to establish the great Roman clan of the Appii Claudii and fought off Sabine incursions in the land lying between the rivers Tiber and Anio. However, Coriolanus' expedition did not succeed in isolating the Hernici and in 486 BC Spurius Cassius Vecellinus succeeded in persuading them to enter into the military alliance with Rome and the Latins on equal terms.

In 484 BC the triple alliance succeeded in freeing Tusculum from the Aequi but could not dislodge them from the Algidus and they continued to dominate the Alban Hills and the region around Praeneste and the lower Anio. In the following decades the war was characterized by small-scale raids and skirmishes, and it is probably to this period that the development of the *manipulus* ('handful') subunit of the Roman legion belongs, rather than during the Samnite Wars a century and a half later. Major pitched battles were few, but the Volsci and Aequi often had the better of these rare large-scale engagements. The Volsci inflicted defeats on the Romans in 494/84 and 478 BC. Later Roman historians pinned the blame on the indiscipline of plebeian soldiers, and there may be an element of truth to this. The unequal nature of Roman society, the few (patricians) dominating the many (plebeians) who supplied most of the military manpower, would continue to disrupt Roman military effectiveness into the early third century BC. In 458 BC a Roman attempt to force the Algidus failed miserably and the army was famously extricated from the encircling Aequi by the *dictator* (emergency chief magistrate) Lucius Quinctius Cincinnatus (the 'Curly Haired') and his hastily-assembled relief force. In 446 BC the Volsci and Aequi devasted the *ager Romanus* right up to the boundary of the city. Yet the tide was beginning to turn.

In 444 BC Ardea, only 20 miles south of Rome and on the Volscian frontier, entered into alliance with Rome and shortly afterwards received a Latin military colony (442 BC; the first since that established at Antium in 467 and which rebelled in 459, perhaps because the Volscians were still the dominant element in the population, having been enrolled with the Roman, Latin and Hernican colonists, rather than be slaughtered or sold into slavery, in an attempt at integration). On 18 June 431 BC, Aulus Postumius Tubertus (the 'Warty', a typically-unflattering Roman *cognomen*), descendant of the victor of

Lake Regillus, finally carried the pass of the Algidus. This was a key stage in the reconquest of Latium. The Aequi, recognising the importance of the pass, enforced a *lex sacrata*, a 'sacred law', to levy troops whose lives would be forfeit to the gods if they showed cowardice in battle. The Volsci sent reinforcements, also raised by a *lex sacrata*, but to no avail. Their casualties were heavy and from this point on the reduction of both peoples was a slow but definite process.

It took another four decades but on the eve of Brennus' incursion Rome, the Latin League and the Hernici had effectively accomplished the reconquest of Old Latium and freed portions of Greater Latium. The Hernican town of Ferentinum was recaptured in 413 BC; instead of receiving a Latin colony, it was returned to the Hernican federation. The Volscians' principle northern stronghold of Velitrae was taken in 404 and colonized in 401 BC. On the Tyrrhenian coast, Antium was defeated, but not captured, in 408 BC; Anxur was subdued in 406 BC and subsequently refounded as the military colony of Tarracina, and the strategic headland of Circeii was colonized in 393 BC. However, the Volsci had not been pushed from Latium and remained a powerful threat.

Their grip on the Alban Hills prised open by defeat at Mount Algidus, the Aequi were ejected from Labici in 418 BC, and their presence on the lower Anio suffered a mortal blow in 393 BC when Tibur was finally recaptured. Nearby Praeneste must have been liberated during this period. Like Ferentinum, Labici did not receive a Latin colony, but was instead quickly annexed by Rome and became part of the *ager Romanus*. Plots of land were distributed to Romans and presumably also Latins and Hernicans, but on accepting they would have become Roman citizens. The examples of Ferentinum and Labici highlight dissatisfaction with the military alliance: citizens of all three allies benefited from the distribution of land, but the real winner was the Latin League for the new colonies were organized as Latin states and thus enrolled in the League, the Roman and Hernican elements laying down their citizenship and becoming Latins.

The Greatest Spoils
While supplying her fair share of troops for the wars against the Volsci and Aequi, Rome received little, if any, aid from her allies in the war against Veii, the most southerly of the Etruscan cities. Located 10 miles to the north of Rome on a rocky eminence, Veii ruled over a large and fertile territory and could thus support a substantial population and from that recruit a powerful army. Much of her wealth stemmed from industry and trade and because of this, as well as any ambitions for territorial expansion, it was critical that she dominated one of the Tiber crossings. Her access to the Tyrrhenian coast, and

the lucrative salt pans at the mouth of the Tiber, was blocked by the strip of the *ager Romanus* that occupied the Etruscan bank of the Tiber, as well as the territory of the unfriendly Etruscan city of Caere. A road, the Via Veientanus, led directly from Veii to the river crossing at Rome, but that route meant Roman control over Veientane commerce and communications. However, Veii was perfectly placed to dominate another of the major Tiber crossings. The valley of the small Cremera River provided a direct route from Veii down to the Tiber and the crossing controlled by the small city-state of Fidenae, only 5 miles upstream from Rome (on the left, or Latin, bank). Fidenae, despite being Latin, thus became Veii's bridgehead, and from there her goods could completely bypass Rome, following the Anio and the route through eastern Latium down to the Greek and Sabellian markets of Campania and southern Italy.

As we have seen, in 504 BC the Sabine chief Attus Clausus, hard-pressed by his Sabine rivals, migrated with his gentilical band to Rome. Clausus was welcomed by the Senate and adlected into the select patrician order. His name was Latinized and he was known from then on as Appius Claudius. The members of his large clan/war band were granted Roman citizenship and formed the new *gens* of the Claudii. They were settled above the Anio and acted as a buffer against Sabine incursions. The Sabines are presented in the sources as Rome's most dangerous enemies at the close of the sixth century BC, and they remained a menace until the middle of the fifth century, occasionally raiding the outskirts of Rome or inflicting a defeat on a Roman army in pitched battle, for example at Eretum in 449 BC. In 460 BC another Sabine, Appius Herdonius, occupied the Capitol in a night attack and attempted to take over the city, but was defeated and killed by the Romans and a force from Tusculum (a rare instance of a Latin city aiding Rome against an opponent other than the Volsci or Aequi). Rather than being identified as a foreign invader, Herdonius was probably a leading Roman of Sabine descent, and the force with which he attempted his coup was a gentilical war band reinforced with slaves, exiles and other malcontents.

Some Sabine bands were attempting to expand down from the region between the rivers Tiber and Anio into the Latin plain, but other incursions were simply plundering missions, and may sometimes have been stimulated by similar Roman raids into Sabine territory. The arrival of the Claudii coincided with defeat of Lars Porsenna's army at Aricia and the loss of Rome's hegemony over the Latins. With the additional manpower of the Claudii, Rome looked northeast to replace the territories lost in *Latium Vetus*. She pushed up the Via Salaria (the 'salt road') to the edge of Sabine territory at Eretum, picking off the Latin (or at least Latin-speaking) city-states of Crustumerium, which may have controlled a Tiber ferry crossing, and probably Ficulea (499 BC). Fidenae also fell and Roman colonists were sent to occupy its small territory and its important river crossing (498 BC). Veii was not cut off from the south by the capture of Fidenae; she could use the Tiber crossing at Lucus Feroniae in the territory of her allies the Faliscans (who spoke a language similar to Latin, but fell firmly under Etruscan influence). But Lucus Feroniae was much further upstream and therefore lacked the close convenience of Fidenae and also its strategic position on the left bank of the Tiber. Veii determined to win back the bridgehead.

Veii's reaction was probably immediate, but the attention of the sources turns to Rome's war against the Latin League, the Battle of Lake Regillus, the subsequent peace and the Romano-Latin-Hernican alliance against the Volsci and Aequi. Full-scale hostilities with Veii are not recorded until 483–474 BC (the First Veientane War). Veii had evidently won back Fidenae by this time and in an attempt to cut, or at least disrupt, her communications, Rome established a fort in the valley of the Cremera. This was manned by the gentilical war band of the Fabii, thus allowing citizen soldiers levied by the Roman state from all the other clans and voting districts to be sent to the Volscian and Aequan fronts. In 479 or 477 BC the Veientanes overwhelmed the Fabii and slaughtered them almost to a man. In the meantime, Veii had established her own fort on the Janiculum Hill. While it is unlikely that Rome was actually besieged, this garrison was a persistent irritation and in 474 BC a forty-year truce was negotiated, no doubt to the advantage of Veii.

The Second Veientane War was fought over possession of Fidenae. At some point, Rome regained control of the city, perhaps on the expiry of the truce, but the Fidenates rebelled, murdered four Roman officials sent to investigate and received military aid from Veii. In a battle outside the city, Lars Tolumnius, the king of Veii, was killed in single combat by Aulus Cornelius Cossus (the intriguing *cognomen* of this hero means the 'Worm'). Cossus was only the second Roman after Romulus, the legendary founder of Rome, to kill an enemy king in single combat and to dedicate the *spolia opima* – 'the greatest spoils' – to Jupiter Feretrius. The spoils included the king's armour and perhaps also his severed head. The Romans later entered Fidenae through a siege tunnel and ransacked the city. The chronology of the war is uncertain, but 428–425 BC is to be preferred. Thus the Second Veientane War closely followed the great victory over the Aequi and Volsci at Algidus (431 BC). As we have seen, the war against the highlanders was to continue for decades, but a crucial corner had been turned, and Rome felt free to turn her manpower against the enemy on her doorstep.

Veii was now confined to the Etruscan bank of the Tiber but Rome still viewed her as an unacceptable rival. The dissatisfaction of the Romans with the Latin colonial system has already been noted, and they looked at the rich territory of Veii with hungry eyes and set out to annex it to the *ager Romanus*. It took ten years, but in 396 BC Veii was finally conquered. It is unclear how exactly the Romans captured the rocky citadel and overcame its recently-improved fortifications – the tale that it was by means of a siege tunnel is a duplication of the capture of Fidenae. Perhaps the city was simply starved into submission. It was during the course of this third and final war that the Romans instituted the *stipendium*, or military pay. Funded by a special tax, this payment was made in kind and in ingots of bronze (the Romans had not yet adopted coinage), allowing the army to stay in the field all year round. Military service was a requirement of citizenship, but the farmers who formed the bulk of the army could not rely on plunder to cover their debts and were always keen to be released from service as soon as possible so they could bring in their crops. When Veii fell, the Roman commander Camillus allowed the troops to sack the city and massacre its inhabitants. The booty was far richer than that taken from any of the cities or towns reconquered from the Volsci and Aequi, and the profits of the conquest were increased when the surviving Veientanes were sold as slaves. The fall of Veii and its logical incorporation into the *ager Romanus* marks the real start of the Roman conquest of Italy.

The addition of the *ager Veientanus* increased Roman territory by about fifty per cent and gave Rome a new northern frontier in Etruria. Rome could perhaps have expanded her territory into the Faliscan country as well, but, after suitable displays of force, she came to terms with Veii's allies, Capena and Falerii (395 and 394 BC). It is indicative of the rivalry between the great Etruscan cities that, with the exception of Tarquinii, Veii did not receive any aid during the long siege.

Chapter 2

The Triumph of Roman Arms

The Enemy of My Enemy

In 389 BC the Volsci, probably united under the leadership of Antium, raised an army and marched north. The Volsci believed Brennus and his Gauls had shattered the power of Rome, but they were wrong. Although routed at the Allia, most of the Roman field army of *iuniores* had escaped to Veii and Camillus, now recalled from his exile in Ardea and appointed dictator, reconstituted the legions with a levy of the most experienced and vigorous *seniores* (men aged 46 and over). At a place called Maecium in the territory of Lanuvium, the Volsci suffered a terrible defeat. They were pursued south and their territory was ravaged.

Camillus (the 'Noble assistant of the priest') then turned his attention to unfinished business with the Aequi. In 393 BC the Aequi captured the new colony of Vitellia in a surprise night attack. Vitellia was established in 395 BC to guard the eastern approaches to the Alban Hills. In 392 BC the Aequi attempted to force their way back into their old Alban stronghold via the Pass of Algidus, but were easily repulsed by the Romans. The Romans were then preoccupied with the effects of a drought in the *ager Romanus* and hostilities with the central Etruscan city of Volsinii (probably as a result of Rome's conquest of Veii and consequent threat to the control of the road through the Ciminus, see below). Like the Volsci, the Aequi over-estimated the effects of the Allia and the occupation of Rome by Brennus' warriors, and they too raised a new army. However, Camillus' warriors, confident from their success at Maecium, defeated the Aequi near to their principle stronghold of Bola and then proceeded to storm the town. It is tempting to view the Aequi of Bola as not dissimilar to their opponents; that is as a settled people of a city-state rather than the roving warriors of the Sacred Spring who stormed into Latium more than a century before. The Aequi surrendered and were prepared to remain quiescent, but the Romans had other plans: the annihilation of their old enemy. This had to wait because of the Tarquinii's attack on Sutrium (below), but in 388 BC the Romans set about their grim business. The obedient Aequi had raised no troops (they probably had very few men left who were of military age) but the Romans acted 'out of hatred' says the historian Livy, 'in order to waste their territories and leave them with no strength to make new trouble'. The terrible campaign was so thorough that the Aequi retreated back into the central Apennines and are not heard of again until 304 BC.

It is not impossible that the Volscian army defeated at Maecium included Latin contingents. A number of Latin cities, some of the League and non-member states like Praeneste and Tibur, now looked upon Rome with wary eyes. They had been unsettled by the annexation of Labici in 418 BC; instead of re-establishing the city as an independent Latin state, it had passed from Aequian to Roman domination. However, Labici's territory, while strategically placed in the Alban Hills to facilitate control of the Algidus Pass, was small and offered Rome little by way of manpower or natural resources. The annexation of the *ager Veientanus*, on the other hand, massively increased Rome's territory. It was fertile, boasted other natural resources such as superior tufa from the Grotta Oscura quarries (soon exploited to encircle Rome with a sturdy wall), and the sale of many of its inhabitants as slaves must have realized a substantial sum.[4] The *ager Veientanus* abutted directly onto the *ager Romanus*, thus creating a unified block. Rome's territory was still inferior to that of the Latin League, but the Latin lands were not unified and, with a few exceptions, the city-states were individually weak. Most vulnerable was the state of Tusculum as it was virtually surrounded by *ager Romanus*. Rome's population was growing rapidly and the distribution of the Etruscan territory in the form of small cultivation plots did not satisfy demand. The fates of Labici and Veii preyed heavily on the minds of the aristocracies and ruling magistrates of the Latin cities, and, when the Roman plebeians demanded the distribution of allotments in the *ager Pomptinus*, many decided to break with Rome.[5]

The Volsci had been chased from parts of the Pomptine plain, but remained its principle inhabitants and so had much to fear from direct Roman expansion into the area, as did the Hernici and Latins. The territory of the recently established Latin colony of Circeii (393 BC) stretched into the Pomptine plain and it feared encroachment, if not direct annexation by Rome. The Hernican territory in the valley of the Trerus was separated from the Pomptine plain by the Monti Lepini, but the Hernici would have been concerned that they too were about to be milked of land. The pro-Roman Latin colony of Signia was too close for comfort. Located on the northern edge of the Monti Lepini to watch the Volsci, it also bordered the western edge of Hernican territory. Rome's growing interest in the world beyond Latium (indicated by her conquest in Etruria, by the establishment of relations with the Greek city of Massilia in southern Gaul and by plans to colonize Sardinia) may also have worried the Hernici, as the Trerus valley formed part of the principal inland route to Campania.[6]

In a complete reversal of the situation in the previous century, Latins, Hernici and Volsci were now allied together against the threat of Roman expansion. Velitrae, re-established as a colony in 401 BC after nearly a century of Volscian occupation, also joined the anti-Roman alliance. Despite the new colony having a substantial number of inhabitants who were originally Roman, they were as jealous of their colony's independence as the rest of its citizens. Velitrae, or at least its territory, still contained a substantial number of Volscians and it is possible that they fought with the Antiates at Maecium.

In 386 BC the Antiates rose up again, their losses of the previous year replenished by a new generation of teenage soldiers and, more importantly, by volunteers from Latin states and the Hernici. The discontented Latins (note that not all of the Latin states went against Rome) and Hernici had yet to openly declare war on Rome, but they refused to send cohorts to serve in the federal army, and, when asked about the presence of their citizens in the Antiate force, claimed they were unable to stop citizens of military age from serving as volunteers wherever they chose. The allied army was defeated at the Volscian outpost of Satricum; Camillus, of course, was one of the commanders of the victorious Roman army. The Latins and Hernici abandoned the field before the battle turned into a complete rout. The Volsci retreated into Satricum and surrendered when Camillus' troops started clambering over its walls. As before, the Romans were soon diverted from the Volscian front by troubles in Etruria, but envoys were sent to the rebellious (as the Romans would have called them) cities to demand reparations. The demands were rejected. The magistrates and aristocrats of the cities involved once again claimed that they could not be held responsible for the actions of private citizens, and as for failing in recent years to send their contingents to fight alongside the legions, well, how could they when faced with the threat of the Volsci?

The Volsci were accused of invading the *ager Pomptinus* in 385 BC and a dictator was appointed to handle the emergency. Aulus Cornelius Cossus, a relative of the hero of Fidenae, levied an army and went south to liberate the area. Whether the Volsci and their allies had really invaded territory earmarked for Roman settlement is debatable. More likely they were already occupying the lands that the Romans desired. Once again the Volsci (presumably led by Antium), Latins of the colonies of Circeii and Velitrae, and Hernici were defeated in battle.

The Romans refused to return the Latins and Hernicans taken captive in the Pomptine campaign. Most were of wealthy and aristocratic families and therefore made excellent hostages. However, the Romans did not yet occupy the area; it was not until 383 BC that commissioners were appointed to divide up the *ager Pomptinus* into allotments. They had to first establish a strongpoint closer to Rome and from which they could keep watch on Antium: the Romans chose to colonize Satricum. Interestingly, this was a Latin colony, but one that benefited the land-hungry citizens of loyal Latin states such as Gabii,

Tusculum, Lanuvium, Lavinium, Aricia and Ardea, as well as 2,000 Romans (henceforth Latin citizens allied to Rome and enjoying reciprocal rights).

Rome's push southwards was delayed by an outbreak of a pestilence in the city and grain shortages (384/383 BC). The Volscians and Latins, including Velitrae, Circeii and previously-loyal Lanuvium, took up arms. The Hernici, though, had had enough. They remained peaceful for twenty years, suggesting that their manpower had suffered a heavy blow in the *ager Pomptinus* and only recovered with the maturation of a new generation.

Rome declared war on Velitrae, but was unable to levy an army on account of the continuing pestilence and the Veliterni raided the *ager Romanus* with impunity. Praeneste now entered the ring on the side of the anti-Roman alliance (383 BC) and attacked Labici and Gabii, the latter being Rome's most faithful Latin ally. Praeneste was a powerful state; after Rome and Tibur she boasted the largest territory in *Latium Vetus*. She was jealous of her independence after long years of enemy occupation. Prior to the invasion of the Aequi, she had vied with Rome for dominance over the other Latins, but was now concerned to protect a more local hegemony. However, Labici lay on her western border and was a constant reminder of the growth of Roman power.[7]

When the plague abated in 382 BC, Rome went on the offensive. She marched on Velitrae and defeated the combined forces of the Veliterni and Praenestini, but no attempt was made to capture the colony itself. The Veliterni were for the time being exhausted, but powerful Praeneste could yet absorb losses and in 381 BC united with the Volsci to capture Satricum, despite the stout resistance of the new colonists. The Romans were incensed when they learned that the colonists had been cruelly treated by their conquerors. Legionaries were immediately levied and cohorts called on from the loyal allies, and the Roman army marched on Satricum. The Volsci and Latins (including newly-rebellious Tusculans and a strong contingent of Praenestini) boldly advanced on the Roman camp and challenged the legionaries to fight. Lucius Furius Medullinus, military tribune with consular power and joint commander of the Roman army, was infuriated and rashly led the soldiers out.[8] The Volsci and their allies then feigned a retreat and deliberately drew the Romans on to unfavourable ground near the Volscian camp, from which another force sallied out and attacked the Romans, probably in the flank or rear. All seemed lost, but steady Camillus led up the Roman reserves in a successful counterattack. The enemy were defeated but Satricum itself remained in the hands of the Volsci. However, Rome established a new loyal Latin colony at Setia, at the east of the Pomptine plain and foot of the Monti Lepini.

Tusculans were discovered among the captives and sent to Rome for interrogation. The Senate decided that Tusculum must be punished. Camillus, having assumed full command of the field army (Medullinus was in disgrace), led the legions through the Alban Hills to the gates of Tusculum. The city submitted, avoiding siege and sack, but it did suffer the fate that haunted the nightmares of all free Latins: annexation to the Roman state. From then on the Tusculans were Roman citizens, subject to Roman law, taxation and service in the legions. The *ager Romanus*, which had long surrounded the city's territory, finally consumed it. The Romans were content to let Tusculum function much as it always had done with its local laws and customs. It retained, therefore, a considerable degree of local autonomy, but as an independent state, with a long and proud history, it had been snuffed out.

The fight at Satricum was indecisive and in 380 BC Rome was convulsed with political and class struggles, so the annual legionary levy was long delayed. Praeneste took full advantage of Rome's lack of an army and ravaged the territory of Gabii and the *ager Romanus* across the River Anio. Eventually the decision was taken in Rome to appoint a dictator and enrol an army. Ten years after the Gallic disaster, Titus Quinctius Cincinnatus led a Roman army to victory at the Allia. While the Roman legionaries were busy helping themselves to the plunder gathered by the enemy, the Praenestini fled back to their home territory where they established a fortified camp, hoping to divert the Roman army away from destroying crops. Such were the risks of waging war within the limited confines of Latium. However, the defences of the camp were considered inadequate to occupy the Romans for long and the raiders retreated into the walls of Praeneste. Cincinnatus, descendant of the curly-haired hero of the Algidus (458 BC), ignored Praeneste for the time being; instead content to capture the eight principle settlements in its territory. He then marched south to Velitrae, which he also captured. This diversion suggests that the Veliterni were fully involved in the raid. Finally Cincinnatus turned on Praeneste. The city surrendered without a blow. Its lofty citadel could have stood siege, but the Praenestini were thoroughly dispirited by Cincinnatus' successes. The dictator pillaged the city, chief among his prizes being a famous statue of the great god Jupiter in his military guise as *imperator*, meaning the 'commander-in-chief' or 'general'. Cincinnatus installed the statue in the Capitoline temple between the shrines of Jupiter and Minerva, along with a gold crown bearing an inscription recording his defeat of Praeneste in battle and the capture of nine of its towns. This act may have earned him an *agnomen* (second *cognomen*) to distinguish him from his famous ancestor – Capitolinus.

Triumph was followed by disaster. In 379 BC Publius and Gaius Manlius, military tribunes with consular power, led the legions into Volscian territory, but were lured into an ambush by a Latin renegade disguised as a legionary. The Volsci and Latins inflicted a brutal mauling on the Romans. It was only the courage of the centurions and legionaries, rather then the inept leadership of its generals, that finally extricated the army. Luckily for Rome, the Volsci and their allies did not follow up this victory, but Praeneste was encouraged to take up arms again, and other Latins followed her lead. The enemy may have conducted operations against Setia, which complained to Rome about its lack of manpower and received a fresh draft of colonists.

Encouraged by Rome's failure to avenge the defeat of the Manlii, the Volsci raided the fringes of the *ager Romanus* in 378 BC, but the Roman historian Livy states that their depredations were minor, like the work of bandits. The Romans, recovered from the shock of the defeat of the previous year, stirred themselves to action and levied a fresh army from the citizenry. Divided into two forces, one part advanced down the coast to Antium and beyond, while the other headed inland towards the Monti Lepini. The Romans devastated all the farms, fields of crops and orchards that they came upon, and rounded up all the animals. Some villages were destroyed, their inhabitants slaughtered or taken as booty (to be kept or sold as slaves), but the main Volscian towns were avoided. In the following year, Antium mustered its forces and united with a Latin army at Satricum. The Latin states involved are not identified, but presumably Praeneste, Circeii and Velitrae sent contingents. Fought over two days, the Latin cohorts, whose fighting style and tactics were essentially the same as that of the legions, caused the Romans particular difficulties, but the enemy were finally broken by the assaults of the Roman cavalry. (Probably an exaggeration; the historical tradition fostered by the noble clans was bound to over-emphasize the heroic deeds of the aristocratic cavalrymen.) The enemy fled into Satricum. The next night they abandoned it for Antium. The Romans were slow to react and the Volsci and Latins made their escape without casualties. The Romans were not equipped for a siege, so after a few days of ravaging the immediate surroundings, they quit Antium and marched home.

Livy marvelled at the persistence of the valiant Volsci in their war with Rome and at their capacity to raise new armies despite heavy defeats. However, in 377 BC Antium, having exhausted her human and financial resources, sought terms with Rome. When her Latin allies, probably led by Praeneste, could not persuade her to turn from this course, they descended on her outpost of Satricum and burned it to the ground, except for the holy sanctuary of Mater Matuta, which was saved, apparently, by the divine intervention of the goddess. The Latins then advanced into the Alban Hills and stormed through the open gates of an unsuspecting Tusculum. However, the Latins found themselves trapped when a Roman relief force arrived. The lower city may have fallen without a blow, but the Tusculans did manage to bar the gates of the upper citadel, and the occupying Latins were subjected to sorties from within the city as well as the assaults of the Roman army. Trapped between two forces, the Latins were worn down. The Romans were in no mood for taking captives and slaughtered them all.

Just as the umpteenth fight at Satricum had broken the Antiates, the disaster at Tusculum proved too much for the Latins and they remained at peace for sixteen years. By force of arms the Romans had made themselves the masters of Latium and southern Etruria (see below), but without the unifying focuses of defence and expansion they were convulsed by social struggles resulting from the unequal balance of power between patricians and plebeians, the land-hunger of poor citizens (rich patricians were seizing public land) and the chronic problem of usury and resulting debt bondage. In 370 BC Velitrae took advantage of Rome's civil preoccupations and consequent lack of an army, raided her territory and even laid siege to Tusculum. When the Romans elected military tribunes with consular power and enrolled an army, the Veliterni were compelled to abandon their attempt on Tusculum and retreated within their own city walls. However, the consular tribunes' attempts to take Velitrae were unsuccessful and the siege dragged on for years, requiring heavy annual levies from the majority plebeian citizens to maintain the blockade.

Velitrae finally capitulated in 367 BC, but this enemy was immediately re-placed by another old foe. We are told that a Gallic army had invaded Latium. The story that the octogenarian Camillus was appointed dictator for the fifth time to deal with the emergency is suspicious. The details of his victory over the Gauls at the Anio are clearly lifted from a campaign conducted in 361 BC in the same location by the dictator Titus Quinctius Poenus.[9] Camillus died of plague in 365 BC, an inglorious end for the hero who, following the Gallic disaster, had reasserted Roman power and prestige with a string of victories. However, it is entirely possible that in 367 BC a band of Gallic mercenaries, perhaps operating out of Apulia, raided Latium (and other parts of central Italy) for booty. Latium had been at peace for a decade, its farms and industries functioning well without the disruption of war and generating produce and wealth, making it a prime target for raiders. This episode, falling immediately before the death of Camillus, could have formed the basis for a fabricated tale of one final great victory. Then again, we cannot be entirely sure that Camillus, Rome's most successful general, was not recalled to office. He could have conducted operations against raiders in the Alban Hills rather than on the Anio, but later Roman historians either confused his campaign with that of Poenus, or deliberately exaggerated Camillus' success.

The real event of importance in 367 BC was the passing of the Licinian Sextian Laws, healing some of the rifts between patricians and leading plebeian families, and effectively creating a patricio-plebeian nobility that vied for honours and spurred on the process of conquest.

The Gallic incursion was followed by reports that the Hernican federation was preparing to reassert itself against Rome (366 BC), but hostilities did not break out until 362 BC. Pestilence returned to the city in 365 BC. As already noted, Camillus was its most prominent victim. Five senior magistrates also succumbed and its effect on the general population was severe. With the epidemic continuing into 364 BC, the Romans attempted to appease the gods with a *lectisternium*, an elaborate feast of supplication involving representations of the gods, but this was followed by a disastrous flood of the Tiber, which was taken as further evidence of divine displeasure. The plague finally abated and preparations were made for the anticipated war with the Hernici (362 BC), but there was resistance to the levy from the debilitated population. Fines were imposed on those who refused to serve, while others were imprisoned, and legions were finally enrolled. The consul Lucius Genucius led the legions into a Hernican ambush, perhaps in the territory of Signia. The consul himself was killed and the remnants of his army pursued back to camp. Here the defeated Romans were rallied by the experienced legate Gaius Sulpicius Peticus, and successfully resisted an attack on the camp.[10] When news of the disaster reached Rome, Appius Claudius Crassus (the 'Fat' or 'Uncouth') was appointed dictator. He had little difficulty in levying a new army and marched to the relief of Peticus' force. The Hernici had also levied reinforcements and organized the best of their warriors into eight cohorts, each 400 men strong. We are told that these elite cohorts were kept apart from the main Hernican battle line, perhaps meaning that they were held in reserve or that they were positioned on the honorific right wing of the army.[11]

In Livy's account of the battle between the Hernici and combined forces of Crassus and Peticus, the fighting is depicted as a contest between the elite cohorts and the Roman cavalry (*equites*). When the cavalry fail to break through the Hernici, they ask Crassus for permission to continue the fight on foot (not an uncommon occurrence in Roman warfare). An epic struggle ensues, but the dismounted cavalrymen are finally victorious; the common soldiers of both sides are reduced to the status of spectators. This reflects the aristocratic tradition. Cavalrymen were generally aristocrats because only the rich could afford to maintain horses. Prior to the writing down of Roman history in extended narratives (from the end of the third century BC), the noble clans and families commemorated the brave deeds (*fortia facta*) of their members in ballads which were sung at feasts, and in funeral orations which referred not only to the deeds of the dead man, but also listed the feats of his most ancient ancestors. These ballads and orations naturally filtered into the later written histories. The role of the Roman cavalry may well have been important in this battle, but the legionaries bore the brunt of the fighting, losing a quarter of their number.

The Hernici withdrew first to their camp 2 miles from the Roman base and then marched for home. They evacuated the camp under the cover of darkness, thus giving the battered Romans a perfect excuse for not mounting a pursuit. However, as the Hernici marched past Signia (in the territory of which the battle was presumably fought), they were attacked by the colonists. The Romans loved a hero and Sulpicius Peticus was elected consul in 361 BC. He continued the war and captured Ferentinum, but the Hernici fought on, sustaining a major defeat in 360 and again in 358 BC, after which they submitted. They appear not to have received aid from Latins or Volsci. The Hernici were 're-admitted' into the old alliance, but as junior members, and part of their territory was confiscated and organized as *ager Romanus*, although Ferentinum was returned to them. It was also in 358 BC that Rome renewed the *foedus Cassianum* with thirty Latin towns and cities. As well as the Hernican conflict, Rome was also conducting wars with Tarquinii and the Gauls, and keen for Latin forces to bolster her manpower, but the Latins were no longer the equal partners of the original alliance. Rome's domination is indicated by Latin acquiescence to the formal annexation of a chunk of the Pomptine territory. Some of the Latins would have been bullied into this unequal alliance but others were perhaps willing, troubled by the renewed Gallic threat, the resumption of Volscian raids and the aspirations of Tibur and Praeneste.[12]

The Wars with Tarquinii

The annexation of Veii's territory pushed the *ager Romanus* north to the foot of the heavily-forested Ciminian Mountains, which dominated the route into central Etruria. It was at this point that the territories (or at least the spheres of influence) of Veii, Falerii and Tarquinii met. Two towns, Sutrium and Nepete, were located at the foot of the mountains and were the keys to the control of the region. Sutrium, some 30 miles north of Rome, commanded the main route north through the Ciminus gap to Volsinii and Clusium and west to Tarquinii. Nepete, lying approximately 6 miles east of Sutrium, was at the very edge of the Faliscan territory, guarding the road to Falerii, and was also a junction on the important routes into Umbria. Sutrium and Nepete may actually have lain beyond the formal boundaries of Veii and Falerii, but the defeat of those cities in 396 and 394 BC made it inevitable that they would fall under Roman domination. Livy records hostilities with Volsinii and its ally Sappinum in 392/91 BC. Volsinii is presented as the aggressor but it is quite possible that she was reacting to a Roman raid up the Tiber valley.[13]

Livy memorably describes Sutrium and Nepete as the barriers and gateways to Etruria: they controlled communications and trade and were natural points of defence or bases for conquest. The territory of Tarquinii, perhaps the most powerful of the Etruscan city-states, extended to the western edge of the Ciminus, and the Tarquinienses naturally feared further expansion by the Romans. As we have seen, Tarquinii was the only Etruscan state to aid Veii, but did so only fleetingly. There was no love lost between the great Etruscan cities and they frequently warred upon each other, but, unlike Caere, Tarquinii could foresee that a Roman victory over Veii would radically alter the balance of power in southern and central Etruria and impact on trade. According to Livy, all of the Etruscan states took advantage of Rome's apparent vulnerability following the Gallic sack, but the only city certainly involved was Tarquinii, though Volsinii may also have participated. In 389 BC the Etruscans besieged Sutrium. It appealed to Rome, and Camillus, fresh from his victories over the Volsci and Latins at Maecium and the Aequi at Bola, was appointed dictator for the emergency and rushed north. He found that Sutrium had fallen, but the Etruscans were too busy celebrating their victory to notice the arrival of the Roman army and the town was immediately recaptured. A substantial number of captives were taken and paraded in Camillus' triple triumph (over Volsci, Aequi and Etruscans), then sold as slaves. The profits helped to replenish the treasury emptied by the demands of Brennus. From his personal share of the spoils Camillus had three gold dishes fashioned, inscribed with his name and perhaps a summary of his victories. These were dedicated to Juno and remained on display in the Capitoline temple until it was destroyed by fire in 83 BC.

The following year saw a Roman incursion into the Tarquinii's territory. The town of Cortuosa was surprised, plundered and burned. Contenebra closed its gates to the invaders and resisted them fiercely but, fighting in relays, the Romans wore down the defenders and eventually stormed the town. Modern San Giovenale, lying some 11 miles to the east of Tarquinii, overlies the remains of an ancient town and excavation has suggested that it suffered violent destruction in the early fourth century BC. It may perhaps be identified with Cortuosa or Contenebra. The consular tribunes (that is military tribunes with consular power, not to be confused with junior military tribunes) who oversaw this campaign decided to hand over the plunder to the state treasury. However, the soldiery had already pocketed most of it and the tribunes could not easily demand its return.[14]

The 'Etruscans' (presumably the Tarquinienses and their allies) captured Sutrium again in 386 BC. Nepete also fell, betrayed to the enemy by an anti-Roman faction in the population. As in 389 BC, Camillus was diverted from warfare against the Volsci. He retook the towns by escalade. Those Etruscans who threw down their arms at Nepete and attempted to surrender were shown no mercy. It was clearly a major victory and severely dented Tarquinii's military capabilities: she did not resume hostilities until 358 BC. However, the Romans still feared trouble on their Etruscan frontier. A legionary garrison was left in Nepete, and one was presumably also installed at Sutrium. In 383 BC the towns were organized as Latin colonies; the Latin colonists would have been drawn from those cities that remained pro-Roman and the number of Roman settlers was substantial. Theoretically independent Latin states, Sutrium and Nepete were in fact firm bastions of Roman power. In 382 BC four of the six military tribunes with consular power remained at Rome, ready to react to any Etruscan move against the new colonies, but all was quiet.

In 358 BC a resurgent Tarquinii, taking advantage of Rome's preoccupations with Tibur and the Gauls, ravaged Roman territory in southern Etruria. Rome's demands for reparations were ignored and the consul Gaius Fabius Ambustus ('the Burned') set out with an army to extract payment. His army was heavily defeated by the Tarquinienses and their Faliscan allies. It was an utter rout. Some of the defeated soldiers escaped and subsequently deserted to Falerii, while 307 of the Romans taken captive were selected for ritual sacrifice in Tarquinii's forum. The other consul, Gaius Plautius Proculus ('the Trampler'), had reduced the Hernici to submission, but news of Ambustus' defeat encouraged the Volscian city of Privernum to raid the newly-established Roman territory in the *ager Pomptinus*, and unruly Velitrae followed her lead. The consuls of 357 BC were assigned commands against Falerii and Privernum respectively. Manlius Capitolinus Imperiosus ('Of the Capitoline and the Masterful') achieved little at Falerii and the city would not give up the deserters. Marcius Rutilus ('the Red') invaded the territory of the Privernates, allowing his legionaries to devastate and plunder freely. The pickings were rich, for the Volsci had been at peace for twenty years and Rutilus, a plebeian, allowed his troops to keep all of the plunder; the state treasury received nothing. The Privernates, so bold in the previous year, preferred not to meet the Romans in the open field and entrenched themselves in a position before their city. Marcius the Red's army doubtlessly outnumbered them and it seems that other Volsci had left them to their fate. The entrenchments were overrun in a single charge led by Sextus Tullius, a senior centurion (*primus pilus*) of considerable renown. Unsurprisingly, Privernum surrendered immediately.[15]

With the situation in the south restored, accounts could be settled with Tarquinii. The proven commander Marcus Fabius Ambustus (architect of an important victory over the Hernici in 360 BC) took to the field in 356 BC. At first it seemed that, like his brother Gaius, he would suffer an ignominious defeat. Etruscan and Faliscan priests stationed in the front rank of the enemy army performed a strange ritual involving snakes and flaming torches. This rite was probably concerned with calling on certain gods to destroy the legions. The Romans had similar rituals, for example *devotio*, which summoned the gods of the Underworld. The Romans were suitably unnerved and when the priests suddenly charged towards them, the legionaries fled in panic to their camp. Ambustus and his officers upbraided the legionaries for their cowardice. They were eager to repent; shame was a powerful motivator for the *virtus* (manly courage and excellence) and honour-obsessed Romans. The legionaries marched out, scattered the enemy and plundered their camp.

The Tarquinienses and Faliscans soon regrouped and, perhaps receiving reinforcements from other Etruscan city-states, advanced into the *ager Romanus* and attacked the salt works (Salinae) on the right bank at the mouth of the Tiber. The enemy set up camp and proceeded to plunder farms and settlements on both banks of the river. Unlike the Etruscan cities, Rome was never a great manufacturing centre and salt production was one of her few industries. Marcius the Red was appointed dictator to save this valuable enterprise; he was the first plebeian to hold the emergency office. Instead of crossing the Tiber by bridge or ferry and then marching his army along the right bank, Rutilus outwitted the Tarquinienses and Falisci by gliding down the Tiber on rafts. Pausing along the way to slaughter bands of raiders, he surprised the main army in its camp at Salinae. It is reported that 8,000 were captured, a figure that may derive from a contemporary record.[16]

Tarquinii and Falerii were now on the defensive. Tarquinii's territory was devastated in 355 BC, and in the following year she suffered a major defeat in a pitched battle. In revenge for the ritual execution of Gaius Ambustus' soldiers, the Romans led 260 (according to Diodorus Siculus) or 358 (Livy) of their Etruscan prisoners of war into the Forum; the unfortunates – probably members of the leading clans of Tarquinii – were beaten savagely with rods and then decapitated. In 353 BC Caere entered the war on the side of Tarquinii. The southern border of her territory was only a few miles above Salinae and the salt works were attacked for a second time. Titus Manlius Torquatus was appointed dictator to deal with the Caeretans, with Cornelius Cossus Arvina as his *magister equitum* ('master of horse'), the dictator's second-in-command. Torquatus derived his glorious *cognomen* from the torque he hacked from the neck of a Gallic champion (see below). Arvina was a descendant of the Cossus who slew Lars Tolumnius and dedicated the *spolia opima*. As has been noted, *cossus* is the Latin for worm; *arvina* means greasy, yet another intriguing *cognomen*.

Caere submitted as soon as Torquatus and Greasy Cornelius appeared with their army. The Caeretans claimed that they had been coerced by Tarquinii, but suspicion arises from the first attack on Salinae in 356 BC. While it is possible that Tarquinii employed her fleet, it seems likely that her army and the troops of Falerii traversed the territory of a sympathetic Caere. Located a mere 21 miles northwest of Rome, the Caeretans must have looked on the growing power of Rome with unease. They had seen Rome's former Latin and Hernican allies defeated and reduced to what was effectively the status of subjects. Caere's reciprocal treaty of friendship with Rome could not protect her indefinitely, but with Torquatus' army at the gates, the Caeretans' defiance evaporated. By reminding Rome of her aid during Brennus' incursion and its immediate aftermath, Caere received lenient treatment and was granted a truce of 100 years. Torquatus then led his army on a campaign of devastation in the Faliscan territory, but deliberately avoided attacking Falerii itself or any other fortified settlement. By destroying farms and crops and livestock, the Romans would have forced the inhabitants of the countryside to seek refuge in the main towns and so increased pressure on dwindling supplies. The Tarquinienses and Faliscans had not the manpower or will to fight off the Romans' incursions and in 351 BC they sued for peace. They were granted truces of forty years. It is also probable that indemnities were exacted, territory confiscated and leading men exiled. If they had not already escaped or died in the fighting since 358 BC, the treacherous legionaries who deserted to Falerii would have been dragged into the Forum and tortured and executed in the traditional fashion – scourging with rods followed by decapitation.

The Heirs of Brennus

Following his capture of Ferentinum, Sulpicius Peticus and his army returned to Rome via the Anio (361 BC). Pausing at Tibur, the consul found the gates of the city barred, a clear indication that the Tiburtes considered Rome to be their enemy. Since her liberation from the Aequi in c. 393 BC, Tibur had remained aloof from the Latin League and her relations with Rome had been strained. After Rome, she possessed the most extensive territory in *Latium Vetus* and, like Praeneste, was determined to reassert her ancient authority in the region. It is probably no coincidence that a Gallic army marched into Latium soon after Peticus was rebuffed from Tibur. The Gauls established their camp a mere 3 miles from Rome, where the Via Salaria crossed over the Anio. The Senate appointed Titus Quinctius Poenus dictator and he enforced an emergency levy; the legions of Peticus may have already disbanded. Poenus established his camp on the opposite bank of the Anio, and there were skirmishes for possession of the bridge, but no major engagement was fought. It was during one of the skirmishes that a Gallic champion came forward and challenged any Roman who was brave enough, to fight him in single combat. The challenge was accepted by Titus Manlius, a military tribune (that is, a legionary officer, not to be confused with the recently defunct office of military tribune with consular power). He defeated the Gaul on the bridge itself. According to Claudius Quadrigarius, a Roman historian of the 80s BC, 'Manlius cut off the Gaul's head, tore off his torque and put it, covered as it was with blood, around his own neck. Because of this act, he himself and his descendents had the *cognomen* Torquatus.' The outcome of the duel shocked the Gauls; their champion was probably a chieftain and accomplished duellist. The Gallic army then withdrew to its camp and subsequently retreated down the Anio to Tibur, where an alliance was negotiated. Tibur reprovisioned the Gauls, who then marched on to Campania. This is order of events given by Livy, but it may be that Tibur had invited or commissioned the Gauls to attack Rome, promising pay and provisions. The historian Polybius believed that the Gallic army had come out of the north, but Livy's reference to Campania suggests the possibility that the Gauls were mercenaries established in the south, although it is possible that having failed in Latium, rich Campania was the next logical target for attack.[17]

In 360 BC the consul Marcus Flavius Ambustus continued operations against the Hernici, while his colleague, Gaius Poetelius Balbus ('the Stammerer'), was assigned the war against Tibur. The Tiburtes recalled the Gauls from Campania and then, seemingly without interference from Balbus, were able to direct the Gauls' raids on Labici, Tusculum and the Alban Hills. Balbus did succeed in confining Tibur's own army within the city by establishing camp nearby, but the Gauls advanced on Rome, and were narrowly defeated just beyond the city's Colline Gate by a scratch force mustered by the dictator Quintus Servilius Ahala. (Another interesting *cognomen*, Ahala means 'armpit', and derived from an incident in 439 BC when one of the patrician Servilii concealed a dagger under his arm and used it to assassinate an aspiring plebeian tyrant.) The Gauls retreated to Tibur, where Balbus' army attacked them. The Tiburtes sallied out to help their allies, but were beaten back through the gates. However, the Tiburtes occupied the Romans long enough for the Gauls to enter the city. When the Tiburtes learned that Balbus had been awarded a triumph, they mocked his victory, denying that they had ever fought a battle with him, insisting he had merely massacred curious townsfolk who had ventured out to watch the flight of the Gauls.

No attempt was made by Rome to capture Tibur, and this should be read as an indication of thr Latin city's strength. In 359 BC the Tiburtes (perhaps without their Gallic mercenaries) mounted a surprise night attack on Rome, but after their initial shock, the Romans easily beat it off. In the following year a new army of Gauls appeared in Latium. The Gallic army is first attested at Praeneste, and then it established a camp at Pedum, a few miles to the south of Tibur. Despite our main source, Livy, not saying so, it is probable therefore that this force was in the employ of Tibur and Praeneste; the latter was probably in alliance with Tibur since 361/0 BC.[18]

With the two consuls fully occupied in Etruria and the Hernican territory, Sulpicius Peticus was appointed dictator. He seems not to have raised new legions but received drafts from the consular armies. As we have seen, in 358 BC the *foedus Cassianum* was renewed with the Latins agreeing to contribute troops, so Latin cohorts would have bolstered his force. The fighting with the Gauls at Pedum was indecisive and, much to the disgust of his soldiers, the dictator ordered them to desist from combat and retire into camp. Peticus preferred to wait for the Gauls to exhaust their supplies. A final general engagement resulted from a skirmish between the Romans and Gallic foragers. Livy attributes the Roman victory to a stratagem of Peticus: prior to the battle, Peticus armed 1,000 muleteers (those responsible for transporting the army's baggage), stiffened their ranks with 100 cavalrymen, and sent them to outflank the Gauls' camp and fall on their rear during the battle. On the other hand, Appian, writing in the second century AD but drawing on sources lost to us, recounts that Peticus instructed his legionaries to launch a devastating 'rolling volley' of *pila* (javelins with long spit-like heads designed to punch through shields and armour at close range), followed by a sudden charge with swords. The first rank of legionaries threw their *pila* at the enemy and then crouched down, followed in rapid succession by the second and third ranks. When the fourth rank had hurled its weapons, all the soldiers rose up, drew their swords, bellowed their war cries and charged.[19]

No hostilities are reported with Tibur in 357 BC, but in the following year the Romans appear to have defeated the Tiburtes in a battle and ravaged their territory. This successful campaign was followed up by the capture of Empulum (355 BC) and Sassula (354 BC), the main satellite towns of Tibur. Before the Romans took over the rest of her towns, Tibur surrendered and received lenient treatment. Praeneste sought terms at the same time, and both cities were granted an alliance with Rome (354 BC).

Gallic allies or mercenaries do not figure in the latter stage of the war with Tibur. The Gauls returned to Latium in 350 BC as raiders. They were defeated by the consul Marcus Popillius Laenas, but it was no easy victory.[20] The consul was seriously wounded and the Gauls occupied what is now Monte Cavo rather than evacuate Latium. In Livy's account of the battle, the Roman legion is described as being organized in three battle lines (each line being several ranks deep): *hastati* ('spearmen') in the first line, *principes* ('best men') in the second, and veteran *triarii* ('third line men') in the third and rearmost line. This has been rejected as anachronistic, as plausible details invented by later Roman historians to flesh out the account of a battle about which nothing was known, except for the identities of the participants and the outcome. However, it seems likely that a reorganization of the legion did occur soon after the shock defeat at the Allia (390 BC), where the Roman's single line was immediately overwhelmed and the need for reserve lines was recognized. While the legion of 350 BC was still in the process of development, it was not dissimilar to the classic legion described by Polybius, the Greek soldier and historian, in the middle of the second century BC. The development of the legion of *ordines* ('lines'; a better description than 'manipular legion', as the single battle line legion of the fifth century BC was already divided into maniples), and reforms in training and tactics, helps to make sense of the rapid recovery of Rome's military fortunes following the Gallic disaster. The multi-line legion, with its ability to reinforce or replace the hard-pressed first battle line of the *hastati* with the *principes*, also explains why the Romans were able to go on conducting wars year after year. Rome's large population – indicated by the size of the city itself and the extent of the *ager Romanus* – meant that her manpower was considerable, but manpower had to be used wisely and be conserved. With the system of interchangeable battle lines, casualties to Roman manpower were reduced and, at least in theory, were not disproportionate to one part of the army, which was arranged by age classes, the *hastati* being the youngest.[21]

Early in 349 BC the Gauls came down from the Alban Hills and plundered the settlements on the Latin plain and coast. At the same time, a fleet of Greek raiders ravaged the coast from Antium to the mouth of the Tiber. The Gauls and Greek pirates encountered each other and fought a hard but indecisive battle somewhere on the coast. Interestingly, they may actually have been allies, the Greeks probably being Syracusans out on a plundering expedition, like that of 384 BC (see Chapter 1), and using the Gauls to draw Roman forces inland, but the Gauls reneged on the agreement, choosing to loot the coastal settlements as well, and perhaps also attempting to seize the Greeks' loot.

Rome needed to raise a strong army to deal with both sets of raiders, but the Latins refused to send any troops. Despite suffering the ravaging of their territories, it was hoped that an isolated Rome would be defeated by the Greeks and Gauls, and that her hegemony in Latium would be broken. But the Latins underestimated Rome's resources and she formed an enormous army from her citizenry. Livy reports ten legions, doubtless an exaggeration; at this time, the regular levy was probably two legions, one per consul. Nonetheless, it is indicative that this was the largest army yet raised by Rome. The army was placed under the supreme command of Furius Camillus, son of the hero of the Volscian and Etruscan wars. The younger Camillus was consul that year, but his colleague had died in office, and the Senate decided to place Camillus in overall command rather than to appoint a dictator. Camillus assigned part of the army to the defence of Rome and divided the remainder between himself and the praetor Lucius Pinarius (the powers of the praetor were second only to those of the consul or dictator). Pinarius was charged with preventing the Greeks from landing on the coast or coming up the Tiber. He accomplished this task admirably. Running dangerously low on fresh water and other sup-plies, the Greeks were forced to sail away. Meanwhile, Camillus led his force into the Pomptine plain, where the Gauls had established a new camp. Camillus had no intention of meeting the Gauls in battle, only of preventing them from continuing their raids. However, a Gallic warrior came up to the ramparts of the Roman camp and challenged any Roman to single combat. The proud warrior issued his challenge through a translator, perhaps a Latin renegade or a Gaul who was familiar with Latin after having served with the Tiburtes. Marcus Valerius, a young military tribune, accepted the challenge. The duel of Marcus and the Gaul entered into legend. It was believed that a raven, sent by one of the gods, aided Valerius by clawing at the eyes of the Gaul. The reality may be that the Gaul wore a helmet decorated with the wings of a raven and, after killing him, Valerius took the helmet for himself and was subsequently known as Corvus ('the Raven'). The Romans were elated by Valerius' success, while the Gauls were enraged, and a fight broke out over possession of the Gallic champion's corpse. This developed into a general engagement in which the Gauls were defeated and they retreated into Campania, where some of them headed for the ports, while others made for Apulia – perhaps where the Greeks had recruited them. Camillus allowed the Gauls free passage out of Latium, preferring not to risk another battle with desperate warriors.

In 348 BC, although aged only 24, Valerius Corvus was elected to his first consulship on account of his bravery. Pestilence returned to Rome that year and another *lectisternium* was held. Consequently there was no campaigning against the rebellious Latins. News of the Romans' successes over the Greeks and Gauls had come to the attention of Carthage, and ambassadors arrived in Rome seeking to negotiate a new treaty of friendship and alliance. Carthage was fighting Syracuse for control of Sicily, and her reawakening of interest in Rome suggests that the Greeks who attacked Latium were indeed Syracusans, thus making Rome her natural ally. The new treaty with Carthage demonstrates the extent of the Latin rebellion; the Carthaginians were permitted to raid any Latin city not subject to Rome, plunder it and take its inhabitants as slaves, but the city would then be returned to Rome. The only Latin states loyal to Rome (or nominally so) and which the Carthaginians were prevented from raiding, are identified as Ardea and the previously-hostile colony of Circeii. Volscian Antium and Anxur (Tarracina) were also to be protected from Carthaginian piracy. This is somewhat surprising, but located on the coast they would have been subject to the attentions of the Greek pirates and benefited from the operations of Lucius Pinarius.

The loyalty of the Antiates did not last for long, though. They had kept the peace for thirty years, but in 348 BC they reoccupied the site of Satricum and set about its reconstruction. In 346 BC they mustered an army drawing on other Volsci, perhaps including a contingent from the Liris valley, and attempted to stir up a wider armed revolt in Latium. Valerius Corvus, in his second consulship, marched on Satricum before further reinforcements reached the Antiates. The Volsci were quickly defeated and fled into the city.

Corvus encircled the city and threatened to storm it, and the Volsci surrendered. Their newly-built city, with the exception of the sanctuary of Mater Matuta, was put to the torch, and the 4,000 fighting men who had survived the battle were taken to Rome, paraded in a triumph, and then sold as slaves. Corvus allowed his legionaries to plunder Satricum before they burned it, but the profits of the sale of the slaves went to the Roman state treasury.

In 345 BC the Aurunci (or Ausones), southern neighbours of the Volsci, made a sudden raid into Roman territory, probably in the Pomptine region. The Romans suspected they were acting as the agents of the Latins, but if they were acting as agents rather than independently, it would be more likely that they were acting for the Volsci. The younger Camillus was appointed dictator and marched into the country of the Aurunci in the hinterland between Latium and Campania. The Aurunci met him in battle and put up such a fight that the dictator called on the aid of the great goddess Juno, in her guise as Moneta, and vowed her a temple in return for victory.[22] The goddess obliged. Camillus returned to Rome triumphant and fulfilled his vow: the temple was dedicated in the following year. Camillus resigned the dictatorship on returning to Rome, but his army was not disbanded. The consuls, Fabius Dorsuo ('Broad- or Humpback') and Sulpicius Camerinus Rufus ('the Ruddy'), took it over and conducted a campaign against the Volsci of the Liris valley, and captured the town of Sora. Along with the advance of Roman arms towards the frontier of Campania, this was a development of great significance. Rome's interest in the area had grown since she annexed part of the neighbouring Hernican territory (the Trerus being a tributary of the Liris). We may presume that the consuls' primary intention was to isolate the eastern Volsci from their brethren in Latium, but Sora was also of strategic importance, commanding as it did the route up the Liris to the country of the Marsi and the Fucine Lake, and this was a region that another great warrior nation sought to dominate.

Chapter 3

Warriors of the Sacred Spring

The First Samnite War

The Samnites were the archetypal warriors of the *ver sacrum* (Sacred Spring). Claiming descent from the Sabines (hence the Samnites and other Oscan speakers were known as Sabelli or Sabellians) they believed that a bull sent by Mamers guided them to their homeland in the southern central Apennines. They divided into four tribes, the Pentri, Caudini, Caraceni and Hirpini. The latter took their name from Mamers' *hirpus* (wolf), which they followed in a subsequent *ver sacrum*. The four tribes cooperated in a military alliance.

In 354 BC the Samnite League sent an embassy to Rome, requesting friendship and alliance between their peoples. According to Livy, the Samnites were prompted to do so because they were impressed by a Roman victory over Tarquinii, but Rome's reduction of the Hernici in 358 BC would have been of more interest to the Samnites; the victory over Tarquinii merely reinforced the growing reputation of Roman military prowess. However, the allies fell out in 343 BC when the Samnites attempted to expand west into northern Campania and the territory of the Sidicini, and Capua, the leading Campanian city-state, appealed to Rome for help against the invaders. The Romans scented an opportunity to massively expand their little empire and renounced the treaty with the Samnite League.

The Romans sent priests called *fetiales* to the border of Samnium, perhaps in the vicinity of Sora, where the chief fetial declared war by symbolically casting a spear into the territory of the enemy. The consul Valerius the Raven (Corvus) was assigned the war in Campania, while his colleague Cornelius the Greasy (Arvina) invaded Samnium. The Raven pushed south to Mount Gaurus, in the hills above Puteoli, drawing the Samnite army away from Capua. The Samnites were defeated after a long struggle, requiring the heroic Valerius to dismount from his horse and lead a counter-attack on foot, and they withdrew from Campania.

Meanwhile, Cornelius the Greasy had advanced into the territory of the Caudini located immediately east of Capua. In the vicinity of Saticula his army was trapped in a heavily wooded defile; this was a favourite tactic of the Samnite mountain men. However, Cornelius' army was extricated by a military tribune, Publius Decius Mus. Tradition asserted that before the Samnites completed the encirclement and closed in, the military tribune led the *hastati* and *principes* of the consular legion (2,400 legionaries) through the woodland to a hill above the enemy; distracted by Mus' sudden appearance on the hill, the rest of the consul's army was able to escape. The dauntless Decius was now surrounded by the full Samnite army (apparently numbering in excess of 30,000 warriors), but during the night the tribune led his legionaries down the hill, broke through the encirclement and reunited with the consul's army. In the morning the Samnites, still disorganized from the confusion resulting from Decius' escape, were surprised by the Romans and soundly defeated. Decius was where the fighting was thickest, claiming that he had been inspired by a dream in which he achieved immortal fame by dying gloriously in battle. It has been suggested that Decius' peculiar *cognomen*, Mus, meaning 'rat', derived from his exploits at Saticula, perhaps because he dared to fight at night, a most unusual enterprise for a Roman commander.

Despite these two heavy defeats the Samnite League was not ready to throw in the towel. A new army of 40,000 men (another exaggeration of the later Roman sources) was raised from the populous tribes of Samnium, and it established a camp by Suessula, a city on the eastern edge of the Campanian plain. The army of Cornelius Arvina had evidently withdrawn from the territory of the Caudini, and it fell to the Raven to fight this last battle of the campaign. He marched from his camp at Mount Gaurus and overcame this new Samnite army as well. Suessula was located at the mouth of a valley that led to the Caudine Forks, an important pass into western Samnium. The defeated Samnites presumably retreated by way of the Forks into the country of the Caudini and Hirpini and thence to their homes, but the Raven did not follow. He was sensible not to. The Suessulans may have informed him that the pass was the perfect spot to trap an army and he had no desire to repeat the error of his colleague.

The consuls returned to Rome to celebrate triumphs (21 and 22 September 343 BC) and news of their victories spread quickly across Italy. The Faliscans were prompted to seek a formal treaty of friendship and alliance (*foedus*) with their old enemy, perhaps fearing that if they simply maintained the forty years' truce imposed on them in 351 BC, the bellicose Romans would find an excuse to declare war and seize their territory. The news also travelled overseas. Ambassadors from Carthage arrived in Rome, keen to bolster the alliance of 348 BC, full of congratulations for the victories over the Samnites and bearing the not inconsiderable gift of a gold crown weighing 25 pounds. However, the war was not over and substantial Roman garrisons were installed in Capua and Suessula to protect them from Samnite incursions.

In 342 BC the Samnites nursed their wounds. The scale of their defeats could not have been as great as Livy's account suggests, but the Romans had administered a serious blow to their military prestige and confidence. Samnite manpower in 225 BC (by which time their territory was very much reduced) is reported by the reliable Polybius as 70,000 infantry and 7,000 cavalry. Afzelius and Cornell have estimated the population of Samnium in the middle of the fourth century BC at around 450,000 persons, and the report of the geographer Strabo that the Samnites had 80,000 infantry and 8,000 cavalry may belong to this period. Strabo's manpower figures would represent somewhat less than 20 per cent of the estimated population. The total number of adult males, including *seniores*, would have been well in excess of 100,000, but these figures are misleading and should be regarded as potential reserves of manpower rather than the number of warriors the Samnite League could mobilize at one time. If the Samnites had lost 30,000 men at Saticula and suffered similarly enormous casualties at Mount Gaurus and Suessula, as Livy's accounts suggest, then their military power would have been utterly broken and their rural economies, which required men to tend crops and herds, would have collapsed.

The strengths of the consuls' armies are not attested. It is uncertain if the practice of enrolling two legions per consular army was yet in effect. It is generally believed that the regular strength of a consular army was raised from one to two legions in 311 BC. However, because the Romans could not draw on any substantial Latin manpower in the 340s BC, it may be that extra consular legions were raised. Campanian levies would have bolstered the Roman legions, and the aristocratic cavalrymen of Capua and the other cities were famed for their martial prowess. The number of soldiers in a consular army may be estimated at 9,000–18,000, that is one or two legions of c. 4,500 (4,200 infantry plus 300 cavalry) and an equal number of Campanians. The Samnite armies were probably of similar size.[23]

The Latin War

No hostilities are recorded between the Romans and Samnites in 342 BC but, in a not-fully-understood series of episodes, the plebeian Roman soldiers garrisoning Campania mutinied and attempted to seize wealthy Capua; the continuing problem of debt certainly influenced the actions of the troops. This coup coincided with political upheaval in Rome, and the prospect of a major war against the Latins and Volsci resulted in a curious about-turn by the Romans regarding the Samnites: in the following year the Romano-Samnite alliance was renewed. The consul Lucius Aemilius Mamercinus invaded Samnium, but it was merely for show. Samnite envoys were received and the price of peace and future co-operation was agreed on. The Samnites paid an indemnity (the cost of one year's pay for the Roman army and three months' rations), while the Romans turned a blind eye to the Samnites' intentions towards the Sidicini. From the territory of the Sidicini the Samnites could restart their assault on lush Campania, but the Romans were content to accept that risk for the time being. The Campanians were greatly disturbed by the mutiny and uneasy about the prospect of Roman domination, and it seemed likely they would join with the Latins.[24]

The mutiny of 342 BC encouraged Privernum to raid the loyal Latin colonies of Setia and Norba, and Antium was raising a new army. In 341 BC the consul Gaius Plautius Venox (or Venno) defeated the Privernates in a single encounter and captured their city. A Roman garrison was installed, probably only temporarily, and the consul confiscated two thirds of the Privernates' territory: the *ager Romanus* was growing ever larger. Venox ('the Hunter') then moved against the Antiates and other Volsci at the now traditional battleground of Satricum. The day's fighting was inconclusive, but instead of resuming the battle on the following day, the Volsci retreated to Antium and left Venox in possession of the field. Pleased with this turn of events, the consul directed his legionaries to gather up the arms the Volscians had lost in the encounter or abandoned when they withdrew from their camp. The weapons were piled up and burned as an offering to Lua Mater (Lua 'the Mother'). Venox may have called on the aid of this goddess during the battle, but it is also possible that the dedication of the spoils to Lua was part of an expiatory ritual.

The consuls of 340 BC were the heroes Decius Mus and Manlius Torquatus. Livy reports that each consul led two legions. Also according to Livy, they effected a union with the Samnite army by a very roundabout route, marching across the countries of the Marsi and Paeligni and finally down into Samnium. The Romano-Samnite force then invaded Campania, establishing a camp outside Capua, where the Latins and their allies had already made their base. Dionysius of Halicarnassus preserves a different tradition. Despite the risks of ambush, the Romans took one of the usual routes from Latium to Campania. This entailed marching through enemy territory, through that of the Volsci and Aurunci if the coastal route was followed, and where the Romans would risk ambush or entrapment at the pass of Lautulae above Volscian Anxur and at Auruncan Sinuessa, where Mount Massicus came down to the sea (this was the route subsequently consolidated as the Via Appia). If the Romans marched down the Trerus valley and the country of the Hernici, they would have had to enter the middle Liris valley, which, despite Roman and Samnite advances, remained Volscian territory. The real difficulty of this route was where it traversed the land of the Sidicini; from their fortress at Teanum the Sidicini controlled the gateway to northern Campania, that is, the passage between the Roccamonfina and Monte Maggiore. However, the Romans entered Campania without opposition, progressing to Casilinum where, as Dionysius informs us, a substantial wooden bridge was thrown across the River Volturnus in the space of three days – an early and perhaps anachronistic example of Roman military engineering. The army then advanced 40 stades – about 5 miles – past Capua, and established a camp on a lofty position, presumably indicating the slopes of Mount Tifatinus. There the Romans waited in vain for the Samnites to join them (this was a fabrication of the Roman sources Dionysius consulted), and all the while the forces of the enemy continued to swell.

Dionysius' account breaks off but Livy's action moves southwest from Capua to the Veseris, a river in the vicinity of Mount Vesuvius. His account of the ensuing battle is cast as a civil war engagement, Romans and Latins, alike in race, military organization and tactics. Both sides were deployed in three battle lines of maniples of *hastati*, *principes* and *triarii* led by tough centurions. Livy digresses to explain how the triple line legion operated:

> When the battle formation of the army was completed, the *hastati* were the first to engage. If they failed to repulse the enemy, they slowly retired through the intervals between the maniples of the *principes* who then took up the fight, the *hastati* following in their rear. The *triarii*, meantime, were resting on one knee under their standards, their shields over their shoulders and their spears planted on the ground with the points upwards, giving them the appearance of a bristling palisade. If the *principes* were also unsuccessful, they slowly retired to the *triarii*, which has given rise to the proverbial saying, when people are in great difficulty 'matters have come down to the *triarii*.' When the *triarii* had admitted the *hastati* and *principes* through the intervals separating their maniples, they rose from their kneeling posture and instantly closing their maniples up they blocked all passage through them and in one compact mass fell on the enemy as the last hope of the army. The enemy who had followed up the others as though they had defeated them, saw with dread a now and larger army rising apparently out of the earth.[25]

The *triarii* were armed with spears (*hastae*) rather than *pila*, but these were probably dual-purpose weapons, suitable for thrusting and throwing.[26]

The Romans were so hard pressed that Decius Mus decided to fulfil the prophecy of his dream in 343 BC. Performing a dark ritual called *devotio*, Mus called on the Gods of the Underworld (the *manes*) to destroy the Latins, but this essentially magical ritual required the immolation of the consul. Mus therefore charged into the ranks of the enemy and entered into legend as a great Roman martyr. Livy was hugely impressed by this act of self-sacrifice, but the dramatic death of Decius Mus is not the climax of Livy's battle narrative. The *devotio* does not trigger the collapse of the Latins; contrast the apparent result of the *devotio* performed at Sentinum in 295 BC (see Chapter 5). In fact, the

Latins are on the point of victory when Manlius Torquatus sends the veteran *triarii* forward with a well-timed charge and they carry all before them.

Torquatus had saved the day, but he was not lauded. Prior to the Veseris (or wherever the battle was fought), probably while in the camp at Capua, the consuls had issued a strict order against legionaries or cavalrymen engaging in single combat; those who disobeyed would be executed. Following the recent mutiny, the consuls were concerned with maintaining discipline and were unwilling to risk unsanctioned duels and skirmishes which could erupt into mass engagements, but Torquatus' own son disobeyed the order. While leading his thirty-man cavalry *turma* on a scouting mission, the younger Manlius encountered a troop of Tusculan cavalry, led by Geminus Maecius, an aristocrat warrior (*bellator*) of wide renown. Tusculum had joined with the Latins in an attempt to win back her independence. Maecius insulted Manlius and challenged him to a duel: notice that our sources always have arrogant and insulting enemies issuing challenges to single combat; good, honest Romans never do that. The younger Manlius killed Maecius, stripped the Tusculan of his arms and armour and rode back to the Roman camp brandishing his spoils. Torquatus congratulated his son and then, unwilling to make an exception, called on a *lictor* to behead Manlius. The summary execution shocked the army, but had the desired effect of reinforcing discipline. Torquatus was hated and feared, but the legionaries followed subsequent orders with alacrity.

Livy's account of the Veseris generally ignores the role of the Samnites, but it seems they routed the Campanians, and pursued them to the enemy camp, which was captured with much slaughter. The Samnites did their fair share. The claim of later Roman historians that they deliberately held back from the fighting, waiting to see who would win, is to be rejected. The Latin contingents, despite the mauling administered by the *triarii*, withdrew in better order. They retreated first to Minturnae and then to Vescia, where they received reinforcements from Latium, the Volsci (but perhaps not from Antium), Aurunci and Sidicini. This is odd. Minturnae and Vescia were in the territory of the Aurunci well to the north of Vesuvius. This has led to the suspicion that Livy or his sources confused the Roccamonfina, the extinct volcano that divided the territories of the Aurunci and Sidicini, with its more famous and active counterpart to the south. However, like his sudden transfer of the action before the battle from Capua to the foot of Vesusius, it may be that Livy simply neglected to report the intervening stages of the Latins' retreat from Vesuvius to Minturnae.[27]

Torquatus marched north – we do not know if the Samnites accompanied him – and soundly defeated the new allied army at a place called Trifanum, located between Minturnae and Sinuessa. The allies surrendered soon after, unable to defend their territories from Roman depredations. The Latins and

Campanians were stripped of territory and the confiscated land was divided into small farm plots to be distributed to Roman plebs; the luckiest received plots in the fertile *ager Falernus*. The Roman frontier was thus carried far south: it now lay on the lower Volturnus in Campania.

Of the Latin states involved in the campaigns of 340 BC, apart from Tusculum (technically Roman), only Lavinium and the colonies of Signia and Velitrae are identified. Lavinium was not punished, because in the end she chose not to send troops to the Latin army and Rome therefore renewed a treaty of friendship and alliance. Of the Volsci, Privernum was presumably unable to act, but Antium took advantage of the consuls' absence in Campania to raid Ardea and Ostia. Ostia was established to guard the mouth of the Tiber following the Greek raids of 350 and 349 BC. It was a small colony of 300 Romans, who retained their citizen status and whose town and territory remained part of the Roman state. Torquatus returned from the Auruncan territory, but illness or his extreme unpopularity prevented him from attacking Antium. A dictator was appointed to conduct the campaign, but he did little more than maintain a camp in Antium's territory for a few months.

Seething at the loss of great swathes of their territories, the Latins lost little time in renewing hostilities. In 339 BC Pedum became the figurehead of Latin revolt. This small city-state lay between powerful Tibur and Praeneste and was perhaps acting under their influence. Tibur, Praeneste, Lanuvium, Velitrae and Antium supplied troops and the attempts of the arrogant consul Tiberius Aemilius Mamercinus to capture Pedum were successfully resisted and he was forced to withdraw. However, this did not prevent him from claiming a triumph; the Senate was unimpressed and refused him the honour. The other consul, Quintus Publilius Philo, had greater success, defeating another Latin army at the Fenectane Plains, the location of which is uncertain. The defiance of Pedum was of extreme irritation to Rome, and the Senate declared that it must be captured, whatever the cost. In 338 BC the full army of Tibur, no doubt reinforced by the soldiers of Praeneste, took up position by Pedum. The forces of the Alban cities of Velitrae, Lanuvium and Aricia united with the Antiates at the River Astura, a little to the south of Antium. We can speculate about their intentions – to draw Roman troops away from Pedum, to attack *ager Romanus* in the Pomptine district or northern Campania, or to link up with eastern Volsci, Aurunci and/or Sidicini. However, as they were completing their muster, the consular army of Gaius Maenius fell on the unsuspecting allies. Their defeat was total and Maenius crowned his victory by capturing Antium. The city's fleet of ships, which had kept it wealthy through piracy and had enabled supplies to be brought in despite the Romans' land operations, were commandeered or destroyed, the bronze rams (*rostra*) of the latter being set up as a trophy in Rome and the monument adopted as a speaker's platform.

The task of defending Pedum and upholding the cause of Latin liberty now fell on Tibur.

In the years following the Gallic sack Camillus was the totem of Roman resurgence. His son took up the baton, ejecting the Gauls from Latium and carrying Roman arms to the frontier of Campania. Now, with the final battle for the control of Latium at hand, Camillus' grandson came to the fore. Lucius Furius Camillus crowned his first consulship with a stunning victory at Pedum. The proud Tiburtes fought hard, but their efforts were undone when the Pedani made an inept sortie from the city and threw the Latin field army into confusion. Camillus took full advantage, routed the Tiburtes and then stormed into Pedum. Except for the reduction of a few other rebel strongholds, the Latin War was over. Latium and northern Campania were reorganized as Roman or allied territory:

> Lanuvium received the full [Roman] citizenship and the restitution of her sacred objects, with the proviso that the temple and grove of Juno Sospita should belong in common to the Roman people and the citizens living at Lanuvium. Aricia, Nomentum, and Pedum obtained the same political rights as Lanuvium. Tusculum retained the citizenship which it had had before, and the responsibility for the part it took in the war was removed from the city as a whole and fastened on a few individuals. The Veliterni, who had been Roman citizens from old times [not strictly true; many Romans had been received into the Latin colony and so gave up their status as Roman citizens], were in consequence of their numerous revolts severely dealt with. Their walls were thrown down, their senate deported and ordered to live on the other side of the Tiber; if any of them were caught on this side of the river, he was to be fined 1,000 asses, and the man who caught him was not to release him from confinement till the money was paid. Colonists were sent on to the land they had possessed, and their numbers made Velitrae look as populous as formerly. Antium also was assigned to a fresh body of colonists [a small Roman citizen colony, not a Latin colony], but the Antiates were permitted to enrol themselves as colonists if they chose [probably Antiates of the ruling class]. Their warships were taken away, and they were forbidden to possess any more; they were admitted to citizenship. Tibur and Praeneste had their domains confiscated, not owing to the part which they, in common with the rest of Latium, had taken in the war, but because, jealous of the Roman power, they had joined arms with the barbarous nation of the Gauls. The rest of the Latin cities were deprived of the rights of intermarriage

(*conubium*), free trade (*commercium*), and common councils with each other. Capua, as a reward for the refusal of its aristocracy to join the Latins, were allowed to enjoy the private rights of Roman citizens, as were also Fundi and Formiae, because they had always allowed a free passage through their territory. It was decided that Cumae and Suessula should enjoy the same rights as Capua. [In fact, only the *equites Campani*, the nobles of Capua, were granted full Roman citizeship; the common folk of Capua and the inhabitants of the other Campanian towns received citizenship without the vote.][28]

In 340 BC the defeated Aurunci entered into a treaty of alliance with Rome. They, accordingly, called on the aid of Rome when attacked by the Sidicini in 337 BC, but the Roman response was so tardy that the Auruncan capital (not named by Livy) was destroyed by the Sidicini, and the Aurunci took refuge in a hastily refortified Suessa Aurunca. The Romans finally moved against the Sidicini in 336 BC. The Ausones of Cales sided with the Sidicini rather than their Auruncan kinsmen, and were defeated in battle along with their allies. The Romans decided to rectify their failure in securing the territories linking Latium and Campania. In 335 BC strategic Cales was captured. Livy ascribes its conquest to Valerius Corvus, aided by the inside knowledge of a Roman prisoner of war who escaped while the Ausones were celebrating a religious festival. The escapee, Marcus Fabius (perhaps the former consul, Dorsuo), advised Corvus to attack while the bulk of the Ausones were still occupied with feasting and drinking. The town was thus captured with little resistance and a mass of plunder was taken.[29]

Located on the main route between Rome and Capua, just above a crossing of the River Volturnus, Cales was the ideal site for a Roman fortress. It was duly colonized in 334 BC by 2,500 men and their families. It is likely that the colonists were not only land-hungry Roman plebs. In return for plots of land and local self-government, these men and their families accepted Latin citizenship and agreed to fight for Rome. At first sight there is little difference between this and the earlier Latin colonies, but Cales was a Latin state established beyond the bounds of Latium. As well as being an outpost of Roman military power, it was also an island of Latin language and culture in hostile territory. Henceforth such colonies were the Romans' preferred means of controlling and Latinizing/Romanizing newly-conquered lands.

Following the practice of the earlier Latin colonies of the triple alliance period where Romans, Latins and Hernici shared in the distribution of land, and taking into consideration the recent invitation to the Volscian Antiates to participate in the small Roman colony planted at Antium in 338 BC (a long time had passed since Volscian rebels undermined the original Latin colony at

Anxur-Tarracina), it is probable that the colonists Rome enrolled at Cales and at subsequent foundations, were selected not only from land-hungry Roman plebs, but from among her allies as well, and perhaps even from her recently defeated enemies. This meant that non-Latins could acquire Latin status. Being a Latin was no longer a mark of ethnic identity; it proclaimed a particular and beneficial legal status. The Latin right (*ius Latii*) allowed the citizens of the new colonies to trade with (*commercium*) or marry (*conubium*) Romans and, if a colonist took up residence in Rome, he could claim the full Roman citizenship.

The Sidicini had still to be dealt with, but the Romans shied away from assaulting the great fortress of Teanum. Their territory was ravaged, but, despite the enemy raising a 'huge army', no pitched battle is reported (334–332 BC). We hear nothing more of hostilities with the Sidicini and it may be presumed that some kind of alliance was negotiated. The Romans were more concerned with the prospect of renewed hostilities with the Samnites. The Samnites had long desired the country of the Sidicini, and Cales lay just beyond the western edge of their territory. The Roman operations were a direct provocation to the Samnites, but embroiled in a war with the Molossian king, Alexander of Epirus, they were prevented from curbing the Romans' imperialism. Sharing in the Lucanians' defeat by Alexander at Posidonia in 332 BC, Samnite power was temporarily shaken. The Romans entered into a treaty of friendship with Alexander, the northern limit of whose territory lay not too far from Campania. He could have been a strong ally or a dangerous opponent to Rome, but shorty afterwards he was defeated and killed by the Lucanians and Bruttii at Pandosia in 331 BC (see Chapter 6).

The war with the Sidicini may have encouraged Acerra in Campania to revolt from Rome. No fighting is reported, but the town was annexed in 332 BC and its inhabitants enrolled as Roman citizens without the vote (*cives sine suffragio*). This lesser citizenship had become a form of punishment rather than a half-way status to full citizenship.

The Samnites' defeat at Posidonia only blunted their military power temporarily. Released from the conflict with Alexander the Molossian, they resumed their expansion into the valley of the Liris and eyed the lower Trerus. This prompted the Volscian town of Fabrateria to send ambassadors to Rome to seek protection against the Samnites (330 BC). Fabrateria was located in the lower Trerus valley and close to the confluence with the Liris – the point to which the Samnites had advanced. The appeal was accepted and these Volscians were enrolled as allies of Rome. The Senate received another embassy also seeking protection from Samnite aggression. The ambassadors were 'Lucani'. However, Livy couples them together with the Fabraterni, and it may be that these Lucanians were actually Volsci, named after a settlement in the Trerus-Liris region called Luca.

The Samnites took heed of the threats but the Romans were immediately involved in a war in Latium with the rebellious Volsci of Privernum and Fundi (330 BC). The Samnites were suspected of encouraging the revolt led by the general Marcus Vitruvius Vaccus of Fundi. Vaccus ('the Bellower') was a well-known figure, even owning a house on the Palatine Hill in Rome. He began his revolt by raiding the territories of Setia, Norba and Cora. Vaccus was confronted by the consular army of Lucius Papirius Crassus and defeated, but his casualties were light and he retreated into the safety of Privernum. The siege of Privernum dragged on into 329 BC and involved both consular armies. Two traditions existed in antiquity concerning the fall of the city. One was that Privernum was taken by storm and Vaccus captured, the other that the towns-folk surrendered and handed Vaccus over to the consuls Aemilius Mamercinus and Gaius Plautius Decianus. Mamercinus (or his descendants) assumed the celebratory *cognomen* Privernas and the Senate granted both consuls triumphs. The joint triumph of Mamercinus and Decianus (whose *cognomen* reveals he was born into the Decii clan but adopted by the Plautii) was delayed until Decianus had overseen the demolition of Privernum's defences and established a strong garrison in the city. Vaccus' execution can be assumed to have occurred at the end of the triumphal procession on 1 March 328 BC.

Following the expulsion of its senate (exiled beyond the Tiber like the magistrates of Velitrae in 338 BC), Privenum was annexed, its inhabitants enrolled as Roman citizens without the vote (*sine suffragio*). Elsewhere in Volscian Latium, the port of Anxur had a colony imposed on it. Like other 'maritime' or 'coast guard' colonies, for example Antium, the 300 adult male colonists retained their full Roman citizenship. The Volscian inhabitants would also become Roman citizens, but without the vote. Known again by its original Latin name of Tarracina, the city may have been implicated in Vaccus' revolt, or was perhaps operating as a base for pirates. Alexander the Great had complained to Rome about Volscian piracy; the Romans might have allowed such activity to continue if they shared in the profits. The main reason for the colonization was Tarracina's strategic position: along with the nearby pass of Lautulae, it dominated the coast road linking southern Latium with the east, where it was squeezed between the sea and the Monti Lepini.

Chapter 4

The Great Samnite War

Provocation

According to Livy, nothing of military or political import occurred in 328 BC. However, the historian does refer to the establishment of the colony of Fregellae as one of the few notable events of the year. In reality this was no minor event; it was the trigger for the outbreak of the Second, or Great, Samnite War.

The appeal of the Fabraterni and the problematical 'Lucani', assuming they were in fact Volsci, gave the Romans the excuse they had long been waiting for: to expand their power in the Liris region. Fregellae was located just east of the Liris, very close to its confluence with the Trerus. This was Samnite territory, taken from the Vólscians by force of arms. The Romans could argue that they established the colony to protect new allies, but that they did so on Samnite territory was the ultimate provocation, and the Samnites were not yet ready for a war in this region. Their attention was again focussed on Campania and on reasserting influence there. Rome had seized a vast chunk of that region, but the Samnites still had allies in the Sabellian city of Nola and even the last remaining Greek stronghold in Campania – Neapolis. There was a sizeable Oscan-speaking element in Neapolis, present since the Sabellian incursion into Campania in the fifth century BC, and the Samnites exerted considerable influence in the city and may have encouraged the raids on the territory of Capua. Even if the raiding of this new part of the *ager Romanus* was not the result of manoeuvrings by the Samnites but motivated simply by the desire for slaves and plunder, it allowed the Samnites and Nola to install a powerful garrison in Neapolis when the Roman Senate demanded reparations and threatened war. As well as the 4,000 Samnite and 2,000 Nolani troops, Tarentum promised to send ships to bolster Neapolis' navy.

In 327 BC the consul Quintus Publius Philo laid siege to Neapolis. The name Philo is notable. It is Greek and means 'beloved' or 'dearest' and is the earliest example of the adoption of a Greek name by a leading Roman, indicating the growing Roman interest in the Greek world – which included southern Italy – and its culture.

Philo took Neapolis in 326 BC. Readers will notice that he had exceeded his year in office but conduct of the siege was not taken over by a new consul. The Senate had made an extraordinary and far-reaching decision. Philo's military powers were renewed, by what the Romans called prorogation, until he succeeded in conquering the city. Philo was therefore the first proconsul. Promagistrates – proconsuls and propraetors – would become more common in later years, the renewal or extension of powers allowing a general to remain in the field beyond the term of his elected office and so avoided disrupting important ongoing campaigns being fought at considerable distances from Rome.

The proconsul did not capture Neapolis by storm, but by a ruse. The common people of Neapolis, mostly Greeks, supported the Samnites and Tarentum (although her aid never materialized), but an element of the Greco-Sabellian aristocracy, perceiving that their authority would be threatened by Samnite or Tarentine domination, decided to throw their lot in with Rome. The aristocrat Nymphius (the name is Oscan) suggested that while the Roman army was preoccupied with the blockade of the city, the Samnite garrison commander employ his troops as marines on Neapolitan vessels and raid the coast of Latium and the Tiber. As the Samnites marched down to the docks, a gate was opened and the Roman army was admitted into the city. The surprised Samnites and Nolani were forced to make their escape as best they could. Neapolis thus became a favoured ally of Rome.

The Romans feared that the Samnites would retaliate by attacking the new colony at Fregellae, and accused them of inciting Privernum, Fundi and Formiae to revolt, but the Samnites were slow to mobilize and the consuls of 326 BC drew first blood by raiding the middle Volturnus region and destroying the Samnite settlements of Allifae, Callifae and Rufrium.

The war was not going well for the Samnites and the forecast appeared gloomy. With the conquest of Latium and northern Campania the Romans had gained a huge reserve of citizen and allied manpower. Just as importantly, the Latin and Campanian plains, along with Roman southern Etruria, were the most fertile and productive agricultural lands in peninsular Italy. Rome had the manpower and the means to feed it, and therefore to keep it in the field for longer. Mountainous Samnium only boasted pockets of fertile land. The country was landlocked and the Romans could attack it from the north and west, but they sought to surround the Samnites completely, making alliances with some of the Lucani and Apuli, thus threatening them from the south and east as well. However, Rome's seizure of Neapolis infuriated Tarentum, the leading Greek power in southern Italy. A rival of the Samnites for the control of the pastures of southern Apulia, she became reconciled with the mountain warriors and prepared to throw her support behind them. Tarentine machinations secured the defection of the Lucani from the Roman alliance, and just to make sure the Lucani did not again stray, the Samnites installed strong garrisons in their towns and fortresses (326 BC).

The Furious Dictator

The Sabellian Vestini also sided with the Samnites in 326 BC. Located in eastern central Italy on the slopes of the Apennines, they were separated from their allies by the territories of the Paeligni and Marrucini. These peoples, along with the Marsi and Frentani, were most probably allied to Rome, or the Romans at least had agreements with them to traverse their lands in order to link up with allies in Apulia and from there threaten the eastern flank of Samnium. The Vestini were therefore well positioned to harass Rome's armies and wreck her grand strategy for the defeat of the Samnites. In 325/4 BC (the traditional Roman chronology is a little out of step, hence the approximate date) the consul Decimus Iunius Brutus Scaeva was assigned the war against the Vestini. Scaeva defeated them in a hard-fought battle, and then stormed their principle fortresses, Cutina and Cingilia. The left-handed consul (hence *scaeva*) was not stupid (*brutus*, the traditional *cognomen* of the Iunii) and did not risk incurring the anger of his victorious legionaries by denying them any of the booty.

Scaeva's fellow-consul was Furius Camillus, but the hero of the Latin War fell ill and Lucius Papirius Cursor was appointed dictator and assumed the command against the Samnites. As consul in 326 BC he had led the successful raid into the valley of the Volturnus. Cursor's master of horse was Quintus Fabius Rullianus (or Rullus), but there was no love lost between them. The dictator was delayed in Rome until the omens for the campaign were declared to be good, but Rullianus was sent ahead with the strictest instructions not to engage the enemy. However, at a place called Imbrinium (location unknown) the ambitious son of Marcus Fabius Ambustus disobeyed orders and inflicted a notable defeat on the Samnites. The decisive moment came when the tribune Lucius Cominius rallied the cavalry, bade them take the bridles off their horses and led them in a mad charge that broke the enemy's ranks. The legions followed up and completed the rout. Rullianus had the spoils heaped up and burnt, as if in offering to a god, but in reality to prevent the dictator from stealing his glory by inscribing his name on the spoils and then dedicating them in shrines, or by displaying them in a triumphal procession.

Cursor was infuriated when he learned of Rullianus' actions. Living up to his *cognomen* (the 'Swift Runner'), the dictator rushed to the camp, arrested Rullianus and was about to have him scourged and executed, when the soldiers intervened and veteran *triarii* formed a protective guard around the master of horse. This enabled him to escape from the camp, but he was pursued by Cursor to Rome. The dictator still insisted that Rullianus should suffer the ultimate penalty for breaking an order and compromising the discipline of an entire army. Cursor was eventually persuaded to relent by the desperate appeals of Rullianus, Marcus Ambustus, the Senate and the Roman populace, but he returned to camp in a foul mood. The army was in an equally surly mood – angry at Cursor for his persecution of Rullianus and irritated by the attacks of the Samnites on their foraging parties. Cursor made a concerted effort to win back the men's affections. With this accomplished, he led them to victory in a pitched battle and so thoroughly ravaged a part of Samnium that the enemy called for a truce. He returned to Rome in triumph, but negotiations to end the war faltered and the Samnite envoys departed from Rome agreeing only to maintain the truce for a year.

Truce Breakers

The Samnites did not maintain the truce. In 323 BC they attacked certain Apuli who were allied to Rome. The Romans sent a consular army into Apulia, but no battle was fought againt Samnite forces. Rather, it seems that the territory of Apulians allied to the Samnites (and therefore most probably the local rivals of the Romans' Apulian allies) was devastated. An incursion was also made in Samnium, but the enemy did not offer battle. Late in 323 or early 322 BC the Samnites mounted their first attack on Roman territory, although they would not have called it that. The country around Fregellae was raided, and the colony itself was perhaps threatened with siege. Realizing that the Roman reaction would be swift and furious, the Samnite League levied a large army from the four tribes and also called on allied contingents.

Livy was aware of two traditions concerning the campaign in Samnium in 322 BC. One held that it was conducted by the aged dictator Cornelius the Greasy and the equally elderly *magister equitum* Marcus Ambustus. The other tradition, which is almost certainly correct, is that the consuls Lucius Fulvius Curvus and Fabius Rullianus (in the first of his five consulships) defeated the Samnites, while Arvina and Ambustus performed duties in Rome. It is worth noting here that Fulvius Curvus was the first consul to emerge from the relatively new citizenry of Tusculum and stands as an example of how former enemies of Rome, once incorporated into the Roman system, could integrate and achieve the highest honours. Of course, this would have been far easier for an aristocrat like Curvus than a lower class individual. The *cognomen* Curvus means crooked or stooped. In a famous passage of his history Livy decried the problems he faced in identifying the victors of this and other campaigns:

> It is not easy to choose between the accounts or the authorities. The records have been vitiated, I think, by funeral eulogies and by lying inscriptions under portraits, every family endeavouring mendaciously to appropriate victories and magistracies to itself – a practice which has certainly wrought confusion in the achievements of individuals and in the public memorials of events. Nor is there extant

any writer contemporary with that period, on whose authority we may safely take our stand.[30]

The outline of the battle ascribed to Arvina and Ambustus, but probably fought by Curvus and Rullianus, is as follows. When the Roman army encamped in an unfavourable position, the Samnites appeared in force and prepared to attack the camp. The Romans abandoned the camp and the retreating legions were harassed by Samnite cavalry and forced to halt. The main body of Samnite infantry came up and a pitched battle was fought. The Samnites had the best of the fighting, and one wing of cavalry swept around the Roman battle line. It did not however attack the Romans in the flank or rear, but plundered the Romans' unattended baggage. The Roman cavalry counter attacked, scattered the Samnite riders, and then proceeded to do what the enemy cavalry should have done: they turned the unprotected flank of the Samnite infantry and attacked them from the rear. The Samnite legions (as Livy calls them) had been on the cusp of victory, but assailed from front and rear, they were destroyed. Some managed to flee but many, including the unnamed Samnite commander, were surrounded and cut down. Livy's battle narrative contains many colourful details, most probably inventions by himself or his predecessors, but the decisive role of the Roman *equites* should not be doubted, as it probably stemmed from the ballad tradition of the noble clans and families, keen to advertise and commemorate the heroic deeds of their scions.

Following the victory in Samnium (the exact location is not revealed), Rullianus proceeded with his legions to Apulia. No details of his campaign exist, except that he captured the strategic city of Luceria, located on the western edge of the Apulian plain and on the frontier with Samnium.

The Samnites were aghast at their defeat. The scale of the preceding Roman victories was probably exaggerated. As was noted in the previous chapter, despite possessing considerable manpower, the Samnites could not sustain thousands of casualties and keep on enrolling fresh armies for the Romans to slaughter. Many fights were probably inconclusive. In some cases victory may have gone to the Romans on account of a technicality, such as being the last to leave the battlefield, even if they had sustained a terrible mauling in maintaining their position. However, the defeat inflicted by Curvus and Rullianus was serious. Not only had the Samnites suffered great losses, but they also believed that their impiety in breaking the truce had turned the gods against them. The piety and superstitions of the ancient Italians should not be underestimated. The *meddices* (chief magistrates) of the Samnite League sought a scapegoat and found it in Brutulus Papius, a noble involved in the attacks on Apulia or Fregellae, but he committed suicide before he could be handed over to the Romans. The sources variously report that his bones were scattered or that his corpse, and those of others identified as the principle truce breakers, were sent to Rome. The Samnites also returned all the Romans they had taken prisoner (indicating that the fighting of 327–322 BC had not been entirely one-sided), as well as all the plunder they had captured. The Samnite fetials (it was usual for Italian states to have a college of priests concerned with the declaration of wars and ratification of treaties) beseeched the Senate to accept these tokens and to resume the truce. Whereas in 325/4 BC the Senate was prepared to negotiate a peace, demonstrating that the victories of Rullianus and Cursor had not broken the Samnites, it was now in a strong position and refused to renew the peace with oath breakers and demanded nothing less than a complete surrender. The fetials could not accede to this and returned home. According to some sources they ransomed the Samnites taken captive by the Romans; they would have been rich and noble Samnites. Defeated common soldiers were not usually held in captivity. They were massacred, enslaved, or set free, perhaps after suffering some sort of humiliation.

Under the Yoke
The consuls of 321 BC were Titus Veturius Calvinus ('the Bald') and Spurius Postumius Albinus ('the White'). They had already shared the supreme magistracy in 334 BC and overseen the colonization of Cales. They were ready to add to the glory of their achievements by delivering a mighty blow to the Samnites and united their armies in Campania. Later Roman historians asserted that enemy soldiers disguised as shepherds lured their force into Samnium. Coming to the Roman camp at Calatia, the disguised Samnites reported that Luceria, so recently captured by Fabius Rullianus, was besieged by the Samnite League. Instead of taking the secure but long route via the Fucine Lake and down the Adriatic coast, the consuls decided to risk the quickest and most direct route to Apulia: through the heart of Samnium via Malventum. At the Caudine Forks, a pass west of Caudium, the Roman army was trapped by the cunning Samnite general Gavius Pontius. The Samnites blocked both ends of the narrow pass and lined the high flanking slopes with warriors. They refused to accept any Roman challenges to fight. Thus denied the opportunity to at least die gloriously, the consuls were persuaded by the senior legate and former consul Lucius Cornelius Lentulus ('the Slow') to surrender in order to extricate the army and so not leave Rome defenceless. Gavius Pontius demanded that the Romans abandon their colonies at Cales and Fregellae; the crafty consuls agreed, but argued that they could not make a formal peace treaty to this effect as no fetials were present, and when they returned to Rome immediately renounced their personal agreement (Latin *sponsio*) with Pontius.

This is mostly the fabrication of embarrassed Roman historians. The consuls were not attempting to relieve Luceria but were embarking on a major invasion of western Samnium. Cicero makes it clear that the combined consular armies were defeated in a regular battle near Caudium – there is no site between Calatia and Caudium really narrow enough for the Samnites to have trapped the Roman army in quite the way described above, but at a location still known as Forchia, the Samnites could have barred the Roman advance. The consuls did surrender and, in return for the extrication of the legions, agreed a formal peace treaty with Gavius Pontius, the terms of which included the evacuation of Cales and Fregellae. To compound their shame, the consuls and their soldiers were stripped of insignia, arms and armour and sent under the yoke wearing only their tunics. This was a humiliation worse than death. The yoke was constructed from two spears thrust into the ground, with a third lashed between them to form a crossbar. Being forced under the yoke indicated that a warrior was utterly defeated, little more than a beast, to be used and abused by his conqueror.

It is reported that Gavius' father, Herennius Pontius, advised against humiliating the defeated Romans, for that shame would encourage them to seek revenge. The wise old man, who had debated philosophy with Plato and Archytas at Tarentum, told his son simply to release the Romans or to kill them all. If released, the Romans would be bound by obligation to the Samnites and this would effectively halt the war. If all the legionaries, *equites* and allied troops were slaughtered, the power of Rome would suffer a considerable blow. The size of the consular armies in 321 BC is uncertain. It may be that each consul had but a single legion, yet each legion of 4,500 would have been accompanied by at least an equal number of Latin (that is, those from the few remaining allied states in Latium and those of the new Latin status from the colonies) and other allies. The army defeated at the Caudine Forks was at least 18,000 strong. The newer Roman citizens, such as the Campani, probably formed separate cavalry contingents (cf. the situation at Sentinum in 295 BC), and their infantrymen may not have been integrated into the legions at this time but were perhaps formed into distinct units.

It is worth noting here that Gavius and Herennius Pontius may have been the ancestors of Pontius Pilatus, better known as Pilate of the New Testament. Pilatus is an interesting *cognomen*, being the Latin for a soldier armed with the *pilum* and it could commemorate some feat that Pilate performed in battle, but another possibility is that it derived from (*ex*)*pilator*, which denoted a pillager.

Decimation

The humiliated army skulked home. The populace of Rome is said to have taken pity on the pathetic legionaries, but that is most unlikely. They would have been treated with contempt and derision; compare the treatment of the legionaries and *equites* captured at Heraclea (Chapter 6). The defeated consuls were soon got rid of and elections were held early. Proven commanders were needed in this time of crisis: the people chose Papirius Cursor and Publilius Philo. The consuls are credited with great victories in 320 BC but these are imaginary, not least the ridiculous claim that Gavius Pontius was captured at Luceria and forced under the yoke.

The Romans kept the peace, refraining from retaliatory raids on Samnium, but the Senate reneged on the terms of the treaty concerning the colonies of Cales and Fregellae, for the Samnites had to take the latter by force, and Satricum in the Liris Valley (not to be confused with the other Volscian Satricum in Latium) was either captured or took the opportunity to revolt and joined with the enemy; a Samnite garrison was installed in the town. It was most probably in the aftermath of the Caudine Forks that Luceria fell to the Samnites. The Sabellian Frentani, whose territory was so crucial for gaining access to Apulia, abandoned their alliance with Rome and sided with their Samnite kin. In Campania and the hinterland linking it with Latium, there were murmurings of discontent with Roman rule: in 318 BC it was necessary for Rome to send a prefect to regulate the affairs of Capua.

Cursor was again consul in 319 BC. He scored a success by capturing Satricum on the Liris and was rewarded by the Senate with a triumph (celebrated on 21 August 319 BC), but the Samnites' grip on Fregellae and the most of the middle Liris region remained tight. The other consul, Quintus Aulius Cerrentanus, reopened communications with Apulia after he defeated the Frentani in a lightning campaign.[31] It seems that they received no support from the neighbouring Samnite Pentri. In the following years warfare was focussed on Apulia, with the Romans seeking to rebuild their coalition of allies and to threaten Samnium from the east as well as the west. Arpi, Rome's principal ally in Apulia, remained loyal and her regional hegemony was strengthened as the legions systematically defeated those city-states and peoples loyal to, or dominated by, the Samnites. Teanum and Canusia in northern and central Apulia fell in 318 BC. Iunius the Ploughman (Bubulcus) advanced south in 317 BC and took Forentum, while his colleague Quintus Aemilius Barbula ('Little Beard'), crossed from Apulia into Lucania and made an example of the unfortunate minor town of Nerulum; the defeated Apulian cities then entered into alliance with Rome. Papirius Cursor finally recaptured Luceria in 315 BC. That year also saw the resumption of direct attacks on the Samnites. Publilius Philo laid siege to Saticula on the border between Campania and Samnium. Attempts by the Samnites to relieve the town were unsuccessful.

The tide was turning against the Samnites. They appear to have done little or nothing to combat the Roman recovery until the siege of Saticula. It is perhaps surprising that they did not attack Campania or make further gains in the Liris valley while the consular armies were occupied in Apulia, but when Saticula fell the Samnites went on the offensive in spectacular fashion. Philo's conquest of Saticula was neatly countered by the capture of nearby Plistica, located a few miles to the northwest on the Roman side of the frontier, and other towns in Campania were captured by the Samnites, most notably Calatia. The Samnites then proceeded to capture Sora on the Liris, aided by a pro-Samnite faction in the strategic town. From Sora they advanced on Greater Latium. In response to this emergency Fabius Rullianus was appointed dictator and he positioned his army (including consular forces taken over from Philo) at the pass of Lautulae, the natural place to halt the Samnite invasion. Roman historians rewrote the outcome of the battle as inconclusive, but the fact is that the legions were broken by the Samnites' furious charge and Rullianus suffered one of the heaviest defeats in Roman history. Aulius Cerretanus, conqueror of the Frentani and Rullianus' master of horse, preferred death to flight. He spurred into the oncoming Samnite ranks and speared an enemy commander, but was then dragged from his mount and killed. Rullianus himself escaped, but he took his fury out on those legionaries unfortunate enough to have also made their way to safety. They suffered decimation, the cruellest of Roman military punishments: every tenth legionary was selected by lot for execution and decapitated in front of his comrades.

The Samnites proceeded to capture Tarracina and raided as far north as Ardea, but they did not venture to attack Rome itself. Encircled by massive fortifications of tufa, Rome was no longer the easy target it had been in 390 BC. However, the Samnites had cut Roman territory in two. Now that the Samnites controlled the coastal route to Latium, the Aurunci were emboldened to revolt and the Campani considered it. In Apulia, Luceria handed herself back over to the Samnites.

Since 321 BC, the Samnites had defeated two major Roman field armies, ejected Rome from disputed territory, caused the defection of her subjects and allies, and even plundered the heart of the Latin plain, yet this was the high watermark of Samnite success in the war, in fact in any of the Samnite Wars. Nothing motivated the Romans more than the need to avenge a defeat and in 314 BC, with the shame of the Caudine Forks and Lautuale burning inside them, the consul Gaius Sulpicius Longus ('the Tall') led the legions – quickly replenished from Rome's considerable manpower – to a pivotal victory over the Samnites at Tarracina and ejected them from Greater Latium. Longus celebrated a well-deserved triumph in Rome on 1 July, his troops parading their spoils and singing the praises of their general. The reconquest of the hinterland followed. The Auruncan and Ausonian strongholds of Ausona, Minturnae and Vescia were betrayed to the Romans by unscrupulous young nobles (as we have seen, the Romans liked to control towns through loyal aristocrats who enjoyed considerable local authority) and the common people were slaughtered. To prevent future revolts, a Latin colony was planted at Suessa Aurunca in 313 BC. Northern Campania, its inhabitants having mostly resisted the urge to break into open revolt, was spared such treatment, but a dictator was appointed to investigate rebellious conspiracies, especially in Capua. Luceria was captured for the third time. The duplicitous Lucerini – as the Romans considered the unfortunates caught between the warring powers – and the Samnite garrison were massacred (314 BC). The decision was made to re-establish the city as a Latin colony. In 313 BC 2,500 male colonists were enrolled. It would be Rome's bastion in Apulia and a thorn in the eastern flank of Samnium.

The legions may have spent the winter of 314/3 BC in the field, still a relatively rare occurrence in an age when armies were largely composed of peasant farmers keen to return home and bring in their crops. The Romans' gains in 314 BC had been substantial, but Fregellae, the cause of the war, remained in Samnite hands. It is uncertain which commander undertook the recapture of Fregellae, but Cursor, in his fifth and final consulship, is a likely candidate. Probably in spring 313 BC, Cursor advanced up the Liris valley, but he found the colony of Fregellae abandoned. The Samnites had retreated to the *arx* of Fregellae, a fortress perched on a hill 500 metres tall and located some 5 miles to the northeast of the colony. This should have posed considerable difficulties to Cursor's army, but according to Livy, the Samnite garrison simply fled. However, in his account of the fighting in 311 BC, Livy has a Roman general exhort his troops by reminding them how Roman valour triumphed over the difficult topography of the *arx* of Fregellae, and thus suggests that its recapture was neither easy nor bloodless. Cursor followed up the reconquest of Fregellae with an incursion into Samnium. Atina, a strongly fortified town to the east of Fregellae in the valley of the River Melfa, was captured and plundered. It is uncertain if the town was subsequently occupied by Rome. It was certainly under Samnite control in the early third century BC. Roman historians would be keen to ignore any Samnite military successes, unless they could be shown to have been achieved by perfidy. However, the Roman attack on Atina was perhaps motivated simply by the need for plunder rather than any great strategic objective to control the valley of the Melfa. The Samnites may have left little of value in Fregellae and especially the *arx*, because such fortresses were occupied only in emergencies. Yet long-term strategy and security in the middle Liris region was of concern to the Romans, and the decision was taken to establish a Latin colony to the south at Interamna

Lirenas (or Sucasinam), close to where the river known now as the Rapido flows into the Liris. This was one of the principal gateways of Samnium, but the Samnites controlled the mighty mountain fortress of Casinum, 5 miles upstream on the Rapido. From here the Samnites could threaten the territories of the Aurunci, Sidicini and northern Campania. Casinum was originally Volscian, but they had long been ousted by the Samnites. Interamna's appellation Sucasinam means 'under' or 'beneath Casinum', and the towering fortress casts a long shadow over the surrounding land and through the course of history: it is now better known as Monte Cassino. The colonization of Interamna was not carried out until 312 BC. The enrolment of 4,000 colonists is indicative of its importance.

Cursor's consular colleague was Iunius the Ploughman. He continued operations in Campania. Calatia, so uncomfortably close to Capua, was wrested back from the Samnites, and Bubulcus presumably also recaptured Plistica. Advancing beyond the bounds of Roman Campania, the consul forced the Nolani, close kin of the Samnites and their key allies on the plain, to surrender. They entered into a privileged alliance with Rome, perhaps with some relief. Like Luceria, Nola was caught between greater powers, and at least now she was on the winning side. The admission (or compulsion) of Nola into the alliance brought another huge swathe of Campania under Roman control. All that remained to be conquered was the south, occupied by the Alfaterni, again close kin of the Samnites and their allies in the war since 317 BC.

As well as Suessa Aurunca, the Romans established a Latin colony in 313 BC at Saticula, securing the sensitive region between Capua and Caudium. The settlers were selected and led to their allotments by three commissioners, the most notable being Valerius the Raven. Another colony was established at Pontia, located in a group of islands to the south of Tarracina in the Tyrrhenian Sea. The islands were Volscian and may have served as a base for their piracy of which Greek rulers, including Alexander the Great, had complained of to Rome. The disaster at Lautulae had demonstrated the vulnerability of the land route to Campania, and the Senate was concerned with maintaining control of the sea route from Latium to the ports of Campania.

The consuls of 312 BC were the sons of two of Rome's greatest heroes. Marcus Valerius Maximus ('the Big') was also known as Corvinus on account of him being the son of the Raven. Publius Decius Mus was the son of the glorious *devotus* of the Veseris, but a serious illness meant that he was confined to Rome and achieved nothing of note during his first consulship. When rumours reached Rome that Etruscans (specific city-states are not named) were preparing for war, Sulpicius Longus was appointed dictator with the Ploughman as his master of horse. It was they, rather than Mus, who oversaw an emergency levy of citizens of all ages, but the anticipated Etruscan attack did not materialize and the army was disbanded. (One wonders if a consular legion had been enrolled for Mus and the emergency levy was to augment this force.)

The military glory of the year went to Valerius Maximus. Livy says only that he fought the Samnites. After the victories of 314 and 313 BC, Livy states that the war was all but over and Maximus was concerned with mopping up operations. However, the *Fasti Triumphales*, an inscribed catalogue of Roman generals who celebrated triumphs set up early in the imperial era, credits Maximus with a victory (or victories) over the Samnites and Sorani. This is problematical as Livy places the recapture of rebellious Sora in 314 BC by the consuls Poetilius Libo ('the Libator') and Sulpicius Longus. According to the historian, the town was taken by a ruse. The consuls initially established their camp very close to the town, and the Sorani maintained a vigilant guard on their walls and, in case they were forced to retreat, they also piled up 'ammunition' (javelins and stones) in the fortress on the *arx* that rose up above the town. A Soran deserter advised the consuls to withdraw some 6 miles from the town as this would encourage the Sorani to lessen their guard. The consuls duly retreated and the Sorani relaxed their watch; some even returned to homes that lay close to the town. Meanwhile, the deserter led ten picked Romans up to the unmanned *arx*. The traitor returned to the lower town during the night and caused panic by declaring that the enemy had seized the *arx*. Scouts were hastily sent up the hill. The ten Romans made as much noise as possible, and probably lobbed some of the stockpiled javelins and stones in the direction of the scouts. The scouts were convinced that a strong force was indeed present, too strong for the *arx* to be recaptured. This served to fuel the uproar in the town, and the noise alerted those who had returned to homes outside the walls. They now hammered at the gates and demanded entry. As they were being admitted, the ten picked Romans made their way down from the *arx* and rushed through one of the open gates. They hacked and slashed their way through the streets. The Sorani were so terrified that they believed both consular armies had stormed into the town. Livy records that the consuls had concealed more substantial forces in woods close to the town, but they play no further part in his account. It seems that the deserter and ten picked Romans caused such chaos under the cover of darkness that the Sorani gave up before the main Roman force arrived at dawn. The town's surrender saved it from being sacked, but the consuls identified 225 of its citizens as the principle players in the rebellion, including a relative of Fabius Rullianus. They were chained and taken back to Rome. The execution of traitors was always good entertainment, and a delighted mass of vengeful plebs filled the Forum to enjoy the scourging and decapitation of the Sorani. The lucky relative of Rullianus was spared.

It is possible that Livy was in error concerning the year Sora was captured and as to the identity of the Roman commander(s). However, it may be that Maximus put down a subsequent rebellion of disgruntled Sorani or defeated a Samnite attempt to retake the town. Following his success at Sora, Maximus was called east to fight the Marrucini. As their name suggests, the Marrucini claimed descent from the war god Mars and probably maintained a tradition that one of his animal pathfinders had led them to their home on the Adriatic coast. The east of the Marrucini country was lapped by the Adriatic Sea, but to the north lay the territory of the Vestini, to the west that of the Paeligni, while to the south was that of the Frentani. The Marrucini therefore straddled part of the crucial route that the Romans relied on to bypass Samnium and send their armies into Apulia. The Marrucini may have been agitated by the passage of unruly Roman forces over the years, but more probably the realization was growing that Rome's imperialism would soon threaten their independence. We have little idea as to what Maximus achieved. A Roman assault on a place called Pollitium is recorded, but its precise location is unknown. It has been suggested that Pollitium was a minor fort or village close to Teate, the only major town of the Marrucini. If so, it is conceivable that Maximus deliberately destroyed Pollitium before moving on Teate, calculating that the example would persuade the Marrucini to surrender in order to save their capital.

The year 312 BC also witnessed the start of controversial censorship of Appius Claudius, a descendent of Attus Clausus, the Sabine warlord who migrated to Rome with his *sodales* in 504 BC. The political and religious aspects of Appius' extended tenure as censor need not concern us here, but his decision to oversee the construction of the Via Appia, a properly surveyed and cut road from Rome to Capua was of great military and strategic importance, enabling the speedy movement of troops and communications between the cities. As the Roman conquests grew, the road was gradually extended across Italy and eventually terminated at Brundisium.

War on Two Fronts: Samnium
Livy's declaration that the Great Samnite War was almost over in 312 BC is wildly off the mark. Early in 311 BC the Samnites recaptured Cluviae. Unable to take the town by storm, the Samnites starved the Roman garrison into submission. The Romans surrendered but received no mercy from the Samnites: the legionaries were scourged and beheaded. Cluviae was located in the most northerly part of Samnium, where a salient of land held by the Samnite Caraceni thrust between the territories of the Frentani and Paeligni, and pointed towards the not too distant frontier of the Marrucini. It is therefore probable that the town was captured by Valerius Maximus following his campaign against the Marrucini. As well as discomfiting the Samnites, it was

perfectly positioned for the Romans to keep watch on the Marrucini, Paeligni and Frentani, and to maintain their route to the Adriatic and Apulia.

Iunius the Ploughman (Bubulcus), in his third and final consulship, was allotted the campaign to regain Cluviae and to punish the Samnites. It is evident from Livy's account that a consular army now comprised two legions, although it is unclear if the increase in the number of consular legions began in 311 BC or if it had started some years before. Some scholars suggest the increase came into effect soon after the disaster at the Caudine Forks, but this cannot be proved. The Ploughman's powerful army stormed Cluviae in a day and massacred the Samnites. The consul then decided to advance deep into the heart of Samnium and to sack Bovianum, the capital of the Pentri. The plunder would amply reward his legionaries for their triumph at Cluviae. However, the Samnites ambushed the army as it marched south:

> Now that nothing could withstand the overwhelming might of Roman arms, neither armies nor camps nor cities, the one idea in the minds of all the Samnite leaders was to choose some position from which Roman troops when scattered on their foraging expeditions might be caught and surrounded. Some peasants who pretended to be deserters and some who had, either deliberately or by accident, been made prisoners, came to the consuls with a story in which they all agreed, and which really was true, namely, that an immense quantity of cattle had been driven into a pathless forest. The consul was induced by this story to send the legions, with nothing but their kits to encumber them, in the direction the cattle had taken, to secure them. A very strong body of the enemy were concealed on either side of the road, and when they saw that the Romans had entered the forest they suddenly raised a shout and made a tumultuous attack upon them. The suddenness of the affair at first created some confusion, while the men were piling their kits in the centre of the column and getting at their weapons, but as soon as they had each freed themselves from their burdens and put themselves in fighting trim, they began to assemble round the standards. From their old discipline and long experience they knew their places in the ranks, and the line was formed without any orders being needed, each man acting on his own initiative. The consul rode up to the part where the fighting was hottest and, leaping off his horse, called Jupiter, Mars, and other gods to witness that he had not gone into that place in quest of any glory for himself, but solely to provide booty for his soldiers, nor could any other fault be found with him except that he had been too anxious to enrich his men at the expense of the enemy.

From that disgrace nothing would clear him but the courage of his men. Only they must one and all make a determined attack. The enemy had been already worsted in the field, stripped of his camp, deprived of his cities, and was now trying the last chance by lurking secretly in ambush and trusting to his ground, not to his arms. What ground was too difficult for Roman courage? He reminded them of the citadels of Fregellae and of Sora and of the successes they had everywhere met with when the nature of the ground was all against them. Fired by his words, his men, oblivious of all difficulties, went straight at the hostile line above them. Some exertion was needed while the column were climbing up the face of the hill, but when once the leading standards had secured a footing on the summit and the army found that it was on favourable ground, it was the enemy's turn to be dismayed; they flung away their arms, and in wild flight made for the lurking-places in which they had shortly before concealed themselves. But the place which they had selected as presenting most difficulty to the enemy now became a trap for themselves, and impeded them in every way. Very few were able to escape. As many as 20,000 men were killed, and the victorious Romans dispersed in different directions to secure the cattle of which the enemy had made them a present.[32]

Livy paints a pretty picture of the consul seizing triumph from the jaws of disaster, but the fact is that he was soundly defeated and that his army, not the Samnites, sustained massive casualties. This is confirmed by Zonaras' account of the battle, itself derived from a lost section of Dio's *Roman History*:

While Iunius was pillaging their territory the Samnites conveyed their possessions into the Avernian woods, so called because on account of their denseness not even the birds fly into them. And having taken refuge there, they stationed some flocks in front of their position without shepherds or guards, and then secretly sent some pretended deserters who guided the Romans to the booty apparently lying at their disposal. But when the latter had entered the wood, the Samnites surrounded them and slaughtered them until completely exhausted.[33]

Yet Bubulcus did manage to escape and extricated at least some of his troops – no mean feat considering the desperate situation he was in – and this formed the seeds for the dramatic victory described by Livy (not necessarily Livy's invention, but quite possibly a recasting of events by his sources). The Ploughman's escape is made clear by his subsequent dedication of a temple in

Rome to Salus, the goddess of salvation, on whose aid he must have called during the battle.

There is a most interesting painted tomb from Lucanian Posidonia that, it has been suggested, may represent this defeat of the Romans. Dating to the latter fourth century BC, one painted panel on Andriuolo Tomb 114 depicts a battle. Two lines of soldiers crouch down and peer over the rims of their round shields. The soldiers in the left line are smaller than those to the right. Behind the soldiers on the left are two hills and emerging from the valley between them are the heads of massively oversized cattle. A lone warrior advances from right to left between the battle lines. The powerful figure is naked but protected by a gold or bronze-faced shield and a bronze helmet with a red crest and black side plumes. He is about to throw a javelin, a 'proto-*pilum*' with a throwing thong, at the line of soldiers to the left. The central figure is not, however, the aristocratic occupant of the tomb, who is depicted on another panel as a richly caparisoned *eques*. The prominent plumes on the helmet of the central figure in the battle scene suggest that the figure represents Mamers (Mars). The side plumes were emblematic of the war god, hence why Italian warriors, including the Romans, frequently adopted such decoration for their helmets. The emphasis on the cattle suggests the ruse employed to lure Bubulcus into the ambush in the 'Avernian' woods. If so, the troops on the right would be the Samnites and their Lucanian allies, and the notably smaller soldiers to the left would be identified as the Romans, and that Mamers intervened on the side of the Sabellians (compare the Roman claim that Mars fought with them at Thurii in 282 BC). However, this is merely supposition, for we have no evidence to suggest that the Lucanians were actively supporting the Samnites in 311 BC, and it is more likely that the painting commemorates a completely unrelated battle in which the occupant of the tomb participated.[34]

War on Two Fronts: Etruria

As in 317 BC, Bubulcus' colleague was Aemilius Little Beard (Barbula). Earlier rumours of Etruscan mobilization proved correct when it was reported that an army from all the Ertuscan states, except Arretium, had laid siege to Sutrium, Rome's most northerly outpost. There had been no hostilities with the Etruscans since 351 BC, but Rome's activities in central and southern Italy clearly demonstrated her imperialist ambitions. The claim that all but one of the Etruscan states was involved is an exaggeration; there is no evidence that Tarquinii, whose forty-year-truce was about to expire, took up arms, or that Caere broke her hundred-year-truce with Rome. Little Beard led his legions to the relief of the colony, but the repulse of the Etruscans was no easy matter. The battle was grim but inconclusive and halted by the fall of night. The Etruscans decided to retreat on account of their heavy casualties. They may not have done so had they been aware that Little Beard's legions were badly mauled and that he had more severely wounded soldiers than could be cared for.

A reinforced Etruscan army returned to Sutrium in 310/9 BC (the traditional Roman chronology is awry here, hence the approximate date), but was defeated by Fabius Rullianus, consul for the second time. He pursued the Etruscans through the Ciminus – he was the first Roman general to force the passage of the heavily forested mountains; the much earlier Roman raid on Volsinii was made by way of the Tiber valley. The consul then ravaged the country north of the Ciminus and defeated a second Etruscan army at Perusia. Rullianus compelled that city, along with Arretium and Cortona, to accept truces of thirty years; all three had presumably supplied contingents to that army that laid siege to Sutrium for the second time or opposed Rullianus at Perusia. Perusia was located on the border with Umbria and Rullianus crossed over the frontier to plunder, batting aside a hastily levied army. Most interestingly, Camerinum, a leading Umbrian state, welcomed Rullianus, revictualled his field army and entered into a formal alliance with Rome. Like Arpi in Apulia, Camerinum must have struggled with other city-states for regional hegemony and viewed the Romans as powerful allies in achieving that aim. Camerinum would also have welcomed Rome's aid against the threat posed by the Senones.

Rullianus was called from the north to fight one final battle with the Etruscans. His daring penetration into northern Etruria and Umbria exposed Rome to danger: the route down the Tiber valley was unprotected. The Etruscan states had suffered such heavy casualties that a new army had to be levied by a *lex sacrata*, a sacred law, which compelled men to serve and to swear an oath to the war god Laran (or their city's patron deity) that they would conquer or die. The lives of those who fled from the battle line were forfeit to the gods. The Etruscans mustered at Lake Vadimon in the Tiber valley, and this suggests that a considerable portion of the troops came from Volsinii. The small lake fascinated the ancients on account of it being almost perfectly round with wandering islands of reeds, and, above all, for its cloudy blue sulphorous water, which suggested the *numina* of the gods. This was clear evidence of its sacredness and an appropriate place for an army raised by *lex sacrata* to make its stand, but according to the nineteenth century traveller George Dennis, the Etruscans must also have been influenced by the lie of the land about the lake:

> Whoever visits the Vadimon, will comprehend how it was that decisive battles were fought upon its shores. The valley here forms the natural pass into the inner or central plain of Etruria. It is a spot, indeed, very like the field of Thrasymene – a low, level tract, about a

mile wide, hemmed in between the heights and the Tiber, which here takes the place of that lake; but the heights rise more steeply and loftily than those by the Thrasymene [Lake Trasimene], and are even now densely covered with wood, as no doubt they were in ancient times, this being part of the celebrated Ciminian forest.[35]

Also, if the Etruscans defeated Rullianus, they could sweep down the Tiber valley and devastate the unguarded *ager Romanus*. It is unlikely that they would make an attempt on Rome itself, but the city was only two or three days' march distant. Livy's stirring account of the battle is worth quoting in full:

> So savage was the feeling on both sides that, without discharging a single missile, they began the fight at once with swords. The fury displayed in the combat, which long hung in the balance, was such that it seemed as though it was not the Etruscans who had been so often defeated that we were fighting with, but some new, unknown people. There was not the slightest sign of yielding anywhere. As the *antesignani* [= *hastati*] fell, those in the second line [*principes*] took their places, to defend the standards. At length the last reserves [*triarii*] had to be brought up, and to such an extremity of toil and danger had matters come that the Roman cavalry dismounted, and, leaving their horses in charge, made their way over piles of armour and heaps of slain to the front ranks of the infantry. They appeared like a fresh army amongst the exhausted combatants, and at once threw the Etruscan standards into confusion. The rest of the men, worn out as they were, nevertheless followed up the cavalry attack, and at last broke through the enemy's ranks. Their determined resistance was now overcome, and when once their maniples began to give way, they soon took to actual flight. That day broke for the first time the power of the Etruscans after their long-continued and abundant prosperity. The main strength of their army was left on the field, and their camp was taken and plundered.[36]

The details were mostly invented by Livy, or by the historians on which he drew, to create a gripping example of how one of the desperate battles of the conquest period was fought. However, the mechanics of the Romans' triple line formation do reflect reality; Livy applies similar line relief or replacement manoeuvres to the other battles of the Etruscan war. Furthermore, Livy implies that the cavalry were to the rear of the Roman battle line for most of the engagement. The relatively narrow battle ground between the Tiber and the high ground to the west may have precluded the cavalry from taking up its usual position on the flanks, and the description of the *equites* dismounting and having to clamber over the dead and wounded to reach the front rank may have derived from the aristocratic ballad tradition. Finally, the description of the Etruscans abandoning their missiles, fighting with swords, and being organized in maniples was perhaps no more than guesswork by Livy. The traditional view fostered by the Roman historians is that the Etruscans fought in a close order phalanx, with hoplite-type shields overlapping, and using thrusting spears as their principal weapon, but it is clear from archaeological finds, mostly from tombs, that the Etruscans employed various javelins, including *pila*. The use of javelins required battle lines to be fairly loose affairs, and the maniple, as employed by the Romans and Samnites, was the most suitable subunit for javelin and sword-armed warriors to fight effectively. So Livy's reconstruction was probably not too far from the truth.

The Last Years of the Great War
While Rullianus was cutting a swathe though Etruria, his consular colleague advanced across the middle Volturnus and seized Allifae from the Samnites. This was the high point of the campaign of Gaius Marcius Rutilus, son of the famed plebeian dictator. As we have seen, Allifae was captured at the start of the war, but perhaps only plundered and destroyed and then abandoned by the Romans. It may be that the Romans did install a garrison in the strategic site – well-placed as it was to control the middle Volturnus region – but later Roman historians would be keen to ignore any Samnite success in retaking the town, especially if achieved in a fair fight and without treachery or ruses.

Rutilus also captured a few other minor forts and villages, but was then defeated in a major battle, presumably fought in the Volturnus region. Many equestrians, military tribunes and a legate were killed, and the consul was badly wounded. The Roman army retreated to a place called Longulae. The Senate decided to appoint a dictator to take over the remnants of Rutilus' army: Papirius Cursor was the senators' choice. However, according to law a dictator had to be named by one of the consuls. Rutilus was stranded in enemy territory and it was well known that Rullianus still hated Cursor. A delegation of former consuls was sent to Rullianus' camp in Etruria to persuade him to name Cursor as dictator. The consul procrastinated for a time, then relented. Now formally appointed, Cursor assumed command of extra legions raised in connection with the Etruscan War, nominated the Ploughman to be his master of horse, and chose Decius Mus and the Raven as his cavalry commanders. The return of Iunius Bubulcus to high command so soon after his debacle in Samnium may seem surprising, but unless a general had been shown to be particularly ineffectual, foolish or cowardly, it was not uncommon for him to regain prominence. Blame for defeats was usually pinned on treacherous enemies or cowardly legionaries – recall how Rullianus decimated his legions after Lautulae.

Cursor advanced to Longulae and found the consul's camp besieged by a powerful Samnite army. The Samnite League had raised the army by a *lex sacrata* and it may be that, as in 295 BC when another army of Samnite *sacrati* was formed, the lives of the warriors were sworn to Jupiter, most powerful of the Italic gods. Livy tells us that the Samnites formed two divisions, one in silver armour, the other in gold. This has been dismissed as invention, but it is possible that warriors who had sworn to conquer or die would line up for battle resplendent in their finest armour and insignia that marked out the bravest men. Like Rullianus at Vadimon, Cursor vanquished these sacred warriors. Commanding the left wing of the Roman army, Bubulcus was keen to atone for his defeat near Bovianum and led a furious opening attack. Aware that the Samnites were *sacri*, he roared to his men that they would sacrifice them now to Orcus, the god of the dead. Cursor's wing followed, not to be out done by the Ploughman's legionaries, but the cavalry sealed the victory when the Rat and the Raven led their *turmae* around the flanks of the enemy.

The Battle of Longulae was a turning point in the Great Samnite War. It was not the last battle; hostilities would continue until 304 BC, and the Samnites would enjoy other successes, as well as endure more defeats, but it was beginning of the end.

In 308 BC Fabius Rullianus and Decius Mus were elected consuls on account of their military successes in the previous year. It was the first of three consulships that they would share. Mus was assigned the Etruscan and Umbrian theatre; Rullianus began his campaigning season with unfinished business in southern Campania. The Alfaterni, allies of the Samnites, remained undefeated. A Roman raid on Nuceria Alfaterna in 310/9 BC was a miserable failure. The Roman troops were transported by sea and landed at Pompeii – one of only two Roman naval operations in the Conquest period. On land the Romans became more concerned with plundering than obtaining their primary objective, and the Alfaterni chased them back to the sea. Now confronted with Rullianus' consular army, the Alfaterni offered to make peace but this was refused. The consul was determined to make his point: the Alfaterni had to endure a period under siege before their surrender was accepted. They were enrolled into the Roman alliance. Rome now controlled all of Campania, either directly or through alliance.

Rullianus took his army north, probably to the middle Liris valley. The Samnites had mustered another army and received reinforcements from the Marsi, previously loyal to Rome. This army was defeated and Rullianus proceeded into the territory of the Paeligni, whose forces were no match for that of the consul. Like the Marrucini and Marsi, the Paeligni were surely aware that alliance with Rome and allowing her armies to traverse their territory would ultimately result in the loss of independence. They may have heard reports that the Romans intended to drive a road through the neighbouring territory of the Aequi and to establish a colony at Alba Fucens, both of which would consolidate Rome's grip on the very heart of Italy. The construction of the military highway, the Via Valeria, began in c. 307 BC. The colonization of Alba Fucens occurred in 303 BC, after the Romans had completed the annihilation of the hated Aequi (see Chapter 5).

In 307 BC Rullianus's *imperium* was prorogued, much to the annoyance of the new consuls, Appius Claudius and Lucius Volumnius Flamma Violens, who were concerned that the proconsul would overshadow their attempts to win military glory. Livy reports that Appius remained in Rome, preferring to hone his civil powers, but this is most probably false, an invention by one or more of Livy's sources that were hostile to the controversial Appius. The so-called *elogium*, an inscription on a statue of Appius set up in Rome by the emperor Augustus (reigned 27 BC–AD 14), lists his magisterial and military accomplishments, and drawing on a more reliable tradition, states that Appius 'captured many Samnite towns'; his first term as consul in 307 BC is the most likely date for this activity. Flamma Violens ('the Raging fire and Violent'!) took his consular army into southern Apulia and Calabria, operating against the Sallentini, presumably allies of the Samnites. He endeared himself to the troops by leading them to victory in a number of pitched battles and making generous distributions of the booty taken from the defeated armies and from the many captured towns (the names of the towns and battle sites are not recorded). The consuls were clearly energetic in their pursuit of glory and in combating the Samnites, but as they feared, it was Rullianus who scored the most notable victory.

The Samnites were determined to win back strategic Allifae, but when advancing on the town they encountered Rullianus and were forced to retreat to their camp. The proconsul surrounded the camp and, following negotiations, the Samnites surrendered. The Samnite warriors were allowed to go free – after they had been stripped of their arms and armour and forced under the yoke wearing only a tunic. This was the same humiliation that Gavius Pontius inflicted on the consular armies at the Caudine Forks. In both episodes, the warriors would have passed under the yoke ungirded. In ancient Italy the belt (*cingulum*) was a symbol of status, manhood and militarism. The Samnites, Lucani, Campanians, Bruttii, Apuli and others proudly wore the bronze belt, and it was therefore regarded as a prized item of plunder. Tomb paintings from Capua and Nola, dating to the later fourth century BC, depict noble Campanian warriors brandishing bronze belts stripped from their conquered enemies. The form of belt worn by the Romans at this time is uncertain, but it's clear from later military punishments, for example in 210 BC when Marcellus made centurions of defeated maniples parade without swords or belts, that the loss of the *cingulum* was also a particular disgrace for the Romans.

It is most probable that the freed Samnites were met with derision when they returned home, and only after redeeming themselves in combat would they have been accepted back into society. But at least they were free. In the negotiations with the unnamed Samnite commander, Rullianus made no provision for the release of the Samnites' 7,000 surviving allies. These unfortunates were to be sold as slaves – war had to be profitable as well as glorious. While sorting the captives it was discovered that a number were Hernican. The Hernici were locally autonomous, but the cities of Anagnia and Frusino wanted real independence from Rome and threw in their lot with the Samnites. Frusino was of no great concern as it was surrounded by the still loyal Hernican states of Aletrium, Ferentinum and Verulae, but Anagnia was located in the north of the Hernican country and on the main route to Rome via the Algidus pass: Rome itself was a mere 40 miles from Anagnia. Samnite control of this crucial route, which would also drive a wedge between Rome and the middle Liris, could not be countenanced. The Hernican war was assigned to the consul Quintus Marcius Tremulus (his *cognomen* translates as 'Trembler') in 306 BC. His campaign was brief, but initially met with little success as the rebel Hernici and their Samnite allies, and perhaps also some Aequi, concentrated on securing all strategic points and severing communications between the consul and his colleague, Cornelius Arvina, who was progressing to the Samnite theatre. Fear grew in Rome and an emergency levy was enforced but the Trembler did not require reinforcements from his colleague or the new levy. The Anagnini and other rebellious Hernici lost their nerve after the consul chased their forces out of three camps in as many days:

> The bargained for a truce of thirty days to enable them to send envoys to the Senate in Rome, and delivered up two months' pay (*stipendia*) and grain and a tunic for every soldier. The Senate sent them back to Marcius, having passed a resolution empowering him to deal with the Hernici as he saw fit. He received their submission on terms of unconditional surrender.[37]

Anagnia and Frusino were annexed to the *ager Romanus*, and their inhabitants enrolled as particularly second-class citizens. They were made citizens without the vote, but even worse, they were denied the usual rights of consorting with, marrying or conducting business with other Roman or Latin citizens. The loyal Hernican states – Aletrium, Ferentinum, Verulae – were invited to become

Roman citizens, presumably with the full citizenship, but they preferred to maintain their distinct identity as allies, enjoying local self-rule and living by their traditional laws and customs. The Hernici would also have known that full Roman citizens were liable to more frequent military service.

Following his success in the Trerus valley, Tremulus took his army into the Liris or Volturnus regions and won a major victory against a Samnite army. Livy reports that he went to the aid of Arvina (son of the original Cornelius the Greasy), who had been trapped and was running out of supplies. However, it is more likely that Arvina was far away in Apulia, as the historian Diodorus Siculus reports the capture of Silvium from the Samnites. The town was stormed after some days, 5,000 captives and a considerable amount of booty were taken. However, the Samnites did succeed in recapturing Sora and also took Caiatia (above the Volturnus) in 306 BC. Tremulus' victory was probably over a force that had been sent to recapture another strategic stronghold, such as Fregellae, Interamna or Allifae. The scale of Tremulus' achievements is indicated by the honours he received on his return to Rome. He was awarded with a triumph (celebrated 29 June) and, most unusually, an equestrian statue of the consul was set up in front of the temple of Castor in the Forum.

The Samnites took Sora and Caiatia by storm and, as was common, the Roman garrisons were massacred and the civilian inhabitants enslaved. Caiatia provided the Samnites with a particularly good base for incursions down the Volturnus and into northern Campania. In 305 BC they raided the rich *campus Stellatis* and *ager Falernus*. These may have been probes in advance of a more substantial invasion: the occupation of this country would drive a wedge between Latium and Campania, as had been achieved in 315 BC. However, the Romans were determined to put an end to the long running war and reacted to the raids by launching a massive assault on western Samnium that resulted in the capture of Pentrian Bovianum and the expulsion of the Samnites from Sora and elsewhere in the middle Liris region. It was the decisive campaign of the war and convinced the Samnites to sue for peace, but it did not run smoothly for the Romans. The principle sources are, as ever, problematical:

> Both consuls accordingly were despatched to Samnium. Postumius [Megellus] marched to Tifernum, Minucius [Augurinus] made Bovianum his objective. Postumius was the first to come into touch with the enemy and a battle was fought at Tifernum. Some authorities state that the Samnites were thoroughly beaten and 24,000 prisoners taken. According to others the battle was an indecisive one, and Postumius, in order to create an impression that he was afraid of the enemy, withdrew by night into the mountains, whither the enemy followed him and took up an entrenched position 2 miles

away from him. To keep up the appearance of having sought a safe and commodious place for a standing camp – and such it really was – the consul strongly entrenched himself and furnished his camp with all necessary stores. Then, leaving a strong detachment to hold it, he started at the third watch and led his legions in light marching order by the shortest possible route to his colleague, who was also encamped in front of another Samnite army. Acting on Postumius' advice Minucius engaged the enemy, and after the battle had gone on for the greater part of the day without either side gaining the advantage, Postumius brought up his fresh legions and made an unsuspected attack upon the enemy's wearied lines. Exhausted by fighting and by wounds they were incapable of flight and were practically annihilated. Twenty-one standards were captured. Both armies marched to the camp which Postumius had formed, and there they routed and dispersed the enemy, who were demoralised by the news of the previous battle. Twenty-six standards were captured, the commander-in-chief of the Samnites, Statius Gellius, and a large number of men were made prisoners, and both camps were taken. The next day they commenced an attack on Bovianum, which was soon taken, and the consuls after their brilliant successes celebrated a joint triumph. Some authorities assert that the consul Minucius was carried back to the camp severely wounded and died there, and that M. Fulvius was made consul in his place, and after taking over the command of Minucius' army effected the capture of Bovianum. During the year Sora, Arpinum, and Cesennia were recovered from the Samnites. The great statue of Hercules was also set up and dedicated in the Capitol.[38]

So Livy reports three battles. The first at 'Tifernum' (probably a mountain in the Montagna del Matese rather than a Samnite town or fortress) was indecisive and Lucius Postumius Megellus retreated to link up with Tiberius Minicius Augurinus ('the Soothsayer'). The combined consular armies then routed the Samnites in two great battles. To crown this success, the Samnite commander, Statius Gellius, was captured. He has been seen by some as the mastermind behind the Samnites' capture of Sora, Caiatia and raids into Campania. The consuls proceeded to capture Bovianum. However, Livy notes another tradition where Augurinus was killed. It was rare for a consul to be killed or severely wounded in battle, unless his army had suffered defeat (compare Marcius Rutilus in 310/9 BC). The feigned retreat by Megellus is also suspicious. Rather than a drawn battle, did Gellius also defeat him? As we have seen, early Roman historians were prone to covering up or watering down Roman defeats.

The *Fasti Triumphales* (register of triumphs) agrees with the other tradition noted by Livy, recording that Marcus Fulvius Curvus Paetinus was elected suffect (replacement) consul. This is an interesting development; it was usual for a dictator to be appointed in a time of military emergency. Paetinus, whose *cognomen* means 'Blinker' or 'Winker', was probably the son of consul of 322 BC from Tusculum. The *Fasti Triumphales* also indicates that Paetinus was awarded a triumph for the defeat of the Samnites. It is possible, then, that Gellius was successful against Megellus and proceeded to inflict a heavy defeat on the army of Augurinus. The situation was retrieved when Paetinus arrived from Rome to take over Augurinus' army. He presumably combined forces with Megellus. That consul would have played his part in the defeat and capture of Gellius and the conquest of Bovianum, but he was such a controversial figure with many political enemies, that it is no surprise that the Senate denied him a triumph. The *cognomen* Megellus, derived from the Greek for 'great', is indicative of the patrician consul's ambitious and overbearing character. It is uncertain who recaptured Sora, perhaps it was a pro-magistrate, and the Romans did not halt there. They advanced southwards and stormed Arpinum, an important hill fortress that the Samnites had seized from the Volsci and held since the middle of the century. The location of Cesennia is unknown, but it was presumably also in the middle Liris region. The dedicator of the statue of Hercules is not known, but it was probably made in connection with the successes against the Samnites and is evidence for the development of a Greek-style cult of Victory.

We may compare Livy's account of the fighting of 305 BC with that of his immediate predecessor, Diodorus Siculus:

> Since the Samnites were plundering the Ager Falernus, the consuls took the field against them, and in the battle that followed the Romans were victorious. They took 20 standards and made prisoners of more than 2,000 soldiers. The consuls at once took the city of Bola, but Gellius Gaius, the leader of the Samnites, appeared with 6,000 soldiers. A hard-fought battle took place in which Gellius himself was made prisoner, and of the other Samnites most were cut down but some were captured alive.[39]

Diodorus goes on to note the recapture of Sora and the conquest of Arpinum and 'Serennia', presumably identical with Livy's Cesennia. Diodorus also refers to a Roman campaign against the Paeligni, apparently prior to the fighting in Campania and Samnium.

Diodorus' account differs considerably from Livy's. There are only two battles. The first is fought in Campania – the consuls having to kick the Samnite invaders out before progressing to Samnium. 'Bola' is not the city of the Aequi, but the error of Diodorus or a copyist for Bovianum. Note how the consuls capture the town prior to fighting Gellius. Diodorus' figure for the size of Gellius' army, as well as the number of Samnite captives taken in Campania, is a fraction of the numbers given by Livy. Even if the consuls' armies lacked Latin or allied contingents, and that is most unlikely, their four legions would have outnumbered Gellius' 6,000 soldiers by four-to-one.

It is difficult to completely reconcile the accounts of Livy and Diodorus (who was also unaware of the suffect consul), but both agree on the capture of Bovianum, the defeat and capture of Gellius, and Rome's successes in the Liris Valley. Having suffered a series of serious defeats, in which many soldiers were killed or captured, unable to maintain their conquests in the Liris or to drive the Romans from Allifae or Luceria, the chief magistrates (*meddices*) of the Samnite League sued for peace. In 304 BC the new consul Publius Sempronius Sophus and his legions traversed Samnium without opposition. In fact, the Samnites provided the army with supplies. Sophus (derived from the Greek for 'wise') recommended that the Senate restore the 'ancient' treaty of alliance with the Samnites. That is the original treaty of 354 BC, presumably with clauses advantageous to Rome, such as recognizing her conquests, alliances and general hegemony in central and southern Italy. The war was over, and the Samnites were fortunate not to have suffered further confiscations of territory beyond those which they had lost during the course of the hostilities. Minus the losses in the middle Liris and at Luceria, Saticula and Allifae, the bounds of Samnium were much as they were in the middle of the fourth century BC, but now Roman colonies and allied states and peoples almost encircled her.

On 5 October 305 BC Fulvius the Blinker led his legions in triumphal procession, wending their way through Rome and up to the temple of Jupiter on the Capitol, where the *triumphator* would perform a sacrifice. We hear no more of Statius Gellius after his capture, but he was doubtless the chief attraction of the procession. Of all the captives and notable spoils being paraded, the war leader of the Samnites would have attracted the most attention, and like most prominent captives, he was presumably dragged off to execution after being displayed to the plebeian masses.

Chapter 5

Tota Italia

Consolidation

When hostilities with the Samnites ceased in 304 BC, Rome's grip on peninsular Italy was already becoming tight. Roman arms had been carried into the Sallentine Peninsula (the heel of Italy), and a Roman garrison had been installed, if temporarily, as far north as Perusia in Etruria. New Latin colonies dominated northern Campania, the Liris Valley, western Samnium and the Samnite-Apulian frontier. Old enemies had been bullied into accepting further long periods of truce or scared into requesting treaties of alliance. For example, in 308 BC Decius Mus coerced Tarquinii into provisioning his consular army and accepting a new truce of forty years' duration. He also cowed Volsinii by storming some of her outlying fortresses and she was forced to seek annual truces to avoid further incursions. It is notable however, that Mus and subsequent Roman generals were unable or unwilling to capture major fortified cities like Volsinii. Fabius Rullianus' incursion into Umbria in 310/9 BC had stirred up considerable resentment. A further victory over the Umbrians is ascribed to Rullianus in 308 BC, but it seems more probable that it was Mus who soundly defeated the Umbrian army that had mustered at Mevania. More Umbrians were taken captive than were killed in the battle and that level of resistance only prompted the Romans to think of further conquests in the region. A treaty of friendship was promptly negotiated with Ocriculum, which was strategically located in the very south of Umbria at the confluence of the rivers Tiber and Nar. In 303 BC both consular armies were sent into southern Umbria to deal with 'bandits' and scored a victory in, of all places, a complex of caves. Ocriculum was clearly on side when, in 300 BC, the Romans embarked on the siege of nearby Nequinum, located in the lower valley of the Nar. Eventually captured in 299 BC through a combination of tunnelling and treachery by Fulvius Paetinus (it is uncertain if he is the same man as the suffect consul of 305 BC), the town was promptly colonized and renamed Narnia, after the river. Nequinum, reminiscent of Latin *nequam*, meaning 'worthless', 'bad' and so forth, sounded ill-omened to Roman ears. With a strong ally in Camerinum to the north, and a major 'bridgehead' at Narnia in the south, the Umbrian states rightly feared further Roman expansion. The Romans were also busy fighting the Sabines, whose territory lay between northeast Latium, the Aequan country and Umbria. It was becoming clear that Rome would not be satisfied until *tota Italia*, all Italy, was under her control.

Rome's behaviour immediately following the Samnite peace in 304 BC was a clear indicator of her intentions. War was declared on the Aequi, now located in the upper valley of the Anio and to the north of the Fucine Lake. Bands of Aequan warriors had fought for the Hernici and Samnites, probably on a mercenary basis, but the Aequi as a whole had not been allied to the enemy. In fact, the Aequi as a nation had probably not fought in any major war since their ejection from Latium, but the Senate had found the necessary excuse to continue the work of extermination that had been carried out so ruthlessly in 388 BC. In 307/6 BC work began on Rome's second great strategic highway, the Via Valeria, running east from Rome it would eventually terminate at lofty Alba Fucens, above the Fucine Lake, at the eastern edge of the Aequan country. This was the perfect location for a colony to dominate the very centre of Italy. Having not fought on any great scale for almost a century, the Aequi dared not meet the Roman invaders in open battle and instead took to their hill-top forts, but the legions were unstoppable: forty hill forts fell in fifty days and no mercy was shown to the defenders. The neighbouring tribes – Marsi, Paeligni, Marrucini and Frentani – were shocked at the speed of the conquest and quickly patched up new treaties with Rome. The Vestini followed suit in 302/1 BC.

Alba Fucens was duly colonized in 303 BC with no fewer than 6,000 adult males, the most powerful yet of Rome's new Latin foundations, and with a huge territory that included country confiscated from the Marsi. The Marsi duly revolted but were soon forced into submission by Valerius Corvus (302/1 BC). The desperate Aequi continued to resist the Roman occupation, providing old generals such as the Ploughman (in 302/1 BC) and the Raven again (300 BC) with easy victories; Bubulcus took less than week to complete his campaign. By 299 BC the resistance of the Aequi had come to an end, and a swathe of their territory in the upper Anio region was reorganized as *ager Romanus* and assigned to the appropriately named voting tribe Aniensis. In c. 298 BC a remnant of the Aequi, known by the disparaging diminutive Aequicoli, were ousted from the town of Carseoli. Lying on the new Via Valeria half way between Latium and Alba Fucens, it was re-established as a Latin colony with 4,000 adult male settlers.

Consolidation of the middle Liris was achieved by re-establishing Sora as a Latin colony (with 4,000 adult male colonists), and Arpinum was incorporated into the *ager Romanus*, its inhabitants becoming citizens without the vote. As we have seen, Anagnia was annexed in 306 BC, and the territory of Frusino was added to the *ager Romanus* either in that year or in 303 BC. Along with the annexations in the Aequan country (to which should be added Trebula

The arx of Sora, key battle site on the middle Liris front during the Second Samnite War. Rome took it from the Volsci in 345 BC, but strategic Sora was captured, or persuaded to rebel, several times by the Samnites. (© *Lawrence Keppie*)

Arpinum is typical of the fortified hill towns fought over in the Samnite Wars. Originally established by the Volscians, it was conquered by the Samnites in the middle of the fourth century BC, and finally captured by Rome in 305 BC and incorporated in the *ager Romanus*. (© *Lawrence Keppie*)

The forum at Alba Fucens, one of the Latin colonies established by Rome to control her new conquests. Founded in 303 BC to dominate the very heart of Italy, its territory was massive, taking in not only Aequan country, but also a chunk of Marsian land. (© *Lawrence Keppie*)

(*Left*) Italian bronze cuirass of uncertain provenance, but dating to the later fourth century BC and inscribed with the Sabellian name, Nonios Bannios (= Novius Fannius). It is conceivable that this cuirass was taken from a Roman by a Samnite commander named Fannius at the Caudine Forks, inscribed with his name and dedicated in a temple in commemoration of the great Samnite victory (321 BC). (© *Author*)

(*Right*) Tomb painting from Capua of the fourth century BC, showing a wealthy Campanian *eques* in a horned helmet and carrying a *scutum*. It is unlikely that a horseman would use such a shield; the *scutum* represents spoils taken by the *eques* in battle, perhaps from a Samnite. (*RHC Archive*)

Tomb painting from Nola, showing Campanian warriors brandishing the spoils stripped from their conquered enemies: bronze belts and a richly decorated tunic. Later fourth century BC. (*RHC Archive*)

Roman legionary (right), with a *scutum*, Montefortino helmet and pectoral armour typical of the mid-fourth to early third century BC, battles an Etruscan noble (left), whose equipment, including the weighted *pilum*, is modelled after a late fourth century BC tomb painting from Tarquinii. (© *Graham Sumner*)

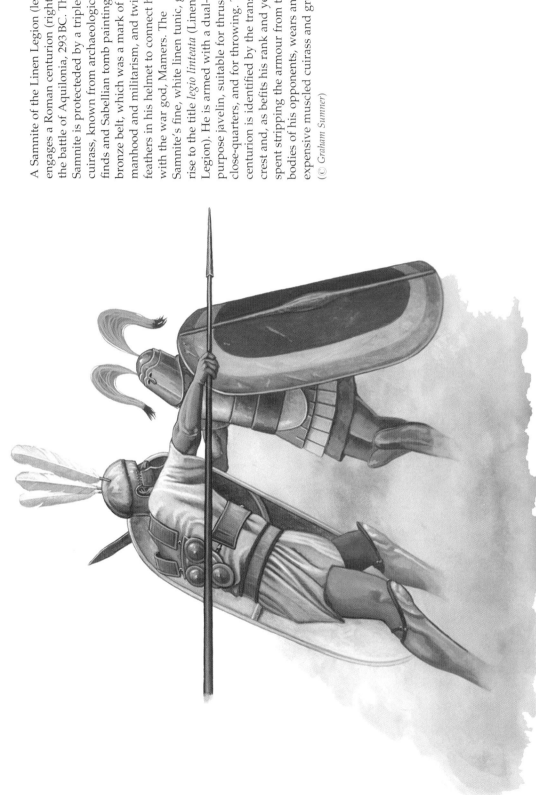

A Sammite of the Linen Legion (left) engages a Roman centurion (right) at the battle of Aquilonia, 293 BC. The Samnite is protecteded by a triple disc cuirass, known from archaeological and finds and Sabellian tomb paintings, the bronze belt, which was a mark of Italic manhood and militarism, and twin feathers in his helmet to connect him with the war god, Mamers. The Samnite's fine, white linen tunic, gave rise to the title *legio linteata* (Linen Legion). He is armed with a dual-purpose javelin, suitable for thrusting at close-quarters, and for throwing. The centurion is identified by the transverse crest and, as befits his rank and years spent stripping the armour from the bodies of his opponents, wears an expensive muscled cuirass and greaves.

(© *Graham Sumner*)

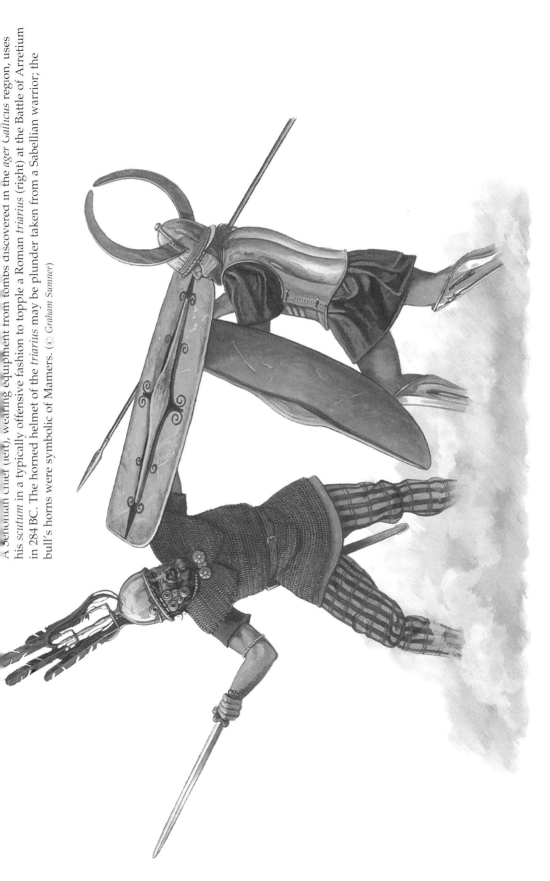

A Senonian chief (left), wearing equipment from tombs discovered in the *ager Gallicus* region, uses his *scutum* in a typically offensive fashion to topple a Roman *triarius* (right) at the Battle of Arretium in 284 BC. The horned helmet of the *triarius* may be plunder taken from a Sabellian warrior; the bull's horns were symbolic of Mamers. (© *Graham Sumner*)

A Latin ally (left), wearing a cuirass made up of small metal plates modelled after the a census scene incised on a bronze box from Latium, uses his *scutum* to swipe at a soldier of the Tarentine levy (right). c. 280–272 BC. The Tarentine is equipped in typical 'hoplite' battle gear, including a long, thrusting spear for phalanx fighting, but is also armed with light javelins for fighting from a distance and perhaps even skirmishing. (© *Graham Sumner*)

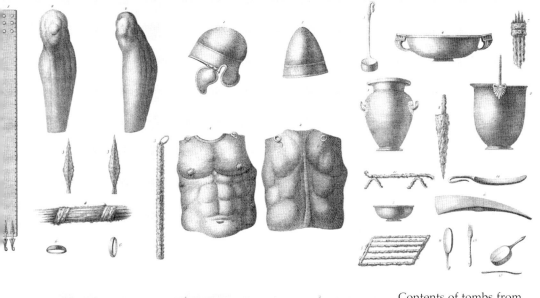

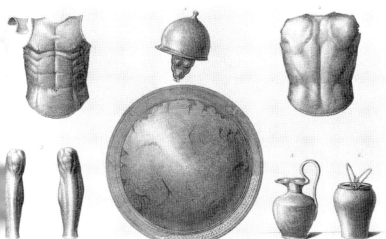

Contents of tombs from Lucanian Posidonia (above) and Etruscan Volsinii (left), showing the bronze panoplies of aristocratic warriors, and also the wares and tools symbolic of their high status. Mid-fourth to early third centuries BC. (*Author's collection*)

Section of a late fourth century BC tomb painting from Posidonia, depicting Mamers fighting with his Lucanian children. It has been suggested that the painting refers to the defeat of Iunius Bubulcus in 311 BC. (© *Krista Ubbels*)

(*Left*) Tarentine silver coinage from the period of Pyrrhus' control of the city, 281–272 BC. All three coins depict a war elephant, suggesting they were minted in celebration of the joint Tarentine-Epirote victory over the Romans at Heraclea. The bottom coin also depicts the murex, from which valuable scarlet dye was obtained, and another source of Tarentum's wealth. The dolphin and rider were symbols of Tarentum, while her strength in cavalry is emphasised by the horsemen, one of whom is crowned by Nike (top). (*Carelli, 1850*)

(*Right*) More coins from the Pyrrhic period in Tarentum. Top and bottom, silver issues reflecting the prowess of Tarentine cavalry, but the top dolphin rider carries a distaff, symbolic of Tarentum's wool production, while under the bottom dolphin rider is a ship's prow, symbolic of Tarentine sea power. The middle coin (gold) bears typical Molossian motifs, the head of Zeus and his eagle, clutching a thunder bolt, but the Tarentines included amphorae symbolic of their important cult of the Dioscuri (cf. the star of the Dioscuri on the shield of the top cavalryman). (*Carelli, 1850*)

Shoulder plates of a fourth centuy BC bronze cuirass of Tarentine manufacture, found in the River Siris. Part of Tarentum's vast wealth stemmed from the export of fine bronze armour, but it is possible that this cuirass was lost by a Tarentine fighting the Lucanians in defence of Heraclea. (*Author's collection*)

Suffenas) and the establishment of the voting tribe Terentia on former Auruncan land, directly-ruled Roman territory dominated west-central Italy. By 290 BC *ager Romanus* would run in an unbroken belt across the peninsula, but before that was achieved Rome had to defeat a grand coalition of Italian peoples led by the resilient Samnites.

The Early Years of the Third Samnite War

As readers will have noticed, ancient Italy was a frighteningly violent land. Just as the Romans fought to drive the Volsci and Aequi from Latium, those peoples now threatened with Roman domination would not give up without a fight. For example, in 302/1 BC the aged but agile Valerius Corvus slaughtered rebellious Etruscans from Arretium and Rusellae as well as Marsian mal-contents. Various Etruscan city-states were to prove troublesome for the next forty years, either individually or in alliance.[40] The Samnites sought to exploit this resistance and cement new alliances.

The Etruscans and Umbrians were threatened not only by the Romans, but also by the Gauls. The Gallic peoples of the Po Valley and Adriatic coast found themselves under pressure from a new wave of Gauls crossing the Alps. Gallic incursions into the peninsula were now as much concerned with conquering new lands for settlement as with the acquisition of plunder. In 299 BC Gauls, probably Senones, invaded northern Etruria, but through negotiations and bribes they were actually persuaded (perhaps in part by the Samnites) to ally themselves with the Etruscans, and instead of pillaging Etruria they marched further south and raided the *ager Romanus*. This caused the Romans to look for allies in the north. The Picentes, whose territory lay between Umbria and the Adriatic Sea, had long been subject to the violent attentions of the Senones who occupied the northern marches of Picenum, and readily entered into alliance with the city well known for her hatred of the Gauls. The Picentes informed the Romans that the Samnites had also been courting them. Between 297 and 296 BC the full extent of the new Samnite alliance became clear: the League had won over Apulians, Umbrians, Etruscans, Senones, Sabines and perhaps part of the Marsi. One suspects that the Picentes chose Rome over the Samnites in 299 BC because the latter had already entered into negotiations with the despised Gauls.

The Third Samnite War broke out in 298 BC, but not because of the Samnites' machinations in the north of the peninsula. In order to bolster its military strength the Samnite League first attempted to persuade the Lucanians to join it. The Lucanians, briefly allied to Rome at the start of the Second Samnite War, were quickly persuaded by Tarentum to renounce that alliance, but appear to have played little if any part in the long conflict. As we have seen, Lucania was subject to a punitive Roman incursion in 317 BC and it has been suggested that a contingent from Posidonia helped the Samnites to defeat Iunius Bubulcus near Bovianum in 311 BC. However, the Lucani appear to have taken advantage of the Samnites' preoccupation with Rome to extend their power into the deep south of Italy and threatened the Greek cities of Magna Graecia. The rapprochement with Tarentum did not last, and in 303 BC the Tarentines called on the aid of their mother city, Sparta (see Chapter 6). However, the Spartan prince Cleonymous was more concerned with establishing his own kingdom than with defending the lands and interests of Tarentum, and the Tarentines turned against him. Prior to the split with Tarentum, Cleonymous had defeated the Lucanians and it may have been then that the Samnite League first made its approach. The ambassadors were rebuffed and the Samnites decided to bring the Lucani over by force. The Lucani then remembered their old friendship with Rome and appealed to the Senate for aid. The consuls of 298 BC, Gnaeus Fulvius Centumalus (meaning 'a Hundred Misfortunes') and Lucius Cornelius Scipio Barbatus drove the Samnites from Lucania and raided the south of Samnium. Interestingly, Centumalus inflicted two defeats on the Samnites by means of ambush:

> When Fulvius Nobilior was leading his army from Samnium against the Lucanians, and had learned from deserters that the enemy intended to attack his rearguard, he ordered his bravest legion to go in advance, and the baggage train to follow in the rear. The enemy, regarding this circumstance as a favourable opportunity, began to plunder the baggage. Fulvius then marshalled five cohorts of the legion I have mentioned above on the right side of the road, and five on the left. Then, when the enemy were intent on plundering, Fulvius, deploying his troops on both flanks, enveloped the foe and cut them to pieces.[41]

> The same Nobilior on one occasion was hard pressed from the rear by the enemy, as he was on the march. Across his route ran a stream, not so large as to prevent passage, but large enough to cause delay by the swiftness of the current. On the nearer side of this, Nobilior placed one legion in hiding, in order that the enemy, despising his small numbers, might follow more boldly. When this expectation was realized, the legion which had been posted for the purpose attacked the enemy from ambush and destroyed them.[42]

Nobilior ('the Most Noble' or 'Oustanding') was an additional *cognomen* of Marcus Fulvius Paetinus, the consul of 255 BC who was famous for his role in the sea battles of the First Punic War, but he did not fight the Samnites and the *cognomen* has been erroneously retrojected onto his relative, the consul of

298 BC. The detail about the legionary cohorts is erroneous; Frontinus, a Roman general of the first century AD, imagined that the legions of the Samnite wars were organized like his own, in cohorts rather than maniples. Note also the misunderstanding concerning the identity of the enemy, here Lucanians, but the passages are of great interest in demonstrating a Roman consul using classically Samnite tactics against the Samnites, and probably also indicative that he preferred not to meet them in formal battle. That impression is strengthened by another anecdote in Frontinus concerning 'Nobilior' = Centumalus:

> Fulvius Nobilior, deeming it necessary to fight with a small force against a large army of the Samnites who were flushed with success, pretended that one legion of the enemy had been bribed by him to turn traitor; and to strengthen belief in this story, he commanded the tribunes, the *primi ordines* [senior centurions] and the centurions to contribute all the ready money they had, or any gold and silver, in order that the price might be paid the traitors at once. He promised that, when victory was achieved, he would give generous presents besides to those who contributed for this purpose. This assurance brought such ardour and confidence to the Romans that they straightway opened battle and won a glorious victory.[43]

That the Samnites were in high morale and the consul needed to motivate the legionaries in such a dubious manner, suggest that the Romans were not immediately successful in the first year of the Third Samnite War. The battle accounts of Livy often suggest that the Romans had to do little more than to turn up to win a battle, but that is far from the reality. Frontinus, like Livy, imagines the Samnites having legions. Considering that the Samnites fought in maniples with similar armament to the Romans and other Italian peoples, it is not impossible that the largest regiments of the armies of the Samnite League were organized in a manner similar to the Roman legions. In fact, we know from an inscription of the late fourth or early third century BC that the Marsi used the Latin word *legio* to describe their military units.

At least one of the consuls of 298 BC also saw service in the on-going and rather desultory Etruscan War, perhaps defeating the army of Volaterra in the field but unable to take the strongly fortified city. News of fresh Etruscan musters reached Rome during the consular elections for 297 BC, but come the opening of the campaigning season, reports from Nepet, Sutrium and Falerii suggested that the Etruscans would not, after all, take to the field and the new consuls attacked Samnium. The patrician Fabius Rullianus and plebeian Decius Mus were consular colleagues for the second time, a sure sign of political alliance. Rullianus began his campaign at Sora and pillaged his way towards Tifernum (in the Montagne del Matese) but his route of advance is uncertain. Rullianus' scouts detected a Samnite ambush in the area of Tifernum. According to Livy, the Samnites 'had drawn their forces up in a secluded valley and were preparing to assail the Romans from above once they had entered it.' Rullianus put his army into a defensive hollow square formation (*agmen quadratum*) and halted short of the ambush site. Realizing that they had been discovered, the Samnites came down to fight a regular pitched battle. Rullianus' son Gurges ('the Glutton' or 'Insatiable') and Valerius Maximus, son of the Raven, opened the fighting with a cavalry charge, perhaps hoping to scatter the Samnites while they were still forming their battle line, but the Roman squadrons were repulsed and they withdrew in shame and played no further part in the battle. Prior to engaging with the infantry, Rullianus ordered his legate Scipio Barbatus to take the *hastati* from the First Legion (the first time Livy identifies a legion by its numeral) and to find a way around the enemy army's position and attack it from the rear. This tactic won the battle. The Samnites stubbornly resisted Rullianus' main body of infantry and the consul had to bring up his second battle line to prevent the first from being overwhelmed, but when Barbatus' *hastati* suddenly appeared behind them the Samnites panicked and attempted to escape. They were under the impression that a second full Roman army was bearing down on them. Livy reports with some disappointment that relatively few Samnites were killed or taken prisoner. The 3,400 dead and 830 captured are a fraction of his usual casualty figures and have the ring of authenticity; records of numbers killed and captured were certainly made and sent to the Senate in dispatches. Commanders would also be keen to discover if they had killed enough to earn a triumph (5,000 enemy dead was the requirement in later centuries). However, the figures may derive from the plausible invention of one of Livy's sources. As we are not told of their release or execution, it is most likely that the captives were sold or kept by the Romans as slaves. The vastly expanded *ager Romanus* and colonial territories required slave labour to work in the fields while the peasant soldiers were on campaign.

Meanwhile, Decius Mus boldly advanced from the territory of the Sidicini to the vicinity of Malventum, the capital of the Hirpini. Mus did not, however, fight the Samnites. He instead intercepted an Apulian army before it linked up with Samnite forces. Once again, Livy's casualty figure is low; he reports only 2,000 Apulians killed.

Mus and Rullianus spent the next four months devastating parts of Samnium, although where exactly is not revealed, concentrating on terrorizing the rural population and destroying farms and crops and herds, but the extent of their devastations is probably exaggerated. Rullianus captured the only notable town. The garrison of Cimetra (its location is uncertain) proved insufficient to save it from the consular army. Of the almost 3,000 defenders, 930 were killed and the rest were added to Rullianus' haul of captives. Rullianus returned to Rome to oversee the election of the consuls for 296 BC, but Mus wintered with his army in Samnium. The *imperium* of Rullianus and Decius was prorogued for six months, allowing the latter to continue his work of devastation in 296 BC. Livy asserts that this activity forced a Samnite army, which had apparently refused to engage in battle, to withdraw completely from Samnium. Livy creates the impression that the Samnites had to go elsewhere to find food supplies, but in reality the main Samnite field army led by Gellius Egnatius had no interest in Mus: it was marching to link up with the new allies in Etruria. It is conceivable that Mus was mostly confined to his winter camp and that he, rather than the Samnites, refused to engage in open battle. One wonders if Mus' winter camp was even in Samnium; perhaps it was located in Apulia or Lucania. Tellingly, once Egnatius had departed, Mus took the opportunity to lead his army on a plundering expedition. Three towns were stormed – Murgantia, Romulea and Ferentinum. They were stripped of valuables, including people. The latter town was clearly not the Hernican settlement and it is conceivably an error for Forentum in Apulia. Maybe it had sided with, or been occupied by the Samnites. If Livy's Ferentinum is in fact Forentum, the otherwise unknown Murgantia and Romulea should also be located in the same general area. However, it may be that there was a Ferentinum located elsewhere in Samnium. Duplicate place names were not uncommon. For example, towns called Ausculum were to be found in Picenum and in Apulia, and there was a Teanum in the Sidicine country and another in Apulia.

Proconsul Rullianus did not return to Samnium in 296 BC. He was called instead to settle disputes among the new Lucanian allies, who were not a unified nation; some might have preferred to side with their Samnite kin, but the presence of Rullianus' army persuaded them to stay loyal to Rome.

The consuls of 296 BC were Appius Claudius and Volumnius Flamma Violens. They had a mutual dislike of each other but were forced to co-operate to combat the worrying presence of Gellius Egnatius in Etruria. The Samnite general's route to Etruria is uncertain. He may have passed through the Marsian country, but in order to rendezvous with his allies in the north (Egnatius is identified by Livy as the mastermind of the grand coalition), he had could not avoid crossing Rome's territory or that of her allies, which stretched from coast to coast. He must have then crossed Sabine and Umbrian territory and entered Etruria from the Upper Tiber Valley, perhaps in the vicinity of Perusia.

The consuls advanced into Etruria and established a camp close to where Egnatius was ensconced, probably Perusia. Livy tells us that Appius' consular legions were numbered I and IV, and were accompanied by 12,000 allies. Flamma's legions bore the numerals II and III and were supported by 15,000 allies; it is uncertain why he had 3,000 more allied troops than his colleague. This is the first time Livy identifies the numerals of all four consular legions and is a rare occurrence of him admitting to the presence of the allies (*socii*). The allies outnumbered the legionaries (18,000 in total), but many of the *socii* could have been drawn from the new Latin colonies. In later centuries the ratio of allied to Roman citizen troops varied from one-to-one to two-to-one.

The size of Egatius' Samnite force is not revealed. He was initially joined by Etruscan contingents (reported by Livy) and probably also by Sabine levies (suggested by the *elogium* of Appius). There were daily skirmishes between the camps but neither side emerged *en masse* to offer formal battle. Eventually, a general engagement did develop when some foragers being led by Egnatius were intercepted. Livy reports a Roman victory, but he admits Egnatius held his ground, and the situation for the Romans became so desperate that Appius dramatically vowed a temple to Bellona, the goddess of war, if she would grant the Romans victory. According to Livy, 7,800 of the enemy were killed and 2,120 taken captive. These were substantial losses (almost 10,000 in total), but despite their 'victory' the consuls were unable to oust Egnatius from Etruria and more Etruscans soon joined him. The Romans too must have suffered very significant casualties and the outcome of the battle was probably indecisive.

When the prorogations of Fabius Rullianus and Decius Mus came to an end, possibly in mid-summer, they had to return to Rome and disband their armies. They appear to have achieved little in the course of their extended campaigns; neither was awarded a triumph. Volumnius Flamma was assigned the Samnite theatre, leaving Appius Claudius with the unenviable task of containing Egnatius' ever-growing army of anti-Roman confederates.

With the proconsular armies disbanded and Flamma still in the north, Samnium was temporarily unattended and Campania exposed. The Samnite general Staius Minatius took full advantage, leading a major incursion down the valley of the Volturnus. The *ager Falernus* and the Auruncan country were pillaged. Thousands of captives were taken, crops and vines destroyed and herds driven off. There was panic in Rome; Egnatius was still undefeated and Minatius' incursion, almost to the Auruncan border with Greater Latium, recalled the catastrophic situation in 315 BC, when the Samnites charged through the pass of Lautulae and seized Tarracina. However, Minatius' army was concerned with plundering and not with occupation. The Samnites made no attempt on Cales or any other Roman strongholds. Virtually unopposed in the countryside, Minatius became careless. Unaware that Flamma had rushed south, the Samnite raiders were intercepted as they left their camp on the Volturnus and headed for home. Almost 7,500 captives were freed, a mass of plunder recovered and Minatius himself was captured along with his warhorse, but despite reports of significant Samnite losses (6,000 killed, 2,500 captured), one suspects that a substantial part of the army made good its escape simply by abandoning the slaves, cattle and less portable plunder, and the Romans may have been forced to abandon their pursuit when the Samnite vanguard returned to support the main body of the army. A period of thanksgiving was declared in Rome. It is notable that, despite this success and the apparent victory in Etruria, no triumphs were awarded in 296 BC; the Senate and consuls realized that their successes were little more than holding actions. The real battle was yet to be fought.

Appius Claudius was hard-pressed in Etruria. He sent increasingly gloomy dispatches to the Senate in Rome reporting that Egnatius continued to receive reinforcements, most notably from the Umbrians and the Gauls. The existing confederate camp was too small to contain the Four Nations, as Appius dubbed them, and a second had to be established. This news, coupled with the scare in northern Campania, prompted the Senate to enforce an emergency levy. This went far beyond the usual conscription of *iuniores*. *Seniores* and even freedmen (that is slaves who had bought their freedom or been released by their masters) were formed into cohorts, each of three maniples, to act as reserves and for the defence of the city. The decision was also taken to guard the Via Appia and approaches to Latium from future raids by the establishment of colonies at Minturnae, where the road crossed the mouth of the Liris, and at Sinuessa (founded in 295 BC). However, these were not large-scale Latin colonies, but small Roman citizen colonies. Despite the fact that a citizen colony required only 300 adult male settlers who would retain their superior Roman status, volunteers were in short supply:

> The tribunes of the plebs were assigned the task of obtaining a plebiscite directing Publius Sempronius [Sophus] the praetor to appoint three commissioners (*triumviri*) to conduct the colonists to these places. Yet it was not easy to find men who would enrol, since they regarded themselves as sent, not to settle on the land, but to serve almost as a perpetual outpost in hostile territory.[44]

Despite the gloomy mood in Rome, life went on as before. The aediles (junior magistrates) were busy prosecuting moneylenders and fining those who were exploiting public land for grazing (indicative of the scale of recent conquests). The curule aediles, the brothers Gnaeus and Quintus Ogulnius, used the possessions seized from the convicted to fund lavish adornments to the shrines on the Capitol. These included a bronze statue group of Jupiter being carried in a chariot drawn by four horses, but more notably they commissioned a statue of Romulus and Remus being suckled by the she-wolf to be set up by the sacred fig tree (*ficus Ruminalus*) associated with Romulus on the Palatine. This demonstrates the belief in the well-known, but probably only fairly recently developed, foundation myth that Rome was established by Romulus and Remus, the twin sons of the war god Mars. The tale has the essential elements of the Sacred Spring – Mars' sacred wolf is elsewhere found as a pathfinder animal, for example of the Hirpini, and the Twins go on to form a war band and carve out a territory in Latium. The Romans were probably aware of the Samnites' belief that they had been led out of the Sabine country by a bull sent by Mamers/Mars, but the Romans could better that boast by asserting they were in fact, through Romulus, the children of Mars and therefore divinely favoured.

The Battle of the Nations

The consuls elected for 295 BC were the old partners Fabius Rullianus and Decius Mus. Both consuls were to take their armies into Etruria and attempt to defeat Egnatius but, to Mus' annoyance, overall responsibility for the command was assigned to the more experienced Rullianus and this made for friction. Volumnius Flamma's *imperium* was prorogued for a full year and he would continue the war in Samnium. He retained the command of two legions. Appius Claudius, who was still in the field, was elected praetor and recalled to Rome to oversee the administration of the city in the absence of the consuls. He might also be called on to organize its defence.

The seriousness of the military situation facing Rome is indicated by the number of experienced military men who were made propraetors and given *imperium*, thus allowing them to command armies, despite them having held no magistracy in the previous year. Postumius Megellus and Fulvius Centumalus were charged with guarding the northern approaches to Rome. Megellus' army was positioned not far from Rome in the *ager Vaticanus*, that is, the land on the far bank of the Tiber including the Janiculum. Centumalus was sent into the Faliscan territory where his army could straddle the important routes into Etruria and Umbria. Scipio Barbatus was also propraetor in 295 BC, but it is uncertain if, like Megellus and Centumalus, he was given *imperium* by the Senate and People of Rome. It is possible that he was originally attached to Rullianus' army as a legate and subsequently imbued with *imperium* by the consul to enable him to command a legion independently of the consular army. If so, this would be the first example of a consul using his powers to invest a private citizen (admittedly a consular) with *imperium*.

There were nine legions in service in 295 BC. As noted above, Flamma continued to command two legions, possibly his consular legions but we cannot be certain. Megellus and Centumalus had at least one legion apiece. Rullianus could have raised two new legions but he chose to enrol only one with an unusual double complement of cavalry; Livy reports this legion had 4,000 infantry, probably rounded down from the standard 4,200, and 600 *equites*. The consul also took over the legions of Appius Claudius, which had wintered on the Umbrian frontier. Mus' consular army had the usual complement of two, presumably newly levied, legions.

Appius Claudius established his winter camp at Aharna in Umbria, just across the Tiber from Perusia. The camps of Gellius Egnatius and his allies were close by and Appius' outnumbered army was confined to its camp. Early in 295 BC Rullianus and Mus arrived with their three legions and 1,000 select Campanian cavalry; it is uncertain if these were Roman citizens from the north of the region, allies from farther south, or a mixture of both. The 12,000 allies attached to Appius' consular army may have spent the winter of 296/5 BC at Aharna, but it is possible that they were dismissed in the autumn of 296 BC. In the precarious military situation Rome needed more troops than ever before, but she could not risk alienating the allies by keeping them away from their homes for too long. Fresh contingents of Latins and other *socii* probably accompanied the consuls. At the subsequent Battle of Sentinum there were more allied troops than Romans but we remain ignorant of the exact number.

If at full strength, the nine legions would have contained 40,800 men, including Rullianus' 300 extra *equites*. The total contributions of the allies, including those in the armies of the proconsul and propraetors, would have at least equalled, and probably exceeded, the number of legionaries. Thus in this critical year Rome had 80,000 to 100,000 men in the field, and more in reserve.

In 296 BC Appius' legions bore the numerals I and IV, but when Rullianus assumed command they were renumbered. At Sentinum, Rullianus' legions had the numerals I and III but we cannot be certain that both were the regiments originally enrolled by Appius, as one may be the legion with extra cavalry that Rullianus recruited from volunteers in Rome. Scipio Barbatus' *imperium* allowed him to assume command of one of Rullianus' three legions and take it over the Apennines to defend Camerinum, Rome's key Umbrian ally. This legion had the numeral II.

The circumstances that took Barbatus and the Second Legion to Camerinum are uncertain. Egnatius certainly moved his army into Umbria, maybe with the intention of forcing Camerinum to join him, or simply to let his plunder-hungry troops sack it, but Barbatus got there before him. A possible scenario is that the consuls received intelligence of Egnatius' intention, but for some reason their armies were unable to march, so Rullianus made Barbatus propraetor and invested him with *imperium*. Barbatus then made a rapid march over the Apennines with *legio* II and established a camp in the vicinity of Camerinum. The consuls followed up when they able to do so.

The propraetor was probably the first of his branch of the Cornelii clan to bear the famous *cognomen* Scipio. It is conceivable that he took the name when elected consul; a *scipio* was a staff that signified magisterial rank. His other *cognomen* tells us that he was bearded (*barbatus*). The *elogium* inscribed on his sarcophagus declares that the bearded propraetor was as handsome as he was brave, but caution was the better part of valour when Egnatius' host loomed into sight. We do not know if Barbatus' small army included allies, but it was clearly no match for the great forces arrayed against it. Fearing his camp would be overrun, Barbatus abandoned the position and made for a hill sited between it and Camerinum. The hill would be easier to defend, but the wily Egnatius anticipated the Roman general and had already sent troops to occupy the summit of the hill. Barbatus failed to send scouts (*exploratores*) ahead to reconnoitre the position. His troops ascended the hill and found themselves face-to-face with Samnite and Gallic warriors. The rest of the confederate army swarmed up behind the Romans. Barbatus, the Second Legion, and any allied cohorts he had, were trapped.

Meanwhile, Rullianus and Mus were following up with their consular forces. As they neared Camerinum, Gallic horsemen rode up to taunt and harass the Roman marching column. The Senonian troopers had freshly severed heads impaled on their spears or hanging from their horses' tack. It is uncertain how long Barbatus and his small army were trapped on the hill, but when the consuls appeared the legion was almost destroyed and the propraetor was surely anticipating death or ignominious capture. Luckily for Barbatus, Egnatius withdrew his troops before they were in turn trapped by the new Roman army. The Samnite general then marched to Sentinum, some 50 miles to the north and made ready to give battle. The Four Nations were again divided between two camps, the Samnites and Senones in one, and the Etruscans and Umbrans in the other. Egnatius planned to engage one consular army with his Samnites, and the Senones would fight the second. While the Romans were fully occupied, the Etruscans and Umbrians would emerge from their entrenchments, skirt around the embattled armies and capture the lightly defended Roman camp located 4 miles away, thus leaving the legions and allied cohorts with nowhere safe to retreat to and vulnerable to attack from the rear. Egnatius may have hoped that this would be enough to cause the Roman army to surrender or flee. Livy informs us that deserters from Egnatius' army brought news of this plan to Rullianus and the consul therefore sent orders to Megellus and Centumalus to leave their positions above Rome and invade the territory of Clusium in Etruria. This diversionary attack has the effect of persuading the Etruscans to hurry back home. They do not feature in Livy's account of the Battle of Sentinum (the principle account), nor do the Umbrians, some of whom may have opted to aid the Etruscans (more natural allies than Samnites or predatory Gauls), while other Umbrian contingents, seeing the coalition weakened, chose to depart to their home towns.

Livy makes it very clear that the consuls were concerned about the great size of Egnatius' army. Unfortunately its actual strength is not reported by Livy or any other source, but it was probably the largest army yet assembled in Italy. One wonders, therefore, if Rullianus' (and perhaps also his colleague's) plan to draw off the Etruscans was actually underway before deserters apparently brought news of Egnatius' dastardly plan. Fulvius Centumalus was especially well placed to march up the valley of the Tiber, or through the Ciminus, to threaten Clusium, once the stronghold of Lars Porsenna. Centumalus' time in the Faliscan country had not been without incident. Even with the propraetor's army on their territory, Rome's perceived weakness encouraged some Faliscans to take up arms and they made an incursion into neighbouring *ager Romanus*, but Centumalus caused the enemy force to disperse by a simple ruse:

> When a force of Faliscans far superior to ours [an exaggeration] had encamped in our territory, Gnaeus Fulvius [Centumalus] had his soldiers set fire to certain buildings at a distance from the camp in order that the Faliscans, thinking that their own men had done this, might scatter in hope of plunder.[45]

Centumalus must have reached the territory of Clusium before Megellus and began the work of devastation. It seems that Megellus arrived to take over this task, allowing Centumalus to march on Perusia and intercept the Perusine and Clusian forces that had returned from Sentinum. The Etruscans were defeated, losing 3,000 men and 20 of their sacred military standards.

The consuls were keen to bring the Samnites and Senones to battle. It was not certain that the propraetors would defeat the Etruscans or that the Umbrians, or even more Gauls, would rejoin Egnatius. Even in its reduced state, the consuls wondered if they had enough men to defeat the army of the Samnite general. For two days the consuls sent troops to harass the enemy. The troops involved would have been cavalry and light infantry, that is, soldiers suited to skirmishing and hit and run tactics. The Samnites and Senones responded in kind, neither side winning any real advantage but, as the consuls intended, Gellius Egnatius was suitably provoked and on the third day he led all of his troops from his camp and offered battle. The Battle of the Nations, as it became known, was at hand; Romans, Latins and Campanians facing Samnites and Gauls.

The actual location of the battle in the territory of Sentinum is uncertain. There is a suitable plain immediately to the north of the town. A small river, now called the Sanguerone, cuts through the centre of the plain. Egnatius' army fought in two divisions. If the battle was fought on this plain, the river might have separated the divisions and the opposing consular armies.[46]

Gellius Egnatius drew up his Samnites on the left wing of the confederate army. Samnite cavalry, although not mentioned by Livy, presumably covered the left flank of their infantry. The Senones formed up on the right, with a very substantial cavalry force protecting their right flank; the infantry on the right flank of any army were vulnerable because this was their unshielded side. Assuming that the Sanguerone separated the Gauls and Samnites, the watercourse protected the unshielded side of the Samnite infantry.

On the Roman side, Rullianus took up position on the right opposite the Samnites with his First and Third Legions. Decius drew up the Fifth and Sixth Legions on the left against the Senones. The Campanian cavalry are reported only on the right flank with Rullianus, but it may be that the 1,000 troopers were shared by the consuls and divided into two *alae* (wings). Unless the legion annihilated at Camerinum was the regiment raised in Rome with the double complement of cavalry, Rullianus should have had 300 more *equites* than his colleague. However, mountainous Samnium was not cavalry country and it is probable that more Gallic cavalry confronted Mus, and Rullianus could have transferred some of his horsemen to Mus.

The positions of the Latin and allied forces at Sentinum is unclear. In Livy's account all of the fighting is carried out by the legionaries and Roman and Campanian *equites*. Livy does refer to *subsidia*, that is, reserves, being brought into action at a critical stage of the battle. These reserves may be the allied cohorts, drawn up behind the legionary battle lines, but the allied cohorts were organized into maniples and interchangeable lines of *hastati*, *principes* and *triarii*, and so could have formed up on the flanks of the legions. Livy's reserves would then be legionary and allied *triarii*, and the allied cavalry *turmae* would have reinforced the Roman and Campanian troopers on the wings.

If the four legions at Sentinum were up to strength, Rullianus and Mus had 16,800 legionary infantry and 1,200 or 1,500 *equites* (18,000–18,300 in total). The force of Latins and allies, perhaps including the 1,000 Campanians, is said to have been greater than the number of Roman troops. We should recall that Appius Claudius and Volumnius Flamma had a total of 27,000 allied soldiers with them in Etruria. It would not be unreasonable to assume that a similar number joined Rullianus and Mus and this would bring the size of the Roman army up to c. 45,000, but the situation was different to that of 296 BC. There were three other Roman armies in the field, all requiring allied contingents, and it may be that the number of allies at Sentinum was only slightly greater than the number of Roman troops, and a total figure of less than 40,000 may be appropriate.

As noted above, Livy does not report or estimate the size of Egnatius' army at Sentinum. He does relate, with considerable disdain, that some of the sources he consulted put forward a grossly exaggerated total for the enemy army:

> Great as the glory of the day on which the Battle of Sentinum was fought must appear to any writer who adheres to the truth, it has by some writers been exaggerated beyond all belief. They assert that the enemy's army amounted to 330,000 infantry and 46,000 cavalry, together with 1,000 war chariots. That, of course, includes the Umbrians and Tuscans who are represented as taking part in the battle. And by way of increasing the Roman strength they tell us that Lucius Volumnius commanded in the action as well as the consuls, and that their legions were supplemented by his army.[47]

An army of this size would be impossible to provision or manoeuvre. However, if the number of enemy casualties, prisoners and fugitives that Livy records is accepted as reasonably accurate, the combined total suggests that Egnatius had at least 38,000 soldiers and the consuls' concerns about the size of his army, even without Etruscans and Umbrians, probably indicates that he had considerably more warriors at his disposal. The total number of troops at Sentinum was probably in excess of 80,000 and may have been as great as 100,000. According to Diodorus, Duris of Samos put the number of enemy casualties at 100,000, perhaps another gross exaggeration but possibly a reflection of the total size of the forces engaged.

*   *   *

The pivotal engagement in Rome's conquest of Italy was probably fought in April 295 BC. It was usual for generals to lead their armies out of their camps at dawn and, considering the vast numbers present, it must have taken some time to arrange the soldiers into battle lines. Something extraordinary happened as the Italian armies faced off:

> As they stood arrayed for battle, a deer, pursued by a wolf that had chased it down from the mountains, fled across the plain and between the two battle lines. The animals then turned in opposite directions, the deer towards the Gauls and the wolf towards the Romans. For the wolf a space was opened between the *ordines*, but the Gauls killed the deer. Then one of the Roman front rankers (*antesignanus*) called out, 'Where you see the animal sacred to Diana lying slain, that way flight and slaughter have shaped their course. On this side the wolf of Mars, unhurt and sound, has reminded us of the race of Mars and of our founder Romulus.'[48]

This was clearly a sign from Mars, progenitor of the Roman race, and Mus' legionaries were elated by the portent of the Gauls' demise. It is, of course, extremely doubtful that a wolf chased a deer between the armies, but it is likely that the Romans saw a wolf that day and it was taken as a good omen. It is also possible that the Gauls, immediately prior to engaging the Romans, sacrificed a deer. Such battlefield sacrifices, carried out before the front rank, were not unusual in the Ancient World. If something went wrong with the ceremony, the opponent observing it would take heart knowing that the gods did not favour their enemy.

Rullianus' strategy was to stand firm and absorb the charges of the enemy. When the Samnites inevitably tired he would launch a decisive counter-charge. He believed that the same tactic would defeat the Gauls: 'They are more than men at the start of a fight, but by the end they are less than women!' He had presumably attempted to convince Mus to adhere to this strategy, yet the other consul was desirous of accomplishing victory more quickly and gloriously and, inspired by the omen of the wolf and the deer, led his maniples forward in an impetuous attack.

The maniples of *hastati* would have closed with the Gauls at the run (*impetus*), pausing only momentarily to hurl their *pila*, roar their war cry (*clamor*), and draw their swords. The centurions and soldiers in the front would have surged ahead, aiming to batter down Gallic warriors with the bosses of their shields, force their way into the ranks and set to work with their cut-and-thrust swords. The soldiers in the rearmost ranks of the maniples would follow up more steadily in good order, drumming weapons against their shields, shouting encouragement to their comrades and perhaps lobbing *pila* over their heads and into the ranks of the enemy.

But the Senones resisted fiercely. They too were armed with *pila*-like missiles, which must have thinned the ranks of the attacking Romans, and their long swords could hack through shields and armour. The two sides were evenly matched in fury and prowess and the infantry action gradually waned. We may presume that Mus called up the *principes* to relieve or reinforce the *hastati*, but when they too failed to break the Senones, the consul looked to his cavalry to hasten victory. Riding from *turma* to *turma* he exhorted the mostly rich and aristocratic troopers: 'Yours will be a double share of glory if victory comes first to the left wing and to the cavalry!'

The cavalry on the left wing would have moved forward to protect the flank of the advancing infantry, but until now, there was no all-out cavalry assault. Mus attached himself to the bravest *turma* (perhaps actually his mounted bodyguard) and led two charges against the Gallic horse. The first charge drove the Gauls back and the second scattered them, exposing the unshielded right flank and rear of their infantry, but the Romans were unable to exploit the opportunity. The war chariots of the Senones had been held in reserve behind the battle line. The sudden and unexpected counter-charge panicked both horses and riders, and the Roman cavalry fled in disorder as the clattering chariots pursued them. Mus was unable to halt their flight, and the fugitives appear to have swept past the flank of their own infantry. The charioteers broke off their pursuit and turned instead on the vulnerable infantry, driving into the intervals between maniples and *ordines*. Many of the *antesignani*, that is the *hastati* or *principes* in the leading battle line, were trampled down. The Gallic infantry took advantage of the chaos and attacked.

With the cavalry in flight and the leading battle line of infantry almost over-run, it seemed that the Roman left might collapse. If the left fell, Rullianus' wing would surely also succumb and with it Rome's hard won conquests in Italy. Decius Mus decided that the time had come for him to follow the example of his illustrious father: he would ride to his death as a *devotus* and through his own sacrifice bring about the destruction of the enemy. Livy has him utter: 'Now I will offer up the legions of the enemy, to be slaughtered along with me, as victims to Tellus [Mother Earth] and the divine Manes [gods of the Underworld].'

Livy informs us that throughout the battle Mus kept the *pontifex*, Marcus Livius Denter, close. Such a senior state priest was necessary to lead a *devotus* through the correct ritual. That Mus had Denter by his side at all times suggests that his decision to perform *devotio* was not spontaneous. The consul's heritage must have led to expectations that he too would perform *devotio* if the situation facing Rome became desperate and Sentinum was such an occasion. It is likely that he informed Rullianus of his intention to devote himself if his initial tactics failed. The legionaries and allies would have been told as well. If they were not prepared, they would most likely panic at the sight of the consul being cut down.

A spear sacred to Mars was laid upon the ground and Mus stood upon it. Denter helped the consul recite the terrible prayer of *devotio*, the same with which the original Decius Mus had devoted himself at Battle of the Veseris. It is possible that Livy or his sources invented this, but it seems likely that it derives from pontifical or other priestly records of religious formulae:

> Janus, Jupiter, Father Mars, Quirinus, Bellona, Lares, divine Novensiles, divine Indigites, you gods in whose power are both we and the enemy, and you, divine Manes, I invoke and worship you, I beg and crave your favour, that you prosper the might and victory of the Roman people and visit on their enemies fear, shuddering and death. As I have pronounced these words on behalf of the Republic of the Roman people, and of the army and the legions and auxiliaries

> ... I devote the legions and auxiliaries of the enemy, along with myself, to the divine Manes and Tellus.[49]

The younger Mus added some grim imprecations to this vow of death:

> I will drive before me fear and panic, blood and carnage. The wrath of the heavenly gods and the infernal gods will curse the standards, weapons and armour of the enemy, and in the same place as I die witness the destruction of the Gauls and Samnites![50]

Denter helped Mus don the ritualistic garb of the *devotus*. This was the *cinctus Gabinius*, a toga hitched in such a way that a man could ride a horse and wield a weapon. The consul was ready to meet his destiny, but first proclaimed Denter propraetor (he had been consul in 302 BC). Thus invested with *imperium*, Denter assumed command of the consular army.

Brandishing the spear of Mars, Mus spurred his way through the broken *antesignani*, charged into the ranks of the advancing Senones and impaled himself on their weapons. The death of a general, the focus of command and authority and leadership, usually triggered the collapse of an army, but the news of Mus' glorious demise, transmitted by Denter, rallied the hard-pressed Roman infantry and they turned on their opponents with renewed vigour. According to Livy, Mus' heroic death had the effect of instantly paralyzing the seemingly victorious Gauls:

> From that moment the battle seemed scarce to depend on human efforts. The Romans, after losing a general – an occurrence that is wont to inspire terror – fled no longer, but sought to redeem the field. The Gauls, especially those in the press around the body of the consul, as though deprived of reason, were darting their javelins at random and without effect, while some were in a daze, and could neither fight nor run away.[51]

The Senones' reaction seems entirely fantastic but is it entirely fictitious? Is it merely the over-egged reconstruction of a patriotic Roman historian or does it have some basis in reality? Livy was keen to describe how the self-sacrifice of Mus brought on the aid of Tellus and Manes and the form that aid took, but were the Senones aware they had killed a *devotus*? It is possible that they did, and their reaction, although exaggerated, was one of shock and caused their advance to halt.

*   *   *

It was suggested above that the Picentes chose alliance with Rome rather than with the Samnite-led coalition because of their hatred of the Senones. The

Senones had encroached on the lands of the proud Picentes for more than a century. The Picentes famously took their name from the sacred *picus* of Mamers that had led them to the east of the Appenines. The association with Mamers/Mars is underlined by considerable archaeological finds of arms and armour that demonstrate the martial nature of ancient Picenum. They were talented smiths, developing elaborate 'pot' helmets and the original Negau-type which were adopted throughout Italy in the sixth and fifth centuries BC and employed by Italic mercenaries serving abroad, for example in Sicily. The 'Woodpeckers' did lose a portion of their northern territory to the Senones, but their success in halting the Gallic advance and holding the remaining country testifies to their military prowess. There is also evidence to suggest that the Picentes knew of the ritual of *devotio* and employed it in battle.

In an excursus about *devotio* following his account of the Veseris, Livy notes that a Roman commander could nominate an ordinary legionary to take his place and die among the enemy. This substitution would eliminate the possibility of the Roman army panicking at the death of its commander, and volunteers were probably not difficult to find. The honour falling on the family of a successful *devotus* would be immense. The use of substitutes should lead us to suspect that *devotiones* were more common occurrences than the sources suggest, but only the successful *devotiones* of great men entered the written record.

Devotio or *devotio*-like practices were not unique to the Romans and Latins, and if the enemy realized that a *devotus* was seeking death, every effort would be made to capture the man alive (cf. the orders of Pyrrhus at Ausculum, below). If the *devotus*, whether a general or a common soldier, failed to die, an expiatory offering had to be made to the gods cheated of the promised sacrifice of the *devotus* and the enemy soldiers. A 7 feet tall statue of the failed *devotus* was buried in the ground and a victim sacrificed over it. Likewise, if the *devotus* was unsuccessful and lost to the enemy the spear sacred to Mars, a pig, sheep or an ox was sacrificed to placate the god.

In 1934 the limestone statue of an Italic warrior was discovered buried in a vineyard near Capestrano. It had not toppled to the ground and gradually been covered over with soil, but was deliberately buried, like a body in a grave. The back of the statue remained in perfect condition, suggesting that it was buried immediately after its production, around 500 BC. The statue is 7 feet tall. The figure wears typical central Italian body armour, the details of which are emphasized with paint: a bronze gorget and disc cuirass, a broad bronze belt and an apron to protect his vulnerable abdomen. His arms are crossed over his chest and he clutches a short sword and a small axe, while javelins with throwing thongs are carved on the vertical supports that hold up the figure. Capestrano is located in what was the territory of the Vestini, but the warrior wears a broad-brimmed Picene helmet with a great crest and the inscription on the statue, not yet deciphered, is in a southern Picene dialect. It has been suggested that the Capestrano Warrior represents a very high status – his rich panoply was far beyond the means of a common soldier – but failed *devotus*.

If the Capestrano Warrior does represent a *devotus*, it would demonstrate that the Picentes employed *devotio*. We can postulate that a Picene *devotio* was essentially similar to a Roman *devotio*: the king, general or lower-ranking substitute invoking the gods, vowing to sacrifice himself and the forces of the enemy, followed by the donning of ritual costume or armour and the lone charge to the death. The opponents against whom the Picentes were most likely to employ this ritual tactic were the Senonian Gauls.[52]

*   *   *

If the Senones were familiar with *devotio* or similar practices from warfare against the Picentes and other Italian peoples, the warriors at Sentinum would have recognized the features of *devotio* in Mus' suicidal charge. The realization that they had unwittingly carried out a sacrifice that would set the gods against them could well have caused their advance to falter. The impact of the divine on ancient Italian warfare should not be underestimated. This was an intensely religious and superstitious age, and even if the Senones were unsure about which gods were being called on to aid the Romans (by this time the Gauls had probably adopted a considerable number of native Italian deities), they recognized ritual practice, knew the powers and whims of the gods and they would have known fear and panic.

That Mus' *antesignani* rallied on witnessing his death demonstrates they had been forewarned that their general might devote himself and, if so, not to panic but rejoice, for the enemy would be doomed. The situation was reversed: Romans turned to pursue Senones, but the Gallic warriors had recovered some of their composure and did not flee pell-mell as the Roman cavalry had. They halted and organized themselves into a strong *testudo* formation. Like the Romans, the Gauls protected themselves with tall shields, well-suited to form the walls and roof of the *testudo* ('tortoise'). The *testudo* is famous from later Roman warfare. If it remained unbroken, it provided excellent protection against missiles and cavalry. Marc Antony's extraordinary retreat from Parthia in 36 BC was facilitated by use of the marching *testudo*. The chieftains of the Senones were experienced enough as commanders to realize the dangers of flight from battle – most casualties occurred during the pursuit of broken troops by cavalry. If they could last out the day in the *testudo*, they should be able to retreat safely under the cover of night. Of course, they may still have hoped for victory. The Samnites continued to fight on the left and if Rullianus was defeated, they would come to the relief of their Gallic allies.

*   *   *

The battle on the Roman right went as Rullianus had predicted. Gellius Egnatius launched his warriors in furious charges at the *hastati*, but the Romans and allies held firm. The classic Roman infantry formation, that is, the three *ordines* of maniples (*triplex acies*), was designed for mobility and attack, the maniples separated by considerable intervals and acting like miniature attack columns. However, one wonders how suitable this open battle formation was to Rullianus' defensive, and presumably static, tactics.

The intervals between the maniples of 'heavy' infantry (not really an appropriate description but nonetheless useful) were protected by bands of 'light' troops called *rorarii*. Known by the end of the third century BC as *velites* ('swift ones'), these were the poorest and usually youngest troops. There were even poorer Roman and Latin citizens, *proletarii*, who were generally exempt from military service, but the *rorarii* had at least the means to afford a bundle of light javelins, a sword, shield and helmet. They could not afford body armour. The *rorarii* fought in swarms, they were not led by centurions and *signiferi* (standard-bearers), but relied on their own initiative. Before the main battle lines enagaged, they would skirmish in front of the army, using hit-and-run tactics to thin the leading ranks of the enemy or to provoke him into a rash and disorderly attack. The later *velites*, and perhaps the earlier *rorarii* as well, wore wolf skins over their helmets to make them conspicuous to senior officers who would take note of acts of valour. Having considerable freedom of movement, these light troops were encouraged to engage in single combat and were eligible for particular military awards (*dona militaria*). When the main battle lines came up, the *rorarii* would retreat to the intervals between the maniples: any enemies advancing into the tempting gap would be stung by their light javelins. It is conceivable that attackers also risked being caught in a 'crossfire' of *pila* from the legionaries in the outside files of the maniples to either side, and that the maniple in the following line, positioned to cover the gap, would charge forward. Samnites were notable for the speed of their charges. Lightly equipped – most Samnite warriors were protected by only a *scutum* (a shield) a helmet, and armed with a couple of dual-purpose thrusting and throwing spears or *pila* – they could rush the intervals and force their way into the flanks and rears of the maniples. Rullianus, who knew too well the devastating effect of the swift Samnite onslaught from Lautulae, may have arranged his maniples of *hastati* without the usual intervals, allowing them to form a continuous wall of shields on which the Samnites could exhaust their missiles, energy and resolve.

The *hastati* would not break and at length the war cries, javelin volleys and charges of Gellius Egnatius' warriors waned. Rullianus judged the time was ripe to attack. He ordered the prefects commanding the cavalry *turmae* to work their way forward and be ready to attack the left flank of Egnatius' army. This suggests that whatever cavalry the Samnite general had was sufficiently weakened or had already retired from the action. The consul then gave the order for the infantry to advance, but this was not yet an all-out charge, only a probe; he was still wary and needed to confirm that the enemy were indeed exhausted. The Samnite maniples were pushed back easily. Rullianus called up reserves he had deliberately held back for this moment. It is uncertain if these were combined legionary and allied *principes* and/or *triarii*, or just allied cohorts, nor is it made clear where he positioned them, but in combination with the legionaries they delivered the hammer blow that caused Egnatius' army to break. Rullianus gave the signal, by trumpet, and the infantry drove forward. Simultaneously the Roman cavalry charged at the Samnites' left flank. The physically exhausted and demoralized Samnites cracked and they fled back to the confederate camp, easy prey for the swift Roman cavalry. The flight of the Samnites meant that the Senones, still holding out in their *testudo*, were completely exposed and the Romans hastened to encircle them.

Meanwhile, Livius Denter was busy riding along the ranks of Mus' army shouting out that the consul had devoted himself, thus making victory certain:

> The Gauls and the Samnites, he said, were made over to Tellus and to the Manes. Decius was haling after him with their devoted host and calling it to join him, and with the enemy all was madness and despair.[53]

The arrival of Scipio Barbatus and Marcius Rutilus with reinforcements from Rullianus' 'rearmost battle line', presumably *triarii*, also helped to rally Mus' army. On learning of Mus' sacrifice the former consuls resolved to 'dare all for the republic' and destroy the Senones' *testudo*. Orders were given to collect up all the *pila*, javelins and spears littering the battlefield, and to bombard the enemy. Initially, the volleys of missiles had little effect, but gradually javelins found their way through small gaps in the wall and roof of shields. Injured warriors dropped their shields and the front of the *testudo* was gradually opened up.

Rullianus, now aware of Mus' death, broke off his pursuit of Egnatius' men and crossed the river to attack the Gallic tortoise. He sent 500 of his picked Campanian horsemen, followed by the *principes* of the Third Legion, to circle around the *testudo* and to make a surprise assault on its rear. 'Make havoc of them in their panic,' he told his men. The unexpected charge of the Campanian *turmae* succeeded in opening gaps in the enemy formation. The 1,200 *principes* forced their way through the openings and split the tortoise apart. Rullianus then returned to the pursuit of Egnatius. Such was the crush at the gates of the camp that many warriors were unable to enter. Gellius Egnatius rallied these men and formed a battle line to meet Rullianus.

On approaching the camp the consul called on the great god Jupiter, in his guise as the Victor. Victory was now certain, but the Roman general knew how dangerous Egnatius and his men would be as they made their last stand. We may also assume that it was late in the day and Rullianus feared that a considerable portion of the enemy would escape under the cover of night, so he vowed to the god a temple and the spoils of battle in return for a complete victory. It seemed to the Romans that Jupiter heard Rullianus, for Egnatius was cut down and his men were quickly swept aside. The Romans and allies then surrounded the enemy camp. The Senones, assailed from front and rear, were annihilated. The Battle of the Nations was over.

The Samnites and Senones lost 25,000 men that day – less than Livy's favourite and exaggerated casualty figure of 30,000 and therefore probably reasonably accurate. Another 8,000 were taken captive, probably mostly those Samnites who had made it into the apparent safety of the camp. At least 5,000 Samnites did escape, but as they headed for home via the territory of the Paeligni, they were attacked. The Paeligni, now of course allies of Rome, killed 1,000 of the Samnite fugitives. Some Gallic infantry might have made good their escape from Sentinum, but most of the warriors in the *testudo* must have been either killed or enslaved – supposing that they were given the opportunity to surrender. It is uncertain what happened to the Senonian cavary and chariots. Did the former rally when Mus' squadrons were panicked by the unexpected attack of the charioteers, or did they continue their flight? Likewise, what happened to the charioteers? Some presumably continued the pursuit of the broken Roman cavalry, but did those that forced their way into the infantry retire before the Romans rallied?

As we have seen, Livy was usually reticent about listing Roman casualties but for Sentinum he made an exception. This was, after all, the greatest battle yet fought by Rome and her losses served to underline the scale and importance of the struggle. Rullianus' casualties were relatively light, 1,700 killed, but Mus' army was severely mauled with 7,000 killed. Sentinum was no easy victory and it was not even the decisive battle of the Third Samnite War. The Samnites would continue the struggle for five more years, and the Etruscans and other peoples remained troublesome, but never again would Rome be faced with such a dangerous coalition of Italian peoples. It also served to bring Rome to the notice of the wider Mediterranean world. The city-states and kingdoms of the Greek East, focussed on the titanic struggles of the Successors of Alexander the Great had, with the exceptions of Magna Graecia and Carthage, paid little attention to events in the West, but now they took note of the new and powerful player on the scene.

*   *   *

Rullianus sent soldiers to search for the body of Decius Mus, but it was not found until the following day. Like his father at the Veseris, Mus was finally discovered under a heap of enemy dead. His corpse was carried to the Roman camp and there was great lamentation. Rullianus immediately oversaw the funeral of his colleague, 'with every show of honour and well-deserved eulogisms,' says Livy. Zonaras, whose account derives from Dio, adds that Mus was cremated but this seems to be based on the assumption that the consul's body was burned with the spoils. In fulfilment of his vow Rullianus had the spoils gathered from the enemy, piled up and burned in offering to Jupiter the Victor. However, only a proportion was given over to the god; the rest was reserved for his legionaries. Rullinaus would have carried Mus' remains back to Rome to be handed over to the Decii for deposit in the family tomb, but it has been suggested that a grave discovered under the altar of the temple of Victoria in Rome belongs to Mus, and that he was honoured with burial there when Postumius Megellus dedicated the temple in 294 BC.[54] The year in which Rullianus dedicated his temple to Jupiter the Victor is not known, but the day and month on which the event occurred is recorded: 13 April, perhaps the anniversary of the day on which the vow was made.

Triumphatores

Rullianus crossed back over the Apennines, leaving Decius Mus' army to keep watch in Etruria (we do not know whom he left in command), and returned to Rome with his legions. On 4 September he celebrated a triumph over Samnites, Gauls and Etruscans. The inclusion of the latter people may be an error. Following his triumph Rullianus was recalled to Etruria to put down the rebellion of Perusia and later historians may have coupled this victory together with the Sentinum campaign. Another explantion is that Rullianus did triumph over Etruscans as well as Gauls and Samnites because he was able to take the credit for Fulvius Centumalus' victory over the Perusini and Clusini. Centumalus was, after all, following Rullianus' orders and fighting under his auspices. The triumphing legionaries were each rewarded eighty-two bronze *asses* (either ingots or rudimentary coins) and a tunic and *sagum* (military cloak) from the spoils not dedicated to Jupiter the Victor. The garments would have been those stripped from the enemy and we can imagine that the finely-made, colourful and embroidered garments of Senone and Samnite nobles were highly prized.

While Rullianus and Mus were campaigning in Etruria and Umbria, Volumnius Flamma was operating in Samnium. Livy reports that the proconsul drove a Samnite army up Mount Tifernus and, despite the difficulties of the terrain he defeated this army and caused its troops to scatter. The circumstances of this victory are uncertain. Did the proconsul defeat a Samnite force that was about to invade Campania, or did he invade Samnium in order to prevent reinforcements from being sent to Gellius Egnatius? Late in the year, seemingly after Rullianus' triumph, Samnite legions attacked the territory of Aesernia in the upper valley of the Volturnus, while others marched down the Liris, simply ignored the new small citizen colony at Minturnae and ravaged the country around Formiae and Vescia. Aesernia was located a little to the north of Mount Tifernus, but we do not know when the Romans captured it. The strategically positioned stronghold probably changed hands many times, and Volumnius Flamma may have captured it following his recent victory on Mount Tifernus. By this time the Decian army, as the survivors of Decius Mus' force were known, had left Etruria and returned to Rome probably to be formally disbanded. The withdrawal of the army encouraged Perusia to take up arms, but Rullianus hastened to the north (with his Sentinum legions?) and inflicted a sound defeat on the Etruscans. Livy reports 4,500 of the enemy killed and, most interestingly, that the 1,740 taken captive were not sold as slaves but ransomed back to their families and clans for 310 *asses* each. This was presumably conceived of as a swifter way to make a profit from the spoils and perhaps also to deliberately empty the coffers of Perusia and hamper the city's future war efforts.

The praetor Appius Claudius assumed command of the Decian army and marched south along the road he had built to drive the Samnite raiders from the Auruncan country. The Samnites withdrew before him and combined forces with their comrades who had advanced down the Volturnus from Aesernia to Caiatia. Flamma, probably based around Capua, joined his legions with those of Appius at Caiatia and together they defeated the Samnites. It was a typically bitter engagement but Livy's casualty figures may be exaggerated – 16,300 Samnites killed and 2,700 taken captive. The number of Roman dead also amounted to 2,700. Appius lost a few more men during the course of the campaign but not to enemy action; these unfortunates were struck by lightning.

Livy ends his account of the year 295 BC with a stirring tribute, but not to the *devotus* Mus or the *triumphator* Rullianus; Livy praises the courage and tenacity of the Samnites, the greatest of Rome's opponents:

> The Samnite wars are still with us, those wars which I have been occupied with through these last four books, and which have gone on continuously for 46 years, in fact ever since the consuls, Marcus Valerius [Corvus] and Aulus Cornelius [Cossus Arvina], carried the arms of Rome for the first time into Samnium.[55] It is unnecessary now to recount the numberless defeats which overtook both nations, and the toils which they endured through all those years, and yet these things were powerless to break down the resolution or crush

the spirit of that people; I will only allude to the events of the past year. During that period the Samnites, fighting sometimes alone, sometimes in conjunction with other nations, had been defeated by Roman armies under Roman generals on four several occasions, at Sentinum, amongst the Paeligni, at Tifernum, and in the Stellate plains [= Caiatia]; they had lost the most brilliant general they ever possessed; they now saw their allies – Etruscans, Umbrians, Gauls – overtaken by the same fortune that they had suffered; they were unable any longer to stand either in their own strength or in that afforded by foreign arms. And yet they would not abstain from war; so far were they from being weary of defending their liberty, even though unsuccessfully, that they would rather be worsted than give up trying for victory. What sort of a man must he be who would find the long story of those wars tedious, though he is only narrating or reading it, when they failed to wear out those who were actually engaged in them?[56]

The Samnites had suffered painful defeats but as Livy emphasizes, they would not give up the fight. Rumours reached Rome that the Samnites had levied three new armies: one to continue the work of Gellius Egnatius and link up with allies in Etruria, another to devastate Campania, while the last would guard Samnium. The rumours were only partly correct. Rather than return to Etruria, early in 294 BC the Samnites seized part of the Marsian territory and installed a powerful garrison in Milionia. This stronghold, the precise location of which is unknown, probably straddled part of the Romans' usual route to the Adriatic coast. The consuls of 294 BC, Postumius Megellus and Marcus Atilius Regulus (probably the son of the consul of 335 BC), were both assigned Samnium as their 'province', that is their sphere of operations, but Megellus fell seriously ill and remained in Rome until August. Regulus invaded northwest Samnium but his route of advance was blocked by a Samnite army. Unable even to forage he was contained in his camp and early one morning, taking advantage of thick fog, the Samnites made a daring raid. Dispatching unsuspecting sentries, they entered the camp by its rear gate, killed Regulus' *quaestor* Opimius Pansa and more than 700 legionary and allied troops (Livy reports the presence of a Lucanian cohort and Latin colonists from Suessa Aurunca).[57] Regulus was forced to retreat back to the territory of Sora. The Samnites followed, but dispersed when Megellus finally joined his colleague at Sora sometime after 1 August (on that day the consul is recorded as dedicating his temple to Victoria in Rome). Megellus proceeded to besiege Milionia, while Regulus marched to relieve Luceria. Regulus' luck did not improve in Apulia. The Samnite army met him at the frontier of Luceria's territory, defeated him in battle and his legions and cohorts retreated into their fortified camp. The following day, only after much cajoling by the consul, senior officers and centurions, was the army persuaded to resume the fight. It seemed that the Romans would again be defeated, but Regulus' loud declarations that he had vowed a temple to Jupiter Stator ('the Stayer') in exchange for victory, and the exemplary leadership of the centurions, encouraged the Romans, who enveloped the Samnites and finally won the fight. The surviving Samnites, 7,800 in number, were not enslaved but stripped and forced under the yoke. They were defeated and humiliated but free to return to Samnium. Regulus was now keen to return to Rome and claim the right to triumph. On route, he intercepted and slaughtered Samnite raiders in the territory of Intermna Lirenas (the Samnites were perhaps making their way down to northern Campania), but when the Senate learned that he had lost almost 8,000 men in the two–day battle near Luceria and, even worse, that he had let the enemy go free, his request for a triumph was rejected.[58]

The Senate and some of the plebeian tribunes who represented the People also denied Postumius Megellus' request for a triumph, but the arrogant and unconventional patrician held one anyway on 27 March 293 BC, perhaps suggesting that he campaigned through the winter months. He had, after all, stormed Milionia, killed 3,200 Samnites and enslaved another 4,700; he captured another Marsian (or Samnite) town called Feritrum and enriched his troops with booty; advancing into Etruria he defeated the army of Volsinii and then he captured Rusellae, no mere hill fort or town like the strongholds of the Aequi or Samnites, but a great fortress city. It had been more than a century since the Romans last captured such a city (Veii). The Etruscans had believed their cities impregnable and the war in Etruria lasted so long simply because the Etruscans could retreat behind their strong walls, just as the army of Volsinii did in 294 BC when defeated in the field by Megellus. It is to be regretted that no details of how exactly Megellus captured Rusellae survive; we know far, far more about the capture of obscure Milionia. However, such was the shock and surprise at his conquest of Rusellae that Volsinii, Perusia and Arretium sued for peace. On supplying the consul's soldiers with clothing and grain, the Etruscans were permitted to seek terms from the Senate. They were granted truces of forty years' duration, but each state was forced to immediately pay an indemnity of 500,000 *asses*. Readers will recall that Fabius Rullianus had extracted 539,400 *asses* from Perusia in ransoms in the previous year.

All Italy

In 293 BC the Samnite League enforced a levy by means of *lex sacrata*: the lives of those men who ignored the summons, or later deserted, were forfeit to

Jupiter. The Samnite army mustered at Aquilonia, the location of which is uncertain, but probably lay somewhere in the north of Samnium, not far distant from Bovianum. Despite heavy losses in recent years, we are told that 40,000 men of military age gathered at Aquilonia. From this great host, 16,000 warriors were formed into an elite corps called the Linen Legion (*legio linteata*), on account of them wearing fine white linen tunics. Like the Etruscan *sacrati* at Lake Vadimon, each warrior of the Linen Legion chose another according to his courage and nobility, and the corps was gradually assembled.

The consuls of 293 BC were Lucius Papirius Cursor, son of the hero of the Second Samnite War, and Spurius Carvilius Maximus. The latter consul took over the legions of Atilius Regulus, which had wintered at Interamna Lirenas. Considering Regulus' losses at Luceria, they must have been substantially re-constituted. While Cursor was levying new legions Maximus advanced against the enemy. Livy reports that the consul captured Amiternum in Samnium. However, no town or stronghold of this name is known in Samnium. It is not impossible that there was an Amiternum in Samnite territory, but it seems that Maximus had in fact captured the well-known Amiternum in the Sabine country. The Sabines had, of course, fought with the Samnites in 296 BC and the Romans had unfinished business with them. Maximus boasted of his success at Amiternum – 2,800 killed and 4,270 enslaved. Cursor could not allow his colleague to hog the glory and led his newly levied army to the otherwise unknown Samnite town of Duronia, which was duly stormed. Cursor did not take as many captives, but killed more of the enemy, and so evened the score with his plebeian colleague. The consuls then joined forces and marched on Aquilonia. They passed through the territory of Atina and devastated it. This former Volscian town had been pillaged by the elder Cursor in 313 BC but was now clearly back in Samnite hands.

Cursor established camp near Aquilonia, but Maximus took his army to nearby Cominium and placed it under siege. The Samnites detached twenty cohorts, perhaps c. 8,000 men, to reinforce the garrison of Cominium. With the Samnite army now substantially reduced in size, Cursor whipped his troops up into a frenzy, formed the army into battle line and attacked. The Linen Legion and the other corps of the Samnite army absorbed the shock of the initial Roman charge, but Cursor had a surprise in store for the enemy. Prior to advancing, the consul had detached three allied cohorts and all the baggage mules from the army. While Cursor engaged the Samnites, the cohorts and mules were to form a column and, raising as much dust as possible, march towards the Samnites' flank. The ruse was highly effective: the Samnites mistook the allies and mules for the consular army of Maximus, arriving victorious from Cominium and about to assail their flank; they panicked and started to break ranks. Cursor had held most of his cavalry behind the infantry, rather than on the flanks, and lanes were opened up between the maniples allowing the Roman and allied *equites* to charge the enemy head on, a rare occurrence in ancient warfare (Valerius Corvus is is reported as employing a similar tactic at Rusellae in 302/1 BC). The right and left divisions of the Roman infantry, respectively commanded by Volumnius Flamma and Scipio Barbatus, followed up the cavalry charge. This was too much for the Samnites. The Linen Legion held out for longer than the other Samnite regiments, but ultimately it too broke. Flamma's division captured the Samnites' camp, while Barbatus led the assault on Aquilonia. With four centurions and a maniple of *hastati*, the handsome and bearded legate formed a *testudo* and captured one of its gates; the Samnites fled out of another. The number of Samnites killed at Aquilonia – in the battle, at the camp, the town and in the pursuit by Roman cavalry – is reported as 23,040. Some did escape to Bovianum, but these were mostly cavalrymen and nobles. The twenty cohorts sent to reinforce Cominium did not arrive in time, nor were they quick enough to return to Aquilonia, where they could have stemmed the rout. The bulk of this force managed to retreat to Bovianum as well, but only because one of the cohorts fought a courageous rearguard action against the rampant Roman cavalry.

As Cursor was victorious at Aquilonia, so too was Maximus at Cominium. The Samnites defended the town with vigour, but when the Romans gained the battlements and forced the Samnites into the marketplace, they threw down their arms and surrendered. Livy reports 4,800 killed and 11,400 made captive. Maximus' army went on to capture three other Samnite towns, Velia and Herculaneum (not to be confused with the more famous cities on the coast of Campania) and Palumbinum. At Herculaneum the Samnites fought a pitched battle before the town and inflicted substantial casualties on the consul's force, but they were ultimately forced inside the town and it was stormed. Around 5,000 Samnites were killed in these engagements, and a slightly greater number were enslaved.

Cursor crowned his success at Aquilonia with the capture of Saepinum, a major hill fortress where the Samnites had deposited the wealth of the surrounding townships and farms. The capture of Saepinum was not easy. The Samnites made frequent sorties from the town to fight in the open, and it was sometime before Cursor could establish an effective cordon and reduce the fortress by siege. Of the defenders 7,400 are reported killed and less than 3,000 taken captive. Cursor had allowed his men to sack Aquilonia, but following his triumph on 13 January 292 BC, all the profits from the capture of Saepinum, and probably also of Duronia, and from the sale of captives were handed over to the Roman state treasury, much to the disgust of the legionaries and their families, who hoped that a donative from the spoils would offset the special tax they paid to sustain the Roman war effort. Carvilius Maximus took note and at his triumph (13 February 292 BC) granted each of his legionaries a donative of 102 bronze *asses*. Centurions and *equites* received double that amount. Maximus still had enough left from the spoils to make a healthy donation to the state treasury and to pay for a temple dedicated to Fors Fortuna. He also had the bronze helmets and other armour stripped from the enemy melted down and used in the production of an immense statue of Jupiter that dominated the Capitol in Rome. This famous statue was so tall that it could be seen from the sanctuary of Jupiter of the Latins (*Latiaris*) on the Alban Mount, 12 miles away.

The numbers of Samnite dead and captives reported for 293 BC may have the ring of authenticity, but the total seems much too great for a nation that had already suffered very heavy losses, and so the figures are probably erroneous or exaggerated. It is true that the Samnites did not sue for peace until 290 BC and in 292 BC even inflicted a notable defeat on the inept consul Fabius the Glutton (Gurges). However, after Aquilonia the Romans were able to traverse Samnium with relatively little opposition, indicating that the Samnites, as a League or as the four individual tribes, no longer had the manpower to adequately defend their territory.

In the winter of 293/2 BC Papirius Cursor wintered with his army in the territory of Vescia, which had been targeted by Samnite raiders. It may have been in this area or northern Campania that a Samnite force defeated Fabius Gurges: 3,000 of his men were killed and many more wounded. Fabius Rullianus exerted all of his influence to prevent Gurges from being recalled to Rome and disgraced, and joined his son's army as a legate. In the 291 BC proconsul Gurges, under the guidance of his father, defeated the Samnites near Caudium, and is even said to have captured the aged Gavius Pontius, though this latter detail is probably a fiction invented to enhance the reputation of the Fabii. Gurges is found next besieging Cominium. Rullianus seems to have left the army by this point, for there was no-one to defend Gurges from the bullying of Postumius Megellus.

Megellus had avoided prosecution for his illegal triumph by serving under Carvilius Maximus as a legate in 293/2 BC. This emboldened him to add to his list of misdemeanours. When the consuls left office early in 291 BC Megellus was appointed *interrex* ('interim king', clearly a relic of the monarchical period) to oversee the election of new consuls: he made sure that he was one of them! Assigned the Samnite War (his colleague fought Etruscans and Faliscans), he cut his way through Samnium, starting in the north at the recently rebuilt Cominium, where he dismissed the unfortunate Gurges, and took the town, apparently killing 10,000 in the process and receiving the surrender of 6,200. He ended his campaign at Venusia on Samnium's southern frontier with Apulia and Lucania. This highly strategic town was conquered and its territory earmarked for distribution to 20,000 colonists. It was a triumphant campaign, but Megellus could not give up his unconventional habits. It was discovered that he was using 2,000 legionaries to clear land on his estate near Gabii in Latium. The use of the legionaries – paid *stipendia* to fight for the state, not to labour for a noble – was illegal, and, even worse, sacrilegious, because the area they cleared included a grove sacred to Juno Gabina. What is more, many of the soldiers died, perhaps of a pestilence that was affecting Rome. This act led to Megellus' prosecution and he was duly found guilty and forced to pay a heavy fine, but one wonders if the disgrace bothered Megellus overmuch. The trial cost the state more than it did him. He deliberately gave all of the booty from his campaign to his legionaries and then dismissed them, forcing the incoming consuls to conduct time-consuming levies.

The section of Livy's great history covering the last years of the Third Samnite War and the completion of the conquest of peninsular Italy in the 260s BC does not survive. We do possess the so-called *Periochae*, epitomes of his lost books, and with other sources we can piece together an outline of events.

The consuls Manius Curius Dentatus and Publius Cornelius Rufinus ('the Red') administered the final blow in 290 BC causing the Samnites to sue for peace. Both consuls earned triumphs but we possess not details of their campaign in Samnium. The 'old treaty' between Rome and the Samnites was renewed, but doubtless the terms were adapted heavily in favour of the victors. The Samnites may also have been required to pay an indemnity; after having had their country stripped bare by Roman pillagers, they would have found it difficult to pay. As well as the great chunk of southern Samnium conquered by Postumius Megellus and organized as the territory of the colony of Venusia, the Romans also stripped from the Samnites the territory between the Liris and the middle and upper Volturnus, the country the Samnites had conquered from the Volscians. Thus Sora and Intermna Lirenas were no longer on the frontier but deep within the *ager Romanus*.

The *cognomen* Dentatus means 'having teeth' and is perhaps indicative of the consul's forceful character, though it may be a typically abusive Roman nick-name, highlighting prominent or buck teeth. He was a *novus homo*, that is a new man, meaning the first of his eminent plebeian family to reach the consulship, but he was already of considerable military renown and this attracted a following of 800 young men – a forerunner of the political gangs that were a feature of the later Republic. After subduing Samnium he turned on the Sabines, still un-punished for their role in the Gellius Egnatius' grand alliance. Rather con-viently, Sabine raiders provided Dentatus with the opportunity to attack:

> When the Sabines levied a large army, left their own territory, and
> invaded ours, Manius Curius by secret routes sent against them a

force which ravaged their lands and villages and set fire to them in divers places. In order to avert this destruction of their country, the Sabines thereupon withdrew. But Curius succeeded in devastating their country while it was unguarded, in repelling their army without an engagement, and then in slaughtering it piecemeal.[59]

Dentatus' victory was as total as it was rapid. He did not merely overrun the Sabine country and the adjoining territory of the Praetuttii (separating the Picentes from the Vestini) on the Adriatic coast, he conquered it. With the exception of territory set aside for the establishment of a Latin colony at Hadria (probably with 4,000 adult male settlers), it was annexed to the *ager Romanus*. Dentatus had almost doubled the size of the *ager Romanus* in a single campaign, an extraordinary achievement. Part of the land was retained directly by the state as *ager publicus* (public land) to be leased out, and the rest distributed in allotments of 7 *iugera* to Roman citizens, but there were complaints that the size of the farm plots was too small. Dentatus dismissed the critics: 'he prayed there might be no Roman who would think too small that estate which was enough to maintain him.' The consul famously refused to receive more than 50 *iugera* for himself – one doubts that Postumius Megellus would have been so modest. There were no objections from the Senate or People to Dentatus being awarded a second triumph in the space of a year. He could justifiably boast that he was uncertain about which was greater, the extent of the land conquered, or the numbers of people subdued.

The Sabines and Praetuttii were enrolled as Roman citizens without the vote. This surge of conquest suddenly carried Roman territory from the Tyrrhenian seaboard to the Adriatic coast. Admittedly, this belt of citizen territory narrowed considerably at the Adriatic, but nonetheless it was un-broken, dividing Rome's northern and southern enemies, who would never again unite. Dentatus is to be numbered among the most important Roman conquerors, for it was through his actions that the conquest of central and upper peninsular Italy was rapidly achieved. His next great conquest would be the country of the Senones.

Dentatus' campaign in the *ager Gallicus* was the result of the on–going war in Etruria. Postumius Megellus' capture of Rusellae did not mark the ceasation of hostilities. In 293–291 BC Rome fought Etruscans (Troilum, otherwise un-known, is the only town identified) and a rebellious Falerii. Troilum was easily subdued by Carvilius Maximus, but the defeat of Falerii was completed by his consular successor, Iunius Britus Scaeva. Brutus also ravaged the territories of Etruscan states, suggesting that treaties had been broken and troops sent to aid the Faliscans. Discontent simmered but it was not until 284 BC that the Romans fought again in Etruria. A Senonian army appeared at Arretium and the consul Lucius Caecilius Metellus rushed north to defend the city, the leading families of which were now firmly allied to Rome. It is uncertain if the Gauls were on a plundering mission, seeking to conquer new land, or if they were employed as mercenaries by other Etruscan states hostile to Rome. Recalling the shame of the defeat at Sentinum, the Senones utterly routed the army of Metellus. The consul and seven of his military tribunes were among the 13,000 Roman and allied casualties. Curius Dentatus was promptly installed as suffect consul. He sent an embassy into the *ager Gallicus* to treat for the return of Roman captives, but a Senonian chief called Britomaris executed the envoys. Dentatus was incensed, invaded the *ager Gallicus*, defeated the Senones in battle and, according to Polybius, drove the tribe out of the region completely. That is an exaggeration, but like his conquest of the Sabines, the reduction of the Senones was achieved with amazing swiftness. The *ager Gallicus* was annexed, but only a small citizen colony was planted on the coast, around 100 miles north of Hadria and called Sena Gallica, after the former inhabitants. It was not until 268 BC and the establishment of a strong Latium colony at Ariminum that the *ager Gallicus* was truly consolidated. The conquest of the Senones meant that the Picentes, nominally allies of Rome, were sandwiched between the Roman-controlled *ager Gallicus* to the north, and *ager Romanus* and Latin territory (Hadria) to the south, while the Sabine country and Roman-dominated Umbria lay to the west. In 269 BC the Picentes 'rebelled'. The war continued into 268 BC but the Picentes were unable to resist both consular armies indefinetly. A battle at Ausculum is highlighted as the decisive engagement. When the fighting was interrupted by an earth tremor (a frequent occurrence in Italy), the consul Publius Sempronius Sophus vowed a temple to Tellus, the earth goddess. This calmed the Roman troops, who promptly took advantage of the Picentes' disarray. The defeated Picentes lost much of their territory to the *ager Romanus* and the inhabitants of those parts became citizens without the vote, clearly a second-class status. Portions of Picenum did remain allied territory, most notable the regions around Ausculum and Ancona (colonized in 387 BC by Dionysius I of Syracuse as a staging post for his Gallic and Italian mercenaries), but to prevent future rebellions a very considerable number of Picentes were also deported west to a new 'Picenum', the *ager Picentinus*, sandwiched between Campania and Lucania. The lowland Sabines were promoted to full Roman citizenship in 268 BC, indicating rapid Romanization, while the Sassinates were conquered in 266 BC, securing northernmost Umbria. Control of the new eastern territories and Adriatic seaboard was further enhanced by the foundation of a Latin colony at Firmum in Picenum in 264 BC.

The completeness of the defeat of the once-great Senones is emphasized by the reaction of the Boii. Fearing that they would be next on the Romans' hit list, they allied themsleves with Etruscans (no particular states are identified) and in a forerunner of the Gallic invasion of 225 BC, decided on a pre-emptive strike against Rome. However, in 283 BC at Lake Vadimon and in the following year at Vetulonia they, and their Etruscan allies, were defeated. Volsinii and Vulci continued the fight against Rome until 280 BC. Caere rose up in 273 BC, but was easily beaten, her territory annexed and her people incorporated as Roman citizens without the vote. In that year the Latin colony of Cosa was planted on the Etruscan coast. In 264 BC a second coastal colony, but of Roman citizens, was established between Ostia and Cosa and named Castrum Novum (New Fortress). The destruction of Volsinii, also in 264 BC, triggered by the rebellion of its large population of slaves and serfs against a minority of pro-Roman ruling families, is to be regarded as the completion of the conquest of Etruria and, indeed, of the conquest of peninsular Italy. But what of the south of Italy? The subjection of Sabellian and Greek southern Italy resulted from the war against Tarentum and the celebrated Pyrrhus of Epirus.

Chapter 6

The Pyrrhic War

Personalities

Few of the Roman consuls and generals of the period 390–290 BC emerge from the pages of Livy, and other ancient sources, as little more than names, although their names (*cognomina*) can be rather extraordinary.[60] Marcus Furius Camillus, saviour of Rome and scourge of the Volsci and Etruscans, is one such example. He always appears in the nick of time to score a great victory, but what of the man himself, his character and personality? Courage, determination, ambition and an able leader of men can be inferred, but those qualities are the marks of all leading Romans of this period. They were born into an intensely competitive aristocracy and were trained to be that way. However, as we progress to the end of the fourth century and into the third century BC, some personalities do emerge. The elder Lucius Papirius Cursor is perhaps the earliest example. A stickler for correct forms and discipline, he also possessed a ferocious temper and bore a long-term grudge against Fabius Rullianus. His *cognomen* reflected his physical prowess. He was a hard drinker – a habit his son seems to have acquired. Cursor was noted for his black humour:

> The praetor [chief magistrate] of Praeneste had shown a lack of courage in bringing his men up from the rear into the fighting line. Papirius, walking in front of his tent, ordered him to be called up, and on his appearance told the lictor to get the axe ready. The Praenestine, on hearing this, stood paralysed with fear. 'Come, lictor,' said Papirius, 'cut out this root; it is in the way of people as they walk.' After almost frightening him to death with this threat, he dismissed him with a fine.[61]

Fabius Rullianus should be mentioned. The unflappable hero of Sentinum was also the cringer who fled from the fury of the elder Cursor and grovelled to the Senate and People to spare his life. He was the man defeated at Lautulae and who cruelly decimated his legions. The *cognomen* Rullianus, meaning boorish, could have reflected the harsher side of his character. Scipio Barbatus is an interesting figure. If the *elogium* inscribed on his sarcophagus in fact dates to the second third of the third century BC, it is possible that it was composed by a member of the clan who knew Barbatus while he lived (he died after 280 BC).

The references to Barbatus' handsomeness and *virtus* may not be a clan boast but a genuine reflection of the man and how he saw himself. Barbatus' reappearance after the debacle at Camerinum indicates he was a political survivor, and his part in the victory at Aquilonia demonstrates how his military talents were appreciated and that he was willing to lead from the front. He may have been the first to use the *cognomen* Scipio. The name is surely another mark of pride and is notably grand.

Appius Claudius has been cited as another emerging personality, an intriguing mixture of iconoclast and old school patrician. The most interesting figure of the period is certainly Postumius Megellus. He was proud and determined, hungry for glory, arrogant and bullying – all surely reflected in his *cognomen*. Above all, he was unafraid to go against convention and the laws of the state to get what he wanted. However, it is ironic that the first real personality in Roman history was an enemy of Rome. He was Pyrrhus of Epirus and much of what we know of him stems from his own memoirs, and the historical and tactical works of members of his court – Cineas and Proxenus. These do not survive, but were used as source material by Greek and Roman historians and biographers, whose works have come down to us. The career and character of Pyrrhus can therefore be reconstructed in detail.

The Restless King

Pyrrhus of Epirus was king of the Molossians, hegemon of the Epirote League, a prince of Illyria, and sometimes king of Macedonia and Thessaly. He was named after his legendary ancestor, Pyrrhus (better known as Neoptolemus), the son of Achilles. Keenly aware of his descent from the hero of the Trojan War, and from the equally belligerent Heracles, another son of the great god Zeus, the energetic Pyrrhus endeavoured to live up to their example and equal their fame by proving himself on the battlefield.

Pyrrhus was born in 319 BC. Only two years later his father, Aeacides, was deposed and the royal family forced to flee Epirus. The infant Pyrrhus was adopted by the Illyrian king, Glaucius, and in 306 BC the king's army restored Pyrrhus to the Molossian throne, but Pyrrhus was again forced to flee when powerful Cassander of Macedon set up a puppet in Epirus (302 BC). The teenager took service with his brother-in-law, Demetrius Poliorcetes ('the Besieger of Cities'), and fought in the wars of the Diadochi – the Successors. The Diadochi were the famed companions of Alexander the Great: Ptolemy, Antigonus Monophthalmus ('the One-Eyed'; father of the Besieger), Seleucus, Cassander and Lysimachus. Their battles for control of their old master's fragmenting empire were titanic in scale. It was in one of these great battles that Pyrrhus established his reputation. At Ipsus, Seleucus' war elephants destroyed the exposed flank of Antigonus' infantry while Demetrius was pursuing Seleucus' broken cavalry. Antigonus was killed and Demetrius' cavalry victory counted for nothing. Despite serving on the losing side, Pyrrhus emerged with distinction for his part in the initially successful cavalry charge (301 BC).

Antigonus saw the promise in the young Pyrrhus prior to the battle and paid him a great compliment. When asked whom he considered to be the best general, Antigonus, a commander to both Philip II and Alexander the Great, replied, 'Pyrrhus – *if* he lives to be old.' The Epirote did become an accomplished tactician and strategist. Hannibal stated that Pyrrhus was his teacher. 'No one has ever shown better judgement in choosing his ground, or in marshalling his forces.' The Carthaginian general also recognized the importance of Pyrrhus' ability to win men over. Pyrrhus possessed that indefinable but essential quality of the great commander: he had charisma and he had it in considerable quantity. His likeable nature and flamboyance drew men and women to him. His energy was boundless and his enthusiasm infectious. In battle he led from the front, conspicuous in his scarlet cloak and horned helmet. He had the ability to galvanize disparate bands under his personal leadership. 'You pick out the big men,' he told his recruiting officers. 'I'll make them brave!' Pyrrhus could also be autocratic – at least outside of Epirus – but it is notable in his chequered career that his Epirote soldiers never abandoned him. They loved him even in defeat.

In his *Life of Pyrrhus* Plutarch wrote that the king 'was adept at turning his superiors to his own advantage.' In 298 BC Pyrrhus was sent to Egypt as a hostage to secure a peace deal between Demetrius and Ptolemy I, but the Epirote was no idle captive. He impressed Ptolemy, charmed Ptolemy's queen Berenice (formerly his concubine), married her daughter (Ptolemy's step-daughter) and returned to Epirus at the head of a Ptolemaic army (297 BC). Pyrrhus grudgingly shared the Molossian kingship with Neoptolemus II, the puppet of Cassander, but it wasn't long before the usurper was assassinated.

Pyrrhus was proud of his Epirote roots, but he was a man of immense ambitions and chafed by the confines of his kingdom. Pyrrhus was never called king of Epirus or of the Epirotes, as the Roman sources erroneously refer to him. He was king of the Molossians, the principal tribe of Epirus, and acknowledged *hegemon* (leader) by the related tribes of the Thesprotians and Chaonians; the three tribes were known collectively as the Epirote Allies. The kings of the Molossians were bound by a strict constitution, which even included clauses allowing the people to depose the monarch and expel his family – as happened to the young Pyrrhus in 317 and 302 BC. Real power lay in the hands of the *prostates*, similar to the ephors of Sparta. The power of the *hegemon* was also constrained. The king had to gain the ascent of the Epirote Alliance before he could call out the army and wage war. The desire of Pyrrhus to conquer foreign territories is understandable. Only outside of Epirus could he rule in the autocratic manner of contemporary Hellenistic kings and Pyrrhus was quick to seize opportunies to acquire territories adjoining Epirus. When Berenice's daughter died, Pyrrhus married Lanassa, the daughter of the Syracusan tyrant Agathocles (295 BC). The island of Corcyra was her dowry, presenting Pyrrhus with an excellent base for operations in the Adriatic and Ionian Seas. His next acquisitions were Ambracia, Amphilochia and Acarnania to the south of Epirus, and Parauaea and Tymphaea to the northeast, on the border with Macedonia (294 BC). Alexander V of Macedon ceded these areas to Pyrrhus. Cassander had died in 297 BC, facilitating the return of Pyrrhus and leaving Macedonia in chaos. Alexander eventually succeeded to his father's throne with Pyrrhus' aid – the Molossian king may have had limited powers, but if persuaded, the Epirote Alliance could supply him with significant manpower, and Pyrrhus was blessed with a silver tongue. Pyrrhus also occupied the island of Leucas, lying off Acarnania. It may have been part of the payment agreed with Alexander V, though it could have formed part of Lanassa's dowry. Thus in only two years Pyrrhus had forged a miniature empire that he could call his own in northwest Greece. He made Ambracia his capital and adorned it lavishly. However, he was not entirely free of constraints in his new lands. The Acarnanians were organized into a league and promised the new king service in defensive wars, but offensive wars were a different manner. If Pyrrhus wished to use their manpower in expansionist enterprises, they would have to be employed on a mercenary basis. He probably had to negotiate similar arrangements in his other territories.

Alexander had barely warmed the seat of his throne when he was murdered by Demetrius (294 BC). The Besieger was also busy consolidating his hold over central and southern Greece, and while he was involved in the siege of Thebes, Pyrrhus raided Thessaly, mostly for profit but perhaps also to avenge his protégé, Alexander. Demetrius abandoned his siege to chase Pyrrhus back to Epirus. The Molossian king then turned his attentions to the north. In 292 BC he married two Illyrian princesses, securing alliances to protect the northern frontier of Epirus but also with an eye to establishing dynastic claims for future expansion. However, his polygamy infuriated Lanassa and she eventually left him for Demetrius, to whom she presented Corcyra (c. 290 BC). The Besieger now occupied Aetolia, threatening Acarnania and Amphilochia. It seemed that Pyrrhus would lose all his recent gains to the more powerful king, but the war presented Pyrrhus with an opportunity he had been waiting for: to claim the Macedonian throne.

Demetrius attacked Epirus in 289 BC. Pyrrhus counter marched against the invader, but somehow the kings managed to bypass each other. This may have been deliberate on the part of Pyrrhus. Calculating that the hardy Epirotes could withstand Demetrius' depredations, he continued his advance south into Aetolia, where Demetrius had left a large force of occupation. If Pyrrhus was successful in Aetolia, Demetrius would have to withdraw from Epirus. The Macedonian Pantauchus commanded the army of occupation in Aetolia. He met Pyrrhus' army at an unspecified location but was shocked at the power of the Epirotes' charge. Fearing defeat, Pantauchus challenged Pyrrhus to single combat in order to reduce the conflict to a battle of champions. If charismatic Pyrrhus was killed, the Epirotes would retreat in dismay. Pantauchus was confident in his strength and courage and he knew Pyrrhus could not resist such a challenge. Pyrrhus accepted, taking heart from his descent from Achilles. The duel became famous:

> At first they hurled their spears, then, coming to close quarters, they plied their swords with might and skill. Pyrrhus got one wound, but gave Pantauchus two, one in the thigh and one along the neck, and put him to flight and overthrew him. However, he did not kill him, for his companions dragged him away. Then the Epirotes, exalted by the victory of their king and admiring his valour, overwhelmed and cut to pieces the phalanx of the Macedonians, pursued them as they fled, slew many of them, and took five thousand of them alive.[62]

Oddly enough, the surviving Macedonians did not take unkindly to Pyrrhus' overwhelming victory. Saddened by a succession of usurpers, the oldest soldiers yearned for a return of the glory days of Alexander the Great:

> This battle did not fill the Macedonians with fury and hate towards Pyrrhus for their losses. Rather, it persuaded those who witnessed his exploits or engaged him in the battle to greatly respect him and admire his bravery and to talk much about him. They compared his aspect and his swiftness and all his motions to those of the great Alexander, and thought they saw him in the shadows, as it were, and imitations of that leader's impetuosity and might in conflicts. The other kings, they said, could only imitate Alexander in superficial details, with their purple cloaks, their bodyguards and the angle at which they held their heads, or the lofty tone of their speech: it was Pyrrhus alone who could remind them of him in arms and action.[63]

The Macedonians were doubtlessly aware that Pyrrhus was the cousin of the great Alexander. Olympias, Alexander's mother, was of the Molossian royal house. News of Pyrrhus' stunning victory would have spread across the Greek East and travelled west by the trade routes to Magna Graecia and Italy. Epirus was, after all, only a short sail across the Ionian Sea. The Romans took an interest in the brave deeds (*fortia facta*) of leading Samnite *bellatores* (the best warriors made the best opponents), and it would not be surprising if they followed the exploits of the distant but immensely glamorous Diadochi. It is possible that Romans or Latin speakers could have carried news of Pyrrhus' duel to Italy. Italian traders and pirates were active in the Adriatic, Ionian and Aegean seas. Rome had established relations with Rhodes in 306 BC and in recent years Demetrius had captured Italian pirates, perhaps operating out of Antium, in his waters. He returned the captives but admonished the Senate, which probably sanctioned the activity in return for a cut of the profits:

> When he sent back to the Romans what pirates he had captured, [he] said that, although he was doing the Romans the favour of sending back the captives because of the kinship between the Romans and the Greeks, he did not deem it right for men to be sending out bands of pirates at the same time that they were in command of Italy, or to build in their Forum a temple in honour of the Dioscuri, and to worship them, whom all call Saviours, and yet at the same time send to Greece people who would plunder the native land of the Dioscuri [Castor and Pollux]. And the Romans put a stop to such practices.[64]

Roman traders and buccaneers (the roles were interchangeable) would have relished the tale of Pyrrhus' single combat with Pantauchus. One can imagine the comparisons with Valerius the Raven, the famous monomachist, who was still alive. The Romans were also fascinated with Alexander the Great, vainly asserting that if he had invaded Italy the likes of the elder Cursor would have vanquished him. This interest in Alexander, the adaptation of the associated Greek cult of Nike into the cult of Victory, and contact with a major player like Demetrius, indicates that the Romans were aware of the personalities and politics of the Hellenistic kingdoms. We should not discount the possibility that when the Romans met Pyrrhus on the field of battle in 280 BC, they knew of his deeds and reputation. Likewise, Pyrrhus may have known of the Romans and their prowess through tales of Sentinum.

*   *   *

Pyrrhus' victory over Pantauchus forced Demetrius to abandon the plundering of Epirus. He raced back to Macedonia to defend its now vulnerable borders and recalled the remnants of his forces from Aetolia, but Pyrrhus discovered the hard way that he was not strong enough to assault Macedonia alone; an alliance had to be forged with Lysimachus of Thrace. Despite the setback in Macedonia, Pyrrhus received a rapturous welcome on his return to Epirus. The Epirotes bestowed an honorific title on their *hegemon*: the Eagle. Pyrrhus knew when to return a compliment and declared, 'Through you I am an eagle. It is by your arms that I am held aloft by swift pinions.' Pyrrhus is later reported as having a pet eagle. It may be that the bird was presented to him at this celebration.

The Eagle invaded Macedonia for the second time in 288 BC, his assault co-ordinated with that of Lysimachus, who attacked from Thrace. The veterans of the Macedonian army remained enamoured with Pyrrhus and, instead of opposing him at Beroea they saluted him as their king. The rumour that Alexander the Great had appeared to Pyrrhus in a dream and approved his enterprise encouraged their defection, as did Demetrius' haughty manner and increasingly unpopular rule. A despairing Demetrius was forced to flee.[65] Pyrrhus was the new king, but Lysimachus demanded that they divide the country. However, Pyrrhus made up for what he lost in Macedonia by ejecting Demetrius' garrisons from Thessaly, where he was also declared king.

Lysimachus had been a bodyguard of Alexander the Great. The conqueror was a military genius and a heroic leader, but he was dangerously unstable and men like Lysimachus bore the brunt of his unhinged behaviour. On one occasion Alexander locked an unarmed Lysimachus in a cage with a hungry lion; mighty Lysimachus killed the beast with his bare hands. Following Alexander's death in 323 BC, he joined the ranks of the Diadochi by seizing the satrapy of Thrace, formerly a province of the Persian Empire. From this base he extended his power north to the River Danube and east to the Taurus Mountains. He even campaigned beyond the Danube, but his adventures were cut short when he was captured and ransomed by a barbarian chief. He taxed his provinces heavily. Wealthy Pergamum and his other Asian territories suffered most from his rapacious demands, but Lysimachus' treasury was the envy of his fellow kings. Pyrrhus could never hope to match Lysimachus' resources and in 284 BC Lysimachus confronted Pyrrhus at Edessa. Despite the numerical superiority of his forces, Lysimachus did not meet Pyrrhus in a formal battle. He chose the more certain strategy of cutting the Eagle's supply lines and watching his army suffer as it ran out of food and fodder. Lysimachus also used his vast wealth to bribe the senior officers of the Macedonian army. With his military and political position completely undermined, Pyrrhus was forced to abandon Macedonia and Thessaly, but his Epirotes and the contingents from the adjoining territories remained loyal. The pragmatic Macedonian soldiery, on the other hand, promptly recognized Lysimachus as their king.

Pyrrhus did not brood on his loss for long. He set about asserting his claims in Illyria, though Lysimachus may have raided Epirus in Pyrrhus' absence, and reconquered Corcyra (possibly achieved in 282 BC). Success was followed by a lull. Dealing with the *prostates* was not to Pyrrhus' liking, reminding him of his limited powers compared to kings like Lysimachus and Seleucus. There was no action, no adventure. 'Like Achilles, he could not endure inaction,' wrote

Plutarch. However, Seleucus invaded Lysimachus' territory in Asia Minor and, early in 281 BC, Lysimachus was killed in battle at Corupedium. The aged Seleucus was assassinted soon after. With the big players out of the game, the Eagle made ready to attack Macedonia and expel its latest new king, Ptolemy the Thunderbolt. But then another, even more tantalizing, opportunity for conquest and glory presented itself. A deputation from Tarentum arrived to request that Pyrrhus lead their city in its struggle against Rome.

Wealthy Tarentum

We have already encountered Tarentum, the greatest and most powerful of the Greek cities in southern Italy. Established in 706 BC by colonists from Sparta, Tarentum commanded the best harbour in southern Italy. Despite this significant advantage, it took several centuries for the city to become the major power in the region. Indeed, in 473 BC Tarentum suffered the greatest defeat yet inflicted on a Greek *polis* (city-state). The victors were the neighbouring Messapians. Tarentum's ruling class of aristocrats was annihilated, but the common people (*demos*) successfully defended the city and then re-established it as a democracy.

The fifth century BC witnessed the consolidation of Tarentum's position as a centre of manufacture and export. The sheltered inner bay of Tarentum, now called the Mare Piccolo, supported the murex. The shell of this gastropod was the basis of a deep scarlet dye much prized in antiquity for its rarity and therefore reserved for the garments of royalty and magistrates. The natural complement to dye production was wool production. Tarentum's pastures were given over to sheep and the weaving of wool into cloth was carried out on a major scale. As well as sheep herding, Tarentum was noted for horse rearing. Her fisheries were abundant (fishermen made up a substantial proportion of the *demos*) and her fields, orchards and vineyards, while not as productive as the rich land of Metapontum (that city produced a great surplus of cereals), were certainly sufficient to meet the needs of the city. Pottery was a very major industry. So too was metal working, Tarentum's bronze implements and ornaments being found far afield. The products of Tarentine gold- and silversmiths were highly sought after, as were the creations of sculptors in limestone and terracotta. Supplying Italian and foreign markets (Sicily, Epirus, Greece, the eastern Mediterranean, the Black Sea and North Africa), Tarentum's income was such that it enabled her to maintain a powerful navy. All of the Greek colonies in southern Italy boasted fleets, but none were as strong as that of Tarentum.

In 433 BC Tarentum established her own colony near the mouth of the River Siris and called it Heraclea. Late in the fifth century BC, or more probably early in the fourth century and in alliance with Dionysius I of Syracuse,

Tarentum assumed control over the Italiote League, that is, the loose defensive alliance of Greek cities in southern Italy, and moved the League's headquarters to Heraclea. Under the leadership of the Pythagorean philosopher Archytas, who was frequently elected *strategos* ('general', the most senior office in the democracy) in the 360s BC, Tarentum's great wealth, coupled with the support of Syracuse and the manpower of the Italiote League, enabled her to dominate southern Italy and hold back the expansion of the Lucanians and older enemies, such as the Messapians. Territorial gains were perhaps made at their expense, and Tarentine political influence was extended into Apulia. The Roman historian Florus was not far wrong when he described Tarentum as 'the capital of Calabria, Apulia and all Lucania.'[66]

Tarentum could levy troops from the members of the Italiote League, but her own manpower in the early to mid-fourth century BC was considerable. As well as the rowers and marines required by the navy, the geographer Strabo reports that Tarentum could call upon 30,000 infantry, 3,000 regular cavalry and 1,200 adaptable light cavalry. The latter were copied by other states and called 'Tarentines'. It has been suggested that these figures include contingents from the Italiote League, but Strabo refers only to Tarentum and the figures are comparable with the similarly sized Greek city of Athens. At the outbreak of the Peloponnesian War in 431 BC, Athens could call on 29,000 infantry (that is, men of the propertied hoplite class) and 1,200 cavalry.

Mercenaries

Tarentum's military power declined in the middle of the fourth century BC following the death of Archytas. She also lost a powerful ally when Dionysius II of Syracuse was deposed and ultimately retreated to exile in Corinth. Dionysius had combated the Lucanians on land, and hunted pirates on the seas. The Italiote Greeks were never a unified bunch, more often at war than cooperating as League members. Tarentum's power was envied and feared. Stripped of her allies, Tarentum's control was limited again to her own territory and the Lucani and Messapii assailed this from west and east. Yet the city continued as a great centre of commerce, trade did not slacken, and she had the funds to seek new allies. Rich Tarentum employed only the best mercenary captains with the most professional armies: Archidamus and Cleonymus of Sparta, and Alexander the Molossian, uncle of Alexander the Great and Pyrrhus. Tarentum's recourse to mercenaries is highlighted in the ancient sources as a mark of her decline, and also of her decadence – assuming that the Tarentines, corrupted by wealth and indolence, were now unwilling to fight. That is nonsense. It was common practice in the Ancient World to enlist the services of proven mercenaries, and the Tarentines fought alongside them, but

Tarentum never again produced a great leader like Archytas, and this made the mercenary commanders difficult to control.

Tarentum's fist appeal was made to her mother city in c. 344 BC. Archidamus, king of Sparta, then occupied with a contract in Crete, did not arrive in Italy until c. 342 BC. He appears to have dealt successfully with the Lucanians, but he was killed fighting the Messapians, and perhaps also Lucanians, at the siege of Manduria in 338 BC. By chance, or more probably by subsequent synchronization, Archidamus died on the same day that Philip II and his teenage son, Alexander the Great, routed the coalition led by Athens and Thebes at the Battle of Chaeronea, establishing Macedonian domination over central and southern Greece. Manduria was situated only a day's march to the southeast of Tarentum, but while her territory might be exposed to the depredations of the enemy, the position of the strongly fortified city on a headland between the Bay of Tarentum and the Mare Piccolo, where she could be supplied from the sea, dissuaded enemies from attempting sieges. Thus Tarentum weathered this setback and considered a suitable replacement for Archidamus.

The Tarentines called next on the services of Alexander the Molossian in 334 BC. Unlike the conscientious Archidamus, Alexander saw an opportunity to carve out an empire in Italy. Tarentum's security benefited from his successful campaigns – he recovered lost ground in Apulia, overran Lucania and, as we have seen, defeated the Lucani and Samnites at Posidonia – but the democracy had unwittingly invited in an even more dangerous enemy. Alexander made his intentions very clear when, after recovering Heraclea from the Lucanians, he transferred the headquarters of the Italiote League to Thurii and encouraged the individual cities to make alliances with him. Metapontum, keen to emerge from Tarentine domination (she had the geographical misfortune to lie between Tarentum and Heraclea) was happy to do this. As noted above, the Greek cities of southern Italy were bitter rivals; only the barbarian threat gave them any unity of purpose. Tarentum immediately withdrew her support from Alexander and may have sought an alliance with the Samnites. With their interests in Apulia and the wool trade, the Samnites were hardly natural allies, and helmets of Tarentine manufacture nailed up as trophies in Samnite sanctuaries may indicate armed conflict with Tarentum (although the helmets could have reached other opponents through trade), but in Alexander they found a common enemy. It was, however, the Lucani and Bruttii who dealt with the troublesome Alexander. (Tarentine financial and material support to these peoples cannot be discounted.) The Molossian, whose vast but fragile territory stretched from southeast Apulia to northwest Lucania, sought to add Bruttium to his empire, but the Lucani were far from subdued.

The Lucani were well-known as an offshoot of the Samnites. It was believed in antiquity that their name derived from *lykos*, the Greek for wolf. This would be an appropriate pathfinder animal, but the etymology is false and the true meaning of their name remains uncertain. Rather than driving out or destroying the peoples they encountered, it is most likely that the Sacred Spring sent out by the Samnites defeated, then dominated, the native population, who were Oscanized and gradually formed into a loose Lucanian nation. By 433 BC the Lucani had advanced as far south as the Gulf of Tarentum and threatened Thurii. The Bruttii were closely related to the Lucani. It was thought that their name derived from the Lucanian Oscan dialect for runaways or exiles, but that is not true. The name may in fact be derived from an Illyrian word for deer. Illyrians had settled in eastern Italy in prehistoric times, and the Messapii spoke an Illyrian dialect, so it would not be surprising to find loan words in other languages in southern Italy. If the Bruttii were named after a deer, this was probably a pathfinder animal (compare the Hirpini and the wolf). It is mostly likely that the Bruttii had their origin in a Sacred Spring sent out by the formative Lucani. They advanced into the toe of Italy and, again, rather than drive out the inhabitants, subdued and Oscanized them. By 357/6 BC, the Bruttian settlements were organized into a league.

In the autumn of 331 BC Alexander was operating in the vicinity of Pandosia. As the weather was foul and the land in the valley of the River Acheron was flooded, Alexander's army was forced to divide into three contingents. The king's division was surrounded by the combined forces of the Lucani and the Bruttian League. Alexander killed the Lucanian *meddix* in single combat, and with a small band of companions burst through the encirclement. Preparing to make his escape across a swollen river, one of his companions, a Lucanian exile, hurled a javelin at Alexander and killed him. The vengeful Lucani and Bruttii hacked Alexander's corpse in two, sending one half to be displayed before the walls of Consentia, which Alexander had captured from the Bruttii, and bombarded the other half with javelins and stones. His mangled remains were eventually reunited, taken to Metapontum, and from there transported to Epirus.

It was not until 303 BC that Tarentum felt it necessary to call upon the services of another mercenary commander. In the intervening period she reasserted her authority over the members of the Italiote League, enjoyed a temporary rapprochement with the Lucanians and focused on trade. When she was not fighting barbarians, Tarentum was selling them goods. However, the rise of Rome and her expansion into the rich markets of Campania and Apulia seriously impinged on the latter and lessened Tarentum's political influence in the South. Tarentum remained neutral in the Second Samnite War, but considering her planned aid to Neapolis and her machinations in removing the Lucani from the Roman alliance, it has been suspected that she gave the Samnites financial support. During one of the fights at Luceria in the Second Samnite War, she offered to mediate between the Romans and Samnites, but the Romans reacted with scorn and this added to her resentment. By the close of the fourth century BC, Tarentum was again struggling against Lucanian expansion. Recalling the satisfactory aid rendered by Archidamus, she appealed again to Sparta, but the Spartan prince Cleonymus turned out to be another Alexander. All went well in the beginning. Arriving in Italy with 3,000 mercenaries carried on Tarentine ships, the dynamic Cleonymus recruited a further 5,000 and won the support of the Messapians and Italiotes, while the Taretines gladly mobilized 20,000 infantry and 2,000 cavalry from the citizen levy. The Lucanians were cowed into accepting an alliance with Tarentum. However, the real alliance was with Cleonymus. Of the Italiote Greek cities Metapontum remained aloof, and Cleonymus used Lucanian troops to ravage its territory, while he captured the city with his mercenaries. A massive amount of silver was extracted and 200 well-born girls were taken hostage. The Tarentines had no love for treacherous Metapontum, but they were appalled by Cleonymus' devious activities. He intended to expand his power in Italy, but decided to first seize Corcyra, the perfect base for piracy and to launch operations in Italy and Greece. While he was so occupied, Tarentum 'revolted'. Cleonymus made a hasty return to Italy and landed in the territory of the Sallentini. According to Diodorus Siculus, after sacking two cities, he was ejected by 'barbarians', that is, the non-Greek peoples of southeast Italy, who stormed his camp. Livy reports that the Romans had a hand in his removal as well, and that seems probable considering Rome's interests in nearby Apulia.

Cleonymus tried to make good his losses by plundering the Adriatic coast of Italy (302 BC), but this expedition came to grief when his forces attempted to raid the city of Patavium in the country of the Veneti. The Patavians divided into two forces; one division defeated Cleonymus' marauders, while the other fell on his lightly defended fleet and destroyed most of the ships. Cleonymus escaped with only one fifth of his fleet. A gravestone from Patavium, dating to about 300 BC, is decorated with a scene of two Venetic horsemen trampling a decapitated enemy. It may commemorate a Patavian who fought in one of the engagements. Livy was of course a native of Patavium and the victory was still proudly celebrated in his day:

> There are now living in Patavium many who have seen the beaks of
> the ships [the bronze rams from the prows used to attack other ships]
> and the spoils of the Laconians which were fastened up in the old

temple of Juno. In commemoration of the naval battle a contest of ships is held regularly, on the anniversary of the victory, in the river that flows through the city.[67]

It is possible that Rome and Tarentum were in alliance at the time of the Cleonymus crisis, but following the Third Samnite War Tarentum was organizing a coalition against the northern upstart. The establishment of the powerful Latin colony at Venusia, approximately 75 miles northwest of Tarentum, was much too close to for comfort. The founding of colonies at Hadria and Sena Gallica on the Adriatic seaboard was most likely another irritant, a threat to Tarentine sea power and trade. The real stimulus for war came in 284 BC. Thurii, hard pressed by the Lucanians, appealed not to Tarentum but to Rome. Relations between Thurii and Tarentum were always strained, so it was perhaps no surprise that the Thurians looked to Rome for aid, recently successful against the Samnites, rather than to Tarentum, who despite her great wealth, had proved incapable of inflicting any lasting blows on the Sabellians. Indeed, it probably seemed to the Thurians that Tarentum courted barbarians for trade and military support. Yet the Romans must have been aware that if they accepted the Thurians' appeal, they would be trespassing in the Tarentines' sphere. Despite the disaster at Arretium, aid was granted to Thurii. It is uncertain what form it took – it may only have been diplomatic, the Lucanians, those erstwhile allies of Rome, scared off with the threat of military action. Whatever the case, it was evidently successful. The grateful people of Thurii set up in the Roman Forum a statue of the plebeian tribune, Gaius Aelius, who had acted against the Lucani. Other Italiote cities now considered seeking the protection of Rome from Lucanian and Bruttian raids. Tarentum reacted by sending agents to Rome's allies, and perhaps also her remaining enemies in Etruria, to stir up discontent. The respected plebeian senator Gaius Fabricius Luscinus was sent to investigate the loyalty of certain allies. Their identity is not revealed, but the senator was arrested by one of the suspect allies and held for a time. One could speculate that the uncooperative allies were Samnites. Indeed, in 282 BC the Samnites rebelled.

In 282 BC the Lucani returned to Thurii, this time with Bruttian reinforcements. The Lucanian general Sthenius Statilius was determined to take the city. Thurii appealed to Rome for a second time. Despite the continuing war against the Etruscans and Boii, Luscinus, now consul and campaigning against the rebellious Samnites, was instructed by the Senate to relieve the city. Still inflamed with the glory of Sentinum and a belief in divine intervention, the Romans asserted that Mars himself fought with them at Thurii. Statilius offered battle on open ground before the city, but his battle line was broken. The Romans poured through the gap and assaulted his camp. The Lucani and

Bruttii who were still in ranks abandoned their posts to defend the camp, but were defeated. The combined number of enemy dead and captives, including Sthenius Statilius, is reported as 25,000. The most remarkable feature of this victory is that the Romans asserted that Mars himself had appeared in the front rank, led the successful charge which sundered the Sabellian line, brought up a ladder and was first to gain the rampart of the enemy camp. This belief was founded on a huge soldier, wearing a plumed helmet, seen to lead the successful attack. On the following day, Luscinus paraded the army and called for the hero to step forward in order that he could be decorated. No one stepped forward. Luscinus then ordered that he be looked for among the dead; his corpse was not recognized, but the helmet was found. The devout Romans, still infected with the glory of Sentinum and belief in divine intervention, decided that this unnaturally tall warrior, wearing the distinctive twin plumes of Mars, must have been the war god. The consul then led his army in a joyous celebration of thanksgiving.

A Roman garrison was installed in Thurii, for her continued protection and to ensure that her pro-Roman aristocrats remained in control. We have seen how Italian aristocrats often preferred to accept Roman overlordship in order maintain their privileges and power at the local level. Rhegium, that strategic Greek city overlooking the Straits of Messana, fearful of Bruttian expansion (Hipponium was a constant reminder of a once great Greek city now completely barbarized), and conscious of the threat posed by the Mamertines just across the straits in Sicily, also admitted a Roman garrison. Similarly, Croton, vulnerable following a violent siege by Agathocles (295 BC), and Locri welcomed garrisons of Roman or allied troops.

Perhaps the Metapontines were tempted to ask Luscinus for aid, but their city lay too close to Tarentum. An inscription demonstrates that around this time, Metapontum employed Campanian mercenaries to bolster her defences. All Campania was under Roman control and this could suggest that the Romans allowed the lucrative mercenary trade to continue, so long as it did not compromise the ability of the Campanian states to fulfil their contributions to the Roman army. Later in the third century, rather than give direct military support, Rome permitted a beleaguered Carthage to recruit new mercenaries from Italy for service against rebellious mercenaries in the Truceless War (241–237 BC), but that was an exceptional episode. We should consider that the mercenaries at Metapontum were not actually from Campania, but were of Campanian descent. War was a frequent occurrence in southern Italy and Sicily; the Italiote cities, Syracusan tyrants and the Carthaginians always needed fighters and some mercenaries took up permanent residence; compare the Gauls based in Apulia in the fourth century BC. The Campanians employed by Metapontum could have been the second or third generation of well-established mercenary company.

Luscinus' activity directly undermined Tarentum's influence. In the autumn of 282 BC a small Roman fleet approached the city – the first we hear of the Roman navy since its role in the disastrous raid on Nuceria in 310/9 BC. The ten warships were presumably involved in Luscinus' campaign, but it is uncertain what they were doing in Tarentine waters. The fleet was much too small to take on Tarentum's navy; maybe the consul hoped to spur the aristocratic faction in the city to seize power and so speedily complete Rome's takeover of the Greek states. The fleet could simply have been on a reconnaissance. When the fleet approached many Tarentines were watching a performance in the theatre overlooking the harbour. Philocaris, a popular demagogue, rose up and declared that the despised Romans were breaking a treaty by sailing beyond the promontory of Lacinium, just south of Croton, and into the Gulf of Tarentum. The date and authenticity of this treaty are disputed. It could date back to Rome's agreement with Alexander the Molossian, decades before Rome could seriously contemplate the conquest of all peninsular Italy. Another possibility is that it dates from the period of Cleonymus' activities, but it is hard to imagine that Rome, fresh from victory in the Great Samnite War, would accept such a constraint on her future activities. In 306 BC Rome had renewed and redefined her old alliance with Carthage. Rome agreed not to interfere in Sicily, but claimed all Italy as her exclusive reserve. It is unlikely, therefore, that in c. 303 BC she would enter into an agreement limiting her scope for action in the south. It may be that the Tarentines were simply infuriated that Rome was now challenging their control of the sea. Broken treaty or not, Philocaris roused the Tarentines to action and they raced down to the wharves to man their warships. The Romans (the ships' crews were likely made up of Antiate Volscians or Neapolitan Greeks) were outclassed and outnumbered. Four of the Roman vessels were sunk and another was captured. The casualties included the Roman commander, and a number of the captives taken by the Tarentines were executed. Thoroughly energized by this victory, the Tarentines moved next on Thurii, forced the small Roman garrison to depart, sacked the city and sent its aristocrats into exile.

A deputation of senators was dispatched from Rome to demand the return of the Roman prisoners, the restoration of the Thurian aristocrats, and payment of suitable compensation to Rome and Thurii. That Rome sent an embassy rather than immediately declaring war on Tarentum has been taken to suggest that she did not, at that time, desire conflict. She was still involved in fighting in Etruria. However, if a successful diplomatic solution was hoped for, why did the Romans choose Postumius Megellus to lead the deputation? He was hardly a diplomatic character. One wonders if Megellus was actually sent to rile the Tarentines. It is true that they had inflicted a defeat on Rome, but in what was really a minor engagement, and although Thurii had received Roman aid and a garrison, she was perhaps not yet a formal ally of Rome. The Senate, aware that its activity in the far south could offer Tarentum just cause for retaliation, may have desired to build a better case for a just war, with Rome as the innocent party, forced to react to Tarentine refusal to make amends.

Megellus' deputation arrived in Tarentum during the raucous Bacchanalia festival (winter 282/1 BC). The former consul and his senatorial companions were jeered by drunken revellers; the Tarentines took an especial delight in insulting the senators' formal togas. The embassy was finally granted a hearing by the city council in the theatre. Here the Romans received similar treatment and Megellus was mocked for speaking Greek with a Latin accent. The council would concede nothing. As the Romans made to leave the theatre, a notorious drunkard called Philonides barred Megellus' way. 'Half Bottle', as Philonides was nicknamed, lifted his tunic and urinated on or, according to some accounts, even defecated on Megellus' toga. The Tarentines found this hugely amusing and burst into applause. Megellus maintained his dignity and declared: 'Laugh while you can. You will be weeping when you wash this garment clean with your blood!'

The sources agree that Megellus was grossly insulted and when the stained toga was displayed to the disgusted populace of Rome, war was finally declared on Tarentum. However, recalling Megellus' haughty and disagreeable character, we should wonder if his treatment by the Tarentines was exacerbated by his behaviour towards them. Even if he was sent to Tarentum to undermine the possibility of a diplomatic settlement, it is most unlikely the Senate imagined that an ambassador would be treated in such a disgraceful fashion. The war was assigned to the new consul, Lucius Aemilius Barbula ('Little Beard').

Tarentum had to find a strong ally, and quickly. She looked across the Ionian Sea to Epirus. While Fabricius Luscinus was battling the Lucanians, Pyrrhus was perhaps involved in winning back Corcyra. The date of this operation is uncertain, but his troops were ferried to the island on Tarentine transports. If the operation took place in 282 BC, Tarentinum may have supplied the ships on a purely commercial basis, but it is possible that a favour was rendered in the hope of securing the services of Pyrrhus in the looming conflict with Rome. When the Tarentine envoys arrived in Ambracia, Plutarch reports they flattered Pyrrhus by telling him 'that they needed a commander of reputation and good sense.' They promised to supply troops and cavalry transports, exaggerated the rich pickings that a war in Italy would offer, and declared that 350,000 infantry and 20,000 cavalry from the Greeks and non-Greeks (Samnites, Lucani, Bruttii, Messapians) would flock to him when he landed in Italy. Plutarch reports that Pyrrhus and the Epirote Alliance were greatly encouraged by this huge number of troops. One would think an experienced campaigner like Pyrrhus would realize that the Tarentines were exaggerating, but Plutarch's figures may have derived from a source which drew on Pyrrhus' memoirs or the writings of his chief minister, Cineas, or his court historian, Proxenus. The Tarentines also promised money. They reduced the silver content of their *didrachms* so that more could be minted and an advance payment was made to the king before he crossed the Ionian Sea. Like his uncle, Alexander, and Cleonymus, Pyrrhus accepted the Tarentine appeal because it provided him with an opportunity to win an empire, but Pyrrhus' aspirations went beyond Italy. He dreamed of conquering Sicily, Carthage and Libya, and then he would reclaim Macedonia. According to Pausanias, Pyrrhus envisaged the struggle with the Romans as a new Trojan War; the descendant of mighty Achilles versus the Roman descendants of the Trojan refugee, Aeneas. However, it is most unlikely that Pyrrhus ever thought this, for, as Pausanias also records, it was Andromache, the Trojan princess, who became the concubine of Neoptolemus-Pyrrhus and she bore him Molossus, founder of the Molossian nation.

As was customary, Pyrrhus consulted the great oracles about the success of the coming war. He received typically ambiguous responses. The priestesses of the oracle at Dodona deciphered the words of Zeus from the wind-rustled leaves of the god's sacred oak tree and the movements of doves on its branches: 'You, if you cross over to Italy, Romans shall conquer.' The response of the priestess of Apollo at Delphi was in a similar vein: 'You the Romans can defeat.' Pyrrhus chose to interpret these dubious responses as indicating that he, and not the Romans, would be victorious. The king decided to hold some or all of the envoys as hostages, just in case the Tarentines had second thoughts about their invitation and hexed his chance for glory in the West.

Having secured the support of the Epirote Alliance, Pyrrhus renounced his claims on Macedonia and obtained in return from Ptolemy Ceraunus twenty Indian war elephants and received the promise of troops.[68] That the other Hellenistic monarchs enthusiastically contributed ships and money to the expedition is indicative not only of Pyrrhus' persuasiveness, but also of the trouble they feared the hugely ambitious and energetic Epirote could cause on his own initiative if he remained in Greece, or that he might form an alliance with a rival monarch. Antiochus, son of Seleucus, and probably Ptolemy II (elder brother of Ceraunus), made a hefty contribution to Pyrrhus' war chest. Antigonus Gonatas, son of the Besieger, was dominant in southern Greece and desired to add Macedonia to his empire. He ensured Pyrrhus' departure from Greece by adding his transport ships to those provided by Tarentum.

Pyrrhus sent an advance force to Tarentum in autumn 281 BC. The 3,000-strong contingent was led by Pyrrhus' senior general, Milo, and his chief minister, Cineas, a suave Thessalian noted for his eloquence and compared with Demosthenes, the great Athenian orator. Its arrival was timely. Having dealt with some Samnites, Aemilius Barbula advanced into the territory of Tarentinum and, in typical Roman fashion, set about devastating it, but the property of rich and aristocratic Tarentines, known to oppose the dominant populist faction, was purposely left untouched. The consul also attacked the Sallentini in Calabria, as they had presumably declared for Tarentum. The strategy was successful. The Tarentines lost their nerve. The leaders of the populist faction were deposed and an aristocrat named Agis was elected *strategos*. He entered into negotiations with Barbula, but when Cineas arrived Agis was replaced with a *strategos* agreeable to the populists and Pyrrhus. Agis was probably executed as a traitor.

Barbula had not the resources to besiege Tarentum and, with winter approaching, retreated to Venusia. It is reported that the Tarentine navy attacked the Roman army, bombarding it with missiles from catapults, but Barbula forced his Tarentine captives to form a screen along the exposed flank of the army. Unwilling to kill their fellow-citizens, the Tarentine sailors abandoned the attack. It is unclear where this happened. Barbula may have marched west along the coast, continuing the devastation of Tarentum's countryside, until he reached the mouth of the Bradanus near Metapontum. There he could turn inland and follow the river valley north in the general direction of Venusia. The Tarentines and Epirotes also attempted to ambush Barbula at a defile, perhaps then in the valley of the Bradanus, but this also failed. For a second time Barbula used the Tarentine captives as a shield and the Roman army was allowed to pass.[69]

Milo established the Epirote headquarters on the acropolis of Tarentum. This was to be expected, but the Epirotes made themselves deeply unpopular when the houses of the wealthy were requisitioned to accommodate officers, and because the uncouth foreign soldiers made sexual advances on the women and boys of the city. Pyrrhus followed in the spring of 280 BC. He brought 20,000 infantry, perhaps all Epirotes; troops from Pyrrhus' other territories and Macedonian reinforcements are not reported until 279 BC. His 3,000 cavalry contained many Thessalians. The plains of Thessaly produced the best horsemen in Greece; some of these men were probably recently recruited mercenaries, but others will have served Pyrrhus since 287 BC. Part of the cavalry was organized into the *agema*, the king's bodyguard of Molossian nobles, and other worthies, such as Macedonians who remained loyal to Pyrrhus. There were also 2,500 archers and slingers, and the twenty war elephants. As it approached the Iapygian Cape, the fleet was hit by a storm and most of the ships were swept towards Sicily and the African coast. Pyrrhus managed to land with only a few troops and marched across Calabria to Tarentum, but Messapians reinforced his reduced ranks (recall Barbula's operation against the Sallentini), and as his scattered transports gradually made their way to Tarentum's harbour, it became clear that the storm losses were in fact minimal.

It is reported that the citizens of Tarentum expected Pyrrhus' soldiers to do all the fighting on land, and were shocked to find themselves pressed into service. That is most unlikely. We have seen how Tarentum was prepared to use her manpower on land – with Cleonymus, and most recently at Thurii and against Aemilius Barbula. Later Roman writers perpetuated a cliché about Tarentum's decadence and moral decline compared to the valiant Pyrrhus and his noble Roman opponents. The fact is that the Tarentines were doughty fighters on land, and would demonstrate their mettle in the battles against the Romans at Heraclea and Ausculum. However, Pyrrhus did feel it necessary to train the Tarentine levy, and because of the ill feeling the Epirotes had already caused, and the recent activities of Agis' party, he deemed it prudent to scatter the Tarentine soldiers throughout his units. The Epirotes fought with pikes in a Macedonian phalanx formation (see below). There is a little evidence that Tarentine infantry was organized along Spartan lines and we would expect them to have fought in a hoplite phalanx formation, but years of fighting the Lucanians, who employed the maniple and *pilum*, may have encouraged Tarentine infantry to fight in a looser formation and make greater use of missiles. We do not know if Pyrrhus trained the Tarentines to fight as phalangites, or if they were to act as lighter troops, in support of the phalanx. The Acarnanians were well-known as light troops, peppering their enemies with javelins in hit-and-run attacks (like the Roman *rorarii/velites*), but they are not reported as serving with Pyrrhus until 279 BC. Pyrrhus later organized Tarentine infantry into a corps of *chalcaspides*. 'White shields' were found in most Hellenistic armies, but their function is unclear, sometimes they appear in the sources as peltasts, that is, light infantry, at other times they fight in the phalanx. This suggests that they were neither dedicated light troops nor heavy, close order infantry, but trained to be adaptable and use a variety of shafted weapons. When they fought in the phalanx, they may have used the spear instead of the longer pike. The same may be true of the *hypaspists*, 'shield bearers', first attested in the army of Alexander the Great, and copied by the Diadochi. At least some of Pyrrhus' Ambraciotes were organized as *hypaspists*, but they do not feature in the war until 279 BC, suggesting the contingent was called upon only after the Epirotes had suffered heavy losses.

Pyrrhus closed Tarentum's theatre and forbade the citizens from meeting in their Spartan-style mess clubs. The theatre and messes, haunts of the more radical democrats, could prove dangerous to the king. The king also executed some Tarentines, and shipped others over to Epirus. Those condemned to capital punishment were presumably traitors who had backed Agis; the deportees being those suspected of favouring reconciliation with Rome, or radicals who might agitate against the king.

Lucanian Cows

Pyrrhus posed a very real threat to Rome's conquests in the south and elsewhere. He might prove even more dangerous than Gellius Egnatius as an architect of a grand alliance of southern and central Italian states and peoples against Rome. It would have been preferable to send both consular armies against him, but in 280 BC Volsinii and Vulci remained undefeated. With those powerful cities situated relatively close to Rome, it was too dangerous for both consuls to march south, and Tiberius Coruncanius took his legions into Etruria. The campaign against Pyrrhus was assigned to the other consul, Publius Valerius Laevinus. The *cognomen* Laevinus translates as 'Other-sided', which might mean the consul was left-handed, but it could also signify an awkward or unfortunate disposition, making it a typically uncomplimentary Roman nickname. In late spring or early summer, Laevinus devastated his way across Lucania and left a strong garrison at an unspecified strategic point 'to prevent its people sending aid to his opponent', but the Lucani were actually waiting to see if Pyrrhus (nephew of the hated Alexander the Molossian) could defeat the Romans before they lent him any aid. Laevinus continued on to the territory of Heraclea, Tarentum's old colony and sure ally, but Pyrrhus was encamped on the plain between the city and the River Siris, which Laevinus had to cross.

The great numbers of allies promised by the Tarentines to Pyrrhus had not yet materialized. The Samnites and Lucani were partly constrained by the presence of Aemilius Barbula, now proconsul, and his army in the vicinity of Venusia, although he would not remain there for much longer; we know he returned to Rome by 10 July to celebrate a triumph over the Samnites, Tarentines and Sallentini. The Sabellians and Italiote Greeks preferred to await the outcome of the battle with Laevinus: if Pyrrhus could defeat the Romans they would join his ranks. This has given rise to a myth that the Romans greatly outnumbered Pyrrhus' soldiers at Heraclea. Laevinus' army was composed of the usual two legions (8,400 infantry and 600 cavalry) and Latin and other allied contingents. If the allies supplied two soldiers for every Roman legionary, Laevinus' army would have numbered c. 27,000. The Latin and allied contribution may not, however, have been so great: in later periods the ratio of allies to legionaries varied from one-to-one to two-to-one. It was not a given that the allies would contribute the greater number of soldiers. Rome certainly had huge reserves of citizen, Latin and allied manpower, but a considerable portion was already deployed. Barbula's two legions had not yet been disbanded; a legion of Campanian half-citizens was now at Rhegium; two legions of full citizens, and allies, were with Coruncanius in Etruria. As we have seen, Pyrrhus' army amounted to 28,500 men (including the 3,000-strong advance force led by Milo and Cineas); Tarentum had more than 30,000 men of military age and the relevant property qualifications in its citizen body, and it is clear that Pyrrhus called up a substantial number of these men; the king had also recruited Messapians. Even if the king had left a powerful garrison in Tarentum to protect it from Barbula and to deter a Tarentine revolution, it is difficult to see how he could possibly have been outnumbered, or why he would choose to confront Laevinus with a smaller army. It is quite possible that the Epirote-Tarentine army outnumbered the Romans and allies.

Pyrrhus sent a messenger with a letter to Laevinus. The letter invited the consul to disband his army. Pyrrhus would then arbitrate between Rome and Tarentum and compel the guilty party to make amends. The king offered Rome his friendship, but also emphasized his skill as a general and the prowess of his army. Pyrrhus allowed Laevinus ten days to make a decision. This was a typical feature of the king's strategy:

> Before Pyrrhus engaged in a war, he always tried to bring the enemy
> to terms; by making clear that otherwise there would be terrible con-
> sequences, by trying to convince them where their own interests lay,
> by demonstrating to them the miseries that must come with the war,
> and by urging every just and reasonable argument against it.[70]

Pyrrhus also hoped that Laevinus would dither and exhaust his supplies, or that reinforcements from the Sabellians and Italiotes would arrive. Laevinus would not play Pyrrhus' game. He replied that he would face trial in the court of Mars – on the field of battle. Laevinus resumed his advance and established camp on the opposite bank of the Siris. One of Pyrrhus' scouts was captured and brought to Laevinus. The consul paraded the complete army for the bemused scout and declared Rome had many more armies like it. He then sent him away with an invitation for Pyrrhus to visit the camp: 'Tell the king that Laevinus, the Roman consul, asks that he send no more spies but to come himself and see with his own eyes the power of Rome.' The king did so. Observing from the other bank of the river, he was surprised by the discipline of the Roman soldiers and their speedy construction of the fortified camp. The king's *philos* ('friend', commander and royal companion) Megacles, was at his side. The Eagle turned to Megacles and said: 'The discipline of these barbarians is not barbarous.'

* * *

Despite his bravado, Laevinus was worried. The king's army was large and Sabellian, Messapian and Italiote reinforcements could yet arrive to bolster it. The consul's own soldiers were awed by the reputation of the warrior king and fearful of his war elephants. They had never seen such beasts before and, having no better name, would come to call them Lucanian cows. Laevinus decided to immediately force a crossing of the Siris and engage Pyrrhus's main army on the plain. He roused the soldiers: Zonaras tells us that Laevinus' speech 'contained many exhortations to courage.' He would certainly have reminded them of the rich plunder that would be taken in the event of victory – always a key motivator.

Laevinus first attempted to cross the Siris by the ford in front of the camp, but Pyrrhus had posted a strong force on other side of the crossing, and while his men held up the Romans, the king arrayed his battle line on the plain. Modern reconstructions of the battle often place the war elephants on the wings of Pyrrhus' army, guarding the exposed flanks of his phalanx, but this is simply assumption. The ancient sources do not reveal the position of the elephants. Only Zonaras mentions they were kept in reserve, and they played no part until the end of the battle, perhaps being deliberately kept out of sight, so their appearance would have the maximum shock effect, or perhaps because they were still on the road from Tarentum and did not reach the battle site until late in the day.

Meanwhile, there was stalemate at the river crossing and Laevinus ordered his cavalry to ride out of sight, as if they were being sent on plundering mission, but they were in fact charged with finding other fords, and once they had gained the opposite bank, to circle around the Epirote position at the ford and attack them from behind. The Roman and allied *equites* were entirely successful. Pyrrhus' men broke in panic when they were unexpectedly assailed, and the legions and cohorts surged across the river.

Having organized his main battle line, Pyrrhus saw an opportunity to crush the head of the column of Roman infantry as it crossed and spurred forward with his elite *agema*, but his charge was intercepted by the Roman and allied cavalry that had chased his men from the ford. The warrior king was in his element, conspicuous in his horned helmet, gorgeous armour and scarlet cloak:

> While personally engaging in combat and repelling all his attackers, he did not become confused in his decisions nor lose his presence of mind. He directed the action as though he were watching it from a distance, but he was everywhere himself, and always managed to be at hand to support his troops wherever the pressure was greatest.[71]

But Pyrrhus was then attacked by Obsidius, the prefect of a contingent of allied Frentani (or possibly Ferentani) cavalry. Pyrrhus' bodyguards closed up around him, but Obsidius broke through them and bore down on the king, grasping his long lance with both hands. Leonnatus the Macedonian, one of Pyrrhus' *philoi*, counter charged the prefect and killed his horse but, even as the horse collapsed under him, Obsidius' lance took the king's mount full in the chest. Some of Pyrrhus' bodyguards dragged him off the stricken horse, while others surrounded Obsidius and cut him down. The Frentani went berserk when he fell and fought madly to retrieve his body. The rest of the Greek cavalry fell back, thinking their king was dead, unaware that Pyrrhus had already mounted another horse (grooms leading spare horses customarily followed their masters into battle) and was being led back by his bodyguards to the infantry. Pyrrhus was surprised by the ferocity of the Frentani's assault. He was hardly a shirker from the dangers of combat, but Pyrrhus would not be able to effectively command his army in this critical engagement if glory-seeking Italian *bellatores* were continually attacking him. He is reported as exchanging his magnificent armour and scarlet cloak (maybe a gift from the Tarentines) for Megacles' 'plain' breastplate, felt cap, such as was worn under a helmet to absorb the force of blows, and brown cloak. One doubts that the panoply of a *philos* was at all plain, but it was certainly not as distinctive as the royal battle gear. The loyal officer was then charged with riding up and down the battle line to hearten the Epirotes and Tarentines and to draw the attention of the Roman and allied *equites*, allowing Pyrrhus to direct the advance of the phalanx without hindrance.

With Pyrrhus' cavalry in retreat, the Roman army completed its crossing of the Siris and deployed into its customary triple battle line. Pyrrhus was impressed with the array of *hastati*, *principes* and *triarii*. The centurions would have stood out because of the transverse crests on their helmets and the glint of their *dona militaria*. At the rear of the maniples stood the *optiones*, the centurions' deputies, equivalent to the *ouragoi* in Pyrrhus' army, and ready to push forward any back-stepping soldiers. The open manipular formation may have made Laevinus' battle line longer than Pyrrhus' line – assuming the king's infantry were formed in a compact phalanx. The king would have deployed his cavalry and light troops to cover the flanks of the phalanx.

The Epirotes fought in the Macedonian phalanx formation. In the middle of the fourth century BC, Philip II of Macedonia developed the formation out of the old hoplite phalanx of eight to twelve ranks. The king replaced spear with pike, reduced the size of the shield and increased the depth of the files, transforming hoplites into phalangites. The basic unit of the Macedonian phalanx was the *speira*. It contained 256 pikemen divided into sixteen files, thus resulting in a frontage of sixteen. *Speirai* were lined up side by side to form a dense hedge of iron pike heads. The best soldiers were positioned in the front and rear ranks. The veteran file-leaders were known as the 'edge of the sword' and could be relied upon to advance fearlessly, even against another wall of pikes. Reliable phalangites were placed in the ranks immediately behind them, for they may have to step forward if their file-leader was wounded or killed. The file-closers were equally steady, and performed the essential function of preventing raw recruits from peeling away from the rear of the phalanx.

The phalangite's great pike was called a sarissa and was some 5 metres long. The sarissas of the first five ranks projected beyond the phalanx, while those of the remaining eleven ranks were held upwards at varying angles and the swaying shafts offered some protection against volleys of missiles. Arrayed almost shoulder to shoulder, the phalangites required both hands to wield their sarissas, and accordingly their shields were strapped to their left forearms and perhaps also supported by a neck strap.

When deployed on suitably level and clear terrain, and composed of well-trained and experienced soldiers, the Macedonian phalanx was a devastating formation. Only the best troops would hold their nerve as the wall of phalangites bore down on them, knowing they could be impaled or trampled. If the sixteen ranks of the phalanx gained full momentum, it would simply plough through battle lines of lesser depth and cohesion, impaling men on pikes and trampling others underfoot. The consul Lucius Aemilius Paullus ('Little Man') fought the Macedonians at the Battle of Pydna in 168 BC. He later admitted that the advance of the phalanx had terrified him:

> He saw that they were swinging down their small shields from their shoulders to cover their front and levelling their sarissas to meet the attack of his shield-bearing troops [legionaries equipped with the *scutum*]. He saw the strength of their interlocked shields and the fierceness of their attack and was both amazed and filled with fear. He had never seen a more terrifying sight. Later he would often speak of that day, of what he saw and his emotions.[72]

Yet like all formations, the phalanx was vulnerable at the flanks, especially the unshielded right, and if its component *speirai* or files were forced to part because of irregular ground or obstacles, the enemy could get in among the ranks and slaughter the phalangites. Sarissas were far too long to be of any use at close quarters. The phalangites also carried short swords, but they were very much weapons of last resort. They were not conditioned to sword fighting as the Romans were.

Pyrrhus may have expected his phalanx to bulldoze through the relatively open Roman formation, but this was his first experience of fighting against maniples organized in *ordines*. He was presumably aware of the Romans' use of interchangeable *ordines* from what the Tarentines and Messapians (Sallentini) had told him, and perhaps from reports of the great battle at Sentinum. This was to be the first confrontation between the legion and phalanx. The courage and determination of the phalangites of the sword's edge and of the *antesignani*, those warriors in the leading ranks of their armies who could actually see their enemy, is evident because they stood their ground despite the alien and terrifying tactics employed by their opponents. The battle lines charged and collided seven times. This is the most intriguing feature of the Battle of Heraclea. The maniples of the Roman army were well-suited to mobile combat, attacking, fighting, pushing and shoving, then breaking off contact, and doing it all over again. The phalanx was suited only to advances, not to retreats. When comparing the merits of the legion and phalanx in the second century BC, the Greek soldier and historian Polybius noted that Pyrrhus, during his Italian campaigns, attempted to make his phalanx more flexible by placing the maniples of his Italic allies between the *speirai*. As Pyrrhus did not receive troops from the Samnites and Lucanians until after Heraclea, it is assumed that Polybius' comment refers to the next battle he fought against the Romans, at Ausculum in Apulia (279 BC). However, it has been suggested that the seven charges at Heraclea (perhaps three by one side, and four by the other), demonstrate that Pyrrhus had already articulated his phalanx with Messapian and perhaps Tarentine maniples (the possibility that the Tarentines fought in a manner similar to the Lucani was noted above). However, this assumes that Pyrrhus' army moved back and forth. It is possible that Pyrrhus' men advanced seven times, the Romans and their allies having to fall back because they could not get to grips with a closely packed phalanx.

The Roman soldiers would have met the phalanx in typical fashion with volleys of *pila*, but the swaying thickets of sarrisas probably robbed the missiles of much of their force. (Of course, the Romans and allies were also bombarded by Pyrrhus' light troops.) As long as the Epirotes maintained their close formation, the Romans would find it very difficult to actually get to grips with the phalangites. Each legionary had to pass through a deadly alley of six sarissa heads before he could attack a file-leader with his sword. Yet the Epirote phalanx could not break through or pin down the mobile maniples. It seemed that the battle would end in stalemate, but then Megacles was killed.

The *philos* had done what his king commanded, inspiring the troops and attracting the attention of Roman and allied cavalrymen while Pyrrhus was directing the advances of the phalanx, but eventually a Roman or Latin *eques* named Decius broke through the bodyguards and killed Megacles. Decius gathered up the distinctive royal helmet and scarlet cloak, and brandished his trophies. Laevinus encouraged his troops to one last effort by riding along the Roman line, displaying a bloody sword and declaring the blood was that of the king. The consul was nowhere near Decius and Megacles and had in fact thrust his sword into the nearest handy corpse, but the deception was effective: the Roman army was exultant and scented victory. The Roman infantry charged forward and Laevinus ordered a contingent of cavalry he had held in reserve to go around the flank of the Epirotes and Tarentines and fall on them from behind.

Like the Romans, the Epirotes and Tarentines believed Pyrrhus was dead. Their spirits plummeted. Only those troops immediately around Pyrrhus in the phalanx knew their king was alive. Realizing that his army was about to crack, Pyrrhus threw off his felt cap, spurred out of the battle line (generals usually remained mounted because it allowed them a better view of the battlefield), and rallied his despairing Epirotes. The king spotted Laevinus' detached force of cavalry and signalled for the war elephants to be brought up from the rear to intercept the *equites*. The Romans' horses became uncontroll-able as soon as they caught the alien scent of the elephants. Some riders were thrown, others clung on as their panicked mounts turned and galloped into the Roman infantry. The advance halted and the chequer-board array of the maniples dissolved into chaos. The Lucanian cows lumbered after the cavalry and crashed into the Roman infantry. Men and horses were trampled or impaled on tusks, and the soldiers in the towers strapped to the backs of the elephants (possibly Pyrrhus' innovation) rained down missiles or lunged at the Romans with long pikes. The Roman army broke and fled.

Pyrrhus sent in his cavalry to complete the rout. The greatest casualties were usually inflicted during the pursuit, as fearful men broke formation, abandoned their weapons and armour, and presented their defenceless backs to bloodthirsty riders. The Romans lost 7,000 men. A further 1,800 were captured, many of them rich nobles serving in the cavalry. Plutarch reports that the pursuit was halted by nightfall, but Zonaras and other sources state that Pyrrhus had to abandon the pursuit at a river when one of the war elephants was injured and its distress infected the other animals. Orosius records that Minucius, a centurion of the *hastati*, cut the trunk from the elephant and so ensured the escape of the Roman army. However, other sources place this episode at Ausculum. This river was not necessarily the Siris, as Laevinus' men then retreated to the safety of an 'Apulian' city, presumably the Latin colony of Venusia.

Wounds to the Front

Pyrrhus' casualties were also substantial. Plutarch reports that most of his 4,000 dead were Epirote, and included *philoi* and veteran officers who could not be easily replaced. This information may derive from Pyrrhus' *Memoirs* via Plutarch's source, Hieronymus of Cardia. Hieronymus was a contemporary of Pyrrhus and consulted the king's writings when he compiled his extensive history about the Diadochi, now only known from fragments.

Pyrrhus' losses demonstrate how ferociously the Romans and the allies fought at Heraclea. Later Roman historians revelled in the tale of Pyrrhus' inspection of the dead on the field of Heraclea. Typical is the account of Florus. Pyrrhus is found marvelling at the corpses of the legionaries:

> The wounds of all of them were on their chests; some shared deaths with their foes, all had their swords still in their hands, a threatening mien still marked their features, and their anger yet lived even in death. So struck was Pyrrhus with admiration that he exclaimed, 'How easy were it for me to win the empire of the world if I had an army of Romans, or for the Romans to win it if they had me as their king!'[73]

Pyrrhus thought it disgraceful that the brave Romans should be left to rot on the plain, and ordered their remains be cremated or buried. The king then asked the Roman captives to join him, but they politely refused. This could all be dismissed as a much later romanticizing invention, but the image of Roman soldiers dying gloriously rather than retreating goes back at least to the third century BC. The poet Naevius, possibly a Roman citizen from Campania, was a veteran of the First Punic War (264–241 BC). A fragment of his epic poem *Punica* reads: '[Romans] would rather die . . . than return in disgrace.' In Plautus' *Amphitruo* (c. 200 BC), the Umbrian playwright has a character describe a battle in Roman terms – the advance from camp, the deployment of the opposing legions into line, the generals' vows to Jupiter, the bloody combat and the heroic deaths of those on the losing side who refuse to retreat. Thus the tradition of Heraclea as a heroic defeat was certainly a feature of the earliest Roman accounts. The poet Ennius, a Messapian who served as an allied centurion in the Roman army during the Second Punic War (218–201 BC), wrote that Pyrrhus set up a dedicatory inscription commemorating his victory at Heraclea in the temple of Zeus in Tarentum. It read: 'Those men who before were unconquered . . . I have conquered and have been conquered by them.' This may be poetic licence, but if Ennius referred to a genuine inscription, it would suggest that the scene of Pyrrhus inspecting the Roman dead and saluting their courage stemmed from the king's own account of the battle, or from a contemporary Greek historian.

* * *

News of the victory spread quickly and representatives from the Samnites, Lucanians, Bruttians and Italiote Greek cities (Croton and Locri dismissed their Roman garrisons) arrived at Pyrrhus' camp. They were now willing to lend him their support but Pyrrhus was irritated and complained he could have done with their support during the battle. However, thinking on his heavy losses and the battles yet to come, he regained his composure and turned on his considerable charm, accepted their aid and rewarded them with a share of the plunder taken from the battlefield and Laevinus' abandoned camp. Another part of the spoils was sent across the Ionian Sea to Epirus and dedicated to Zeus at Dodona. Part of the dedicatory inscription still exists: 'King Pyrrhus and the Epirotes and the Tarentines to Zeus Naius [took these spoils] from the Romans and their allies.' Note that Messapian allies are not referred to. Pyrrhus sent his flamboyant battle armour, evidently recovered from Decius, as an offering to the shrine of Athena at Lindus on Rhodes.

The Samnites, Lucani and Bruttii supplied Pyrrhus with infantry and some cavalry. The Italiote Greeks could not supply great numbers of infantry or cavalry, but they could offer their fleets to conduct naval operations and to transport troops, the surpluses of grain and other foodstuffs produced on their territories to feed Pyrrhus' army, and hard cash to pay his soldiers. Their financial contributions were very huge. Inscribed records from the treasury of the temple of Zeus Olympius at Locri Epizephyrii, demonstrate that from c. 280 to 275/4 BC the city contributed almost 300 tonnes of silver to 'the king . . . for the common cause'. On the basis of the average rates of pay received by Greek mercenaries in this period, it has been calculated that Locri's contribution was enough to maintain an army of over 20,000 for six years! The total amount amassed by Pyrrhus from Locri and the other Italiote cities now on side – Metapontum, Croton, Heraclea, Caulonia, and presumably Thurii – must have been immense. It is unlikely that Pyrrhus shared any of this with the Tarentines; he might even have expected them to pay and supply the Samnites and other Sabellians.

With his army substantially reinforced, Pyrrhus advanced through Lucania and into Campania. Pyrrhus hoped that Campania would defect to him, but the plundering of his Epirotes and Thessalians won him no friends. He found Capua occupied by the reconstituted army of Laevinus and turned his attention to Neapolis, but his friendly advances were rebuffed. Pyrrhus then advanced into Latium by way of the Liris and Trerus river valleys. Along the way, the Samnite contingent took the opportunity to attack Fregellae. Pyrrhus progressed to at least Anagnia, 40 miles from Rome, but some sources claim he reached Praeneste, and from its high citadel he could see Rome. The king's objective was probably not to attack Rome. It was too strongly defended; he had not, after all, attempted to besiege Capua or Neapolis. He probably intended to devastate Latium and form an alliance with Volsinii and Vulci, but while still at Anagnia or Praeneste, he received intelligence that Tiberius Coruncanius had defeated the Etruscans and was leading his legions south. Despite the protestations of his allies, especially the Samnites, Pyrrhus retreated back the way he had come. In northern Campania he found the route blocked by Laevinus. The consul's army was now larger than it had been at Heraclea. There had been an extraordinary levy of *proletarii* in Rome, that is those poor Roman citizen who did not possess enough – or any – property to qualify them for legionary service. The *proletarii* did not, however, replenish the ranks of Laevinus' legions; they strengthened the garrison of Rome. In 216 BC, the *volones*, slave 'volunteers' purchased to quickly replace some of the legionary losses of the disaster at Cannae, were equipped from the spoils taken from the Gauls at the Battle of Telamon in 225 BC. The *proletarii* of 280 BC could have been equipped with the vast hauls of arms and armour taken from the Samnites at Sentinum, Aquilonia and Cominium. There may also have been an emergency levy of *assidui*, those qualifying for legionary service, in order to reconstitute Laevinus' army, but the consul may have taken over the legions of Aemilius Barbula at Venusia.

Facing Laevinus for a second time, Pyrrhus declared that the legions were like the Lernaean hydra: if one of its heads was cut off, another two grew in its place. The king now had an inkling of Rome's huge reserves of manpower and the agricultural produce that sustained it. In northern Campania, the king was struck by the richness of the land; he was of course traversing the most fertile region of peninsular Italy. The Romans also controlled the second most fertile regions – the Latin plain and southern Etruria. In 280 BC Scipio Barbatus conducted a census of adult male Roman citizens. Their number is recorded as 287,222 and probably includes 'half-citizens' that is, those without the vote like the Campanians and Sabines. Also, not all the men would serve as legionaries or *equites* in the field. Some were too old (*seniores*) and others were too poor (*proletarii*), but would guard Rome and the other settlements of the *ager Romanus*. However, the figure, to which should be added hundreds of thousands of Latin citizens and other *socii*, gives an indication of what Pyrrhus was up against.

Despite the size of their armies, neither Pyrrhus nor Laevinus wished to fight a pitched battle. The Eagle was concerned that if he paused to fight, Coruncanius might appear and he would be caught between two Roman armies. Laevinus was in disgrace, and his enemies in the Senate, especially Fabricius Luscinus, had lambasted him. He could not risk a second defeat. Both generals formed their armies into battle line. Pyrrhus ordered his men to raise an immense war cry. They did so, clashing weapons against shields, and the elephants and trumpeters added to the cacophony. The Romans responded with a great *clamor*. Pyrrhus did not then attack, but departed for Tarentum. Laevinus did not stop him. Technically, the victory belonged to Laevinus as he remained in possession of the field, but it was hardly a glorious episode and in no way offset his failure at Heraclea. He was ordered by the Senate to spend winter with his legions at Saepinum in Samnium. This was partly to combat the Samnite rebellion, but it was also a punishment. The shamed consul and his defeated soldiers would not pollute Rome with their presence.

One-Eyed Fabricius and Blind Claudius

In autumn 280 BC three consulars arrived at Tarentum to negotiate the release of the Romans captured at Heraclea. They were Quintus Aemilius Papus and Publius Cornelius Dolabella ('the Little Pickaxe'), both victorious generals, especially Dollabella, who had won the second Battle of Lake Vadimon, but Pyrrhus was most taken with the third ex-consul, Fabricius Luscinus.[74] The king's experiences in Campania and Latium, and the realization that Rome possessed vast resources, persuaded him to seek a diplomatic conclusion to the war. His immediate rapport with one-eyed (*luscinus*) Fabricius encouraged him to believe that peace terms could be quickly negotiated. The king paroled a number of the Roman prisoners as a gesture of good will, and Cineas accompanied the envoys back to Rome. Pyrrhus was confident that Cineas could persuade the Senate to come to terms. He declared that Cineas' eloquence had won him more cities than he had taken by the spear. Cineas offered peace and military alliance with Pyrrhus (tellingly a personal alliance with the king, not the Epirote Alliance), but the Romans had to recognize the independence of Tarentum and the Italiote Greeks, and had evacuated their conquests in Samnium and Lucania.

Some senators were apparently tempted, but the majority were possessed of the spirit that defined Rome following the disasters at the Caudine Forks and Lautulae: there would be no peace. Appius Claudius now bearing the *cognomen* 'Caecus' because he had gone blind, articulated the resolve of the Senate. Rome would not be dictated to by a foreign enemy, he said. Pyrrhus would be driven out of Italy. His defiant speech became famous and was still drawn on for inspiration by Romans in the first century BC. His mission a failure, Cineas returned to Tarentum with the Roman prisoners. Pyrrhus asked what manner of men the senators were. Cineas replied: 'They are like kings.'

In the winter Luscinus returned to Tarentum to seek the release of the prisoners. Pyrrhus was more interested in negotiating an end to the war, and attempted to win over the Roman with promises of wealth and gold and the promise of a high command in the king's army. 'If I were to serve you,' joked the incorruptible senator, 'those men who now advise and honour you would surely find me preferable and have me for king!' Pyrrhus was amused and again paroled a number of prisoners, so they could attend the Saturnalia (festival of the god Saturn) on 17 December, but he refused to release them completely until peace was agreed.

Battle Narratives

Frustrated by the Romans' refusal to come to terms, Pyrrhus prepared for a new campaign. In spring 279 BC he invaded Apulia, captured many towns and received the submission of others. The towns are not named, but his targets were presumably allied to Rome. There is no report of him attacking Venusia. The Eagle advanced north of the River Aufidus but was confronted by the Romans at Ausculum. Both consular armies were present, led by Publius Sulpicius Saverrio and Publius Decius Mus, the son of the consul who devoted himself at Sentinum.[75] There was an expectation among the Roman and enemy troops that he would follow the path of his father and grandfather. Pyrrhus' soldiers were terrified at the prospect of *devotio*, but the king steadied them: 'How can one man by dying prevail over so many? Incantations and magic are not superior to weapons and men.' He ordered that if any man in the ritual toga of a *devotus* was sighted, he was to be taken alive. The king then sent a message to Mus warning him not to attempt the act. The consul responded that he had no need to perform *devotio* because Pyrrhus would be conquered in other ways.

Plutarch's account of the Battle of Ausculum reveals that it was fought over two days. On the first day, the consuls offered battle on rough, wooded terrain, and a deep river with steep banks appears to have secured one flank of the Roman army. Pyrrhus' phalanx could not maintain formation on this ground, nor could his war elephants or cavalry operate effectively. The king's army sustained heavy casualties and gladly broke off fighting at sunset. During the night, Pyrrhus sent troops to occupy certain points on the rough ground. These had presumably played an important part in the day's fighting, though Plutarch does not tell us what they were; high points, which the Romans had fortified, or a ford on the river seem possible. For some reason, Pyrrhus' occupation of these key points forced the Romans to come down to more level ground which favoured Pyrrhus' phalanx and elephant tactics. Pyrrhus had chosen his ground well. Somehow the king forced the Romans to close up their maniples, and they could not roam about the battlefield with their usual fluidity. They would have to meet the phalanx in close order. Experienced in more open forms of combat and lacking long pikes, the Romans were at a distinct disadvantage in a head-on confrontation, but Plutarch stresses that the legionaries and allied troops were more concerned about the Lucanian Cows, fighting desperately to break into the phalanx before the elephants came into play. After using up their *pila*, the Romans hacked at the long shafts of the sarissas with their swords, but made little impact, and were under a continual hail of missiles from Pyrrhus' slingers. The Roman army began to fall back where Pyrrhus himself was leading the attack; the king was seriously wounded in the shoulder by a *pilum*, and carried from the field, but then the elephants came up and the Romans fled. The majority of the army made it back to the camp, but 6,000 were killed. Plutarch makes no reference to Decius Mus attempting *devotio*.

Following Hieronymus, who had copied the figure from Pyrrhus' *Memoirs*, Plutarch reports the king's casualties as 3,505, heaviest among the men he had brought over from Greece. Pyrrhus was despondent. When congratulated on his victory he declared: 'If we are victorious in one more battle with the Romans, we shall be utterly ruined.' This eventually gave rise to the modern expression 'Pyrrhic victory', used to describe a victory that costs the winner more than the loser. The ancients called such a victory Cadmean:

> All of Pyrrhus' victories were Cadmean. For the Romans, though defeated, were in no way humbled, since their dominion was so great. Pyrrhus, on the other hand, had suffered the damage and disaster that commonly go with defeat.[76]

Pyrrhus' losses grew because he had nowhere to shelter or treat his wounded. The Apulian contingent led by Arpi arrived too late to form up in the Roman battle line and instead attacked Pyrrhus' lightly defended camp. After emptying it of portable valuables, they set fire to everything that remained and slaughtered the baggage animals. The king treated his men as best he could. The Romans remained secure in their camp; Pyrrhus would not risk assaulting it and eventually withdrew back to Tarentum.

*   *   *

Dionysius of Halicarnassus' *Roman Antiquities* contains a detailed but fragmentary account of the battle. It is fascinating but problematical and here I will only highlight information that supplements Plutarch.

Dionysius tells us that Pyrrhus' right flank were Macedonian infantry, Italian mercenaries hired by Tarentum (perhaps the contingents of the Italiote cities), Ambracian *hypaspists* and Tarentine *chalcaspides* (White Shields). These contingents fought as a phalanx. Beside the Tarentines were a mixed force of Lucani and Bruttii. At the centre of the army were the Epirote phalangites and 'mercenaries' from Aetolia, Acarnania and Athamania. These latter contingents fought as light troops. The Samnites, clearly the largest of the allied contingents, formed the left wing of the army. They were equipped with the tall *scutum*. Samnite, Thessalian, Bruttian and Italian mercenary cavalry secured the right wing of the army. The Ambracian, Tarentine and Greek 'mercenary' squadrons (the Macedonian cavalry is described as mercenary) secured the left. The light troops and nineteen war elephants (suggesting that one was indeed killed at Heraclea) were divided into two groups and positioned behind each wing 'in a position slightly elevated above the plain'. Pyrrhus himself commanded the *agema* of 2,000 picked horsemen, held in reserve behind the main battle line. The combined infantry contingents numbered 70,000 (16,000 from Epirus and elsewhere in Greece), and somewhat more than 8,000 cavalry.

The Roman imperial general Frontinus clearly used a different source. In his *Stratagems* he reports the Samnites and Epirotes formed the right flank, traditionally the strongest and most prestigious in an ancient army. The Bruttii, Lucani and Messapians were on the left, also important because they would face the strong enemy right, but the Tarentines, as the least reliable troops, were placed in the centre of the battle line. Frontinus has the cavalry as well as the war elephants held in reserve. The strength of the army is given as 40,000. Frontinus also puts the strength of the Roman army at 40,000. Of course, four legions were present, accounting for 18,000 (16,800 infantry and 1,200 *equites*), and suggesting 22,000 Latin and other allied troops. Dionysius makes the Roman army much bigger, reporting 20,000 legionaries (possibly rounded up from 18,000, or Dionysius assumed the legions were c. 5,000-strong as in his day) and 50,000 other troops including Campanians, Umbrians, Volscians, Marrucini, Peligni and Ferentani, and 8,000 cavalry. Frontinus' figures are to be preferred over Dionysius', but the information of the latter on the makeup of the armies is probably accurate.

As mentioned above, Polybius reports that while in Italy Pyrrhus alternated the maniples of his Italian allies, meaning the Samnites and Lucanians, with the units of his phalanx in order to create a less rigid battle line and match the flexibility of the legion, but this would have resulted in a far more composite formation than is described by Dionysius and Frontinus.

There remains the problem of Decius Mus. Was he killed at Ausculum and, if so, was he killed as a *devotus*? In the first century BC Cicero wrote that Mus did die at Ausculum, but he was vague as to the manner of the consul's death, whether in regular combat or as a *devotus*. Even if a stray javelin or sling bullet had killed Mus, his heritage would have led people to believe he had actually performed *devotio*. However, in 265 BC the consul Fabius Gurges was killed in the fighting at Volsinii and a Decius Mus was elected suffect and assumed command of the Etruscan war. Of course, this could be another Decius Mus, a son or brother of the consul of 279 BC; we do not know the *praenomen* (first name) of the suffect, but if it was the same man, we could postulate that he had attempted *devotio* at Ausculum, but the ritual was never completed because Pyrrhus' troops would not kill him. Perhaps Mus promised to end the uprising of the serfs at Volsinii by finally fulfilling his vow to the gods of the Underworld?

Men of Mamers

Despite winning the battle, Pyrrhus was not winning the war. The consul, or consuls, remained in Apulia. The king knew Rome would speedily replace her losses and he was dejected. Relations with the Tarentines and allies had soured and Pyrrhus was eager to abandon the war for a new and more fruitful adventure. He was presented with two opportunities. The throne of Macedonia was vacant: Ptolemy the Thunderbolt was dead, killed in a battle against migrating Gauls, but the Eagle chose not to fly home and reclaim his crown. When Pyrrhus returned to Tarentum he found waiting for him a deputation of Greeks from Sicily. It was well-known that Pyrrhus was the son-in-law of Agathocles (it did not matter that he and Lanassa were long divorced), and the Syracusan-led embassy invited him to lead them against Carthage, which had steadily extended her power across Sicily following the death of Agathocles in 289 BC. With a Carthaginian fleet blockading Syracuse and an army threatening her landward walls, it was only a matter of time before the whole island was ruled by Carthage. Pyrrhus seized this opportunity, the chance to be a liberator, to win fresh glory, and to establish a base from which to launch an assault on Carthage. But he had to first seal a truce with Rome. The king's personal physician unwittingly brought this about.

Fabricius Luscinus and Aemilius Papus were elected as the consuls for 278 BC. They had proved an effective pairing in 282 BC and it was hoped they would finally defeat Pyrrhus. The consuls took command of the army that had wintered in Apulia; Luscinus was familiar with the men and the country, having served as a legate under the consuls of 279 BC. Like Pyrrhus, he was wounded at Ausculum. This may have strengthened the rapport between the king and the consul. When Pyrrhus established his camp close by, his physician, Nicias, contacted Luscinus and offered to poison the king. The consul was appalled and immediately alerted Pyrrhus. Nicias was executed and Pyrrhus released all of his Roman prisoners, but the consuls refused to accept them as the king's gift. They were exchanged for an equal number of captives – Tarentines, Samnites, and perhaps also Epirotes. We know that the Romans did have some Epirote prisoners because at some point during the war, an Epirote held at Rome was made the legal owner of a patch of land in the city. This enabled the *fetiales* to belatedly perform the ritual declaration of war against Pyrrhus and Epirus by casting a spear into enemy territory! The freed Romans did not receive a warm welcome. They were taunted as 'Pyrrhus' ugly little presents'. All were demoted. Proud *equites* were forced to fight on foot, and legionaries were reduced to the status of slingers. They were not even allowed within the camp, but a man could redeem himself and be restored to his former status if he was witnessed killing two enemies in single combat and if he could produce the spoils he stripped from them.

The Nicias incident allowed Pyrrhus to arrange a temporary truce with Rome, and he was soon preparing to depart for Sicily. The king was aware that in autumn 279 BC Rome had renewed her alliance with Carthage; the revised treaty included promises of mutual military aid against Pyrrhus. Carthage would provide Rome with transport ships, enabling the Romans to widen their operations against Pyrrhus and keep him occupied in Italy and thus away from Sicily. In 279/8 BC Carthaginian ships landed 500 legionaries at Rhegium, which had been taken over by its mutinous garrison. Despite their small number, the Romans attacked the city and destroyed timber stockpiled for ship building, lest it be used by the rebels or fall into the hands of Pyrrhus. However, the consuls and Senate could see the attractions of avoiding another costly battle with Pyrrhus by allowing him to depart for Sicily. Without his forceful personality, the anti-Roman alliance would crumble and Rome's enemies could be tackled one by one. Unsurprisingly, the Tarentines were angered and dismayed at Pyrrhus' decision to break off the war in Italy, but Pyrrhus was not going to abandon what he now considered his Italian possessions or the cash he milked from them. The Tarentines were aghast, but the king dismissed their complaints. According to Plutarch, 'he ordered them to keep silent and await his convenience.' Pyrrhus sailed for Sicily in sixty or seventy Tarentine vessels. His expedition force was small, comprising only 8,000 of his loyal Epirotes and Greeks. Milo retained the rest of the army to garrison Tarentum and the other Italiote cities.

Pyrrhus' sojourn in Sicily was spectacular but ended in failure. The Eagle landed at Tauromenium, which immediately accepted his leadership and reinforced his army. Catana followed suit. The king's army was still small but he continued on to Syracuse. The Carthaginian besiegers took fright and departed, and their fleet sailed away before it was trapped between the Tarentine fleet and the 141 Syracusan warships bottled up in the Great Harbour. Pyrrhus was saluted as king of Sicily and assumed command of Syracuse's 10,000 soldiers and substantial navy. Additional contingents from Acragas and Leontini increased the size of his field army to 30,000 infantry and 2,500 cavalry. The year 277 BC was perhaps the most brilliant in Pyrrhus' career. He picked off Carthage's strongholds one by one. Enna was the first to fall. At Mount Eryx Pyrrhus called on the aid of Heracles and led his *philoi* in the assault. The king was first over the wall and killed many Carthaginians, but he suffered no wounds. Heircte and Panormus followed. Only Lilybaeum remained, a strongly fortified harbour at the western extremity of the island, but Pyrrhus dealt first with the Mamertini, the 'men of Mamers', Sabellian mercenaries who had served Agathocles. They are identified as either Campanians (perhaps actually descendents of Campanians long established in Sicily) or as (descendents of) a Sacred Spring sent out by the Samnites. Discharged from Syracusan service on the assassination of Agathocles in 289/8 BC, they seized Messana, using it as a base to dominate the northeast of the island. Pyrrhus defeated them in several pitched battles and they scuttled back to Messana. He then resumed the campaign against the Carthaginians, but Pyrrhus abandoned the siege of Lilybaeum after two months. The city was almost impregnable on its landward side and Pyrrhus had not the patience to wait for a blockade by sea to take effect. He wanted to take the war across the Mediterranean to Carthage, but his popularity with the Sicilian Greeks had not lasted for long. Pyrrhus had seized estates for his *philoi*, executed prominent men and appointed Epirote magistrates to govern the cities. Like the Italiote Greeks, the Sicilians discovered that Pyrrhus was no liberator. When the king demanded more troops, ships and rowers, and cash for an invasion of North Africa, they revolted. The Greeks formed alliances with the Mamertines and even Carthage, which was encouraged to send a fresh army to Sicily. Pyrrhus defeated it, but Sicily was already lost to him and requests for help from Tarentum and the Samnites persuaded him to return to Italy.

Later in 276 BC the king made an alliance with Hieron, his most loyal Syracusan general, which enabled Heiron to take control of Syracuse, and then sailed for Italy with 110 warships and numerous troop transports and cargo vessels. As the fleet approached Rhegium, a Carthaginian battle fleet intercepted it. Seventy of Pyrrhus' warships were captured or destroyed. Only twelve warships escaped without damage, but all of the transport ships docked safely at Locri.

As we have seen, Locri provided Pyrrhus with immense sums of cash. The exactions continued during Pyrrhus' absence in Sicily and this, combined with successful Roman campaigns in Bruttium and Lucania, prompted the city to revolt. In 277 BC Cornelius Rufinus captured Croton (below). A pro-Roman faction in Locri organized the slaughter of Pyrrhus' garrison, but the city again switched sides at the arrival of Pyrrhus' battered fleet. Pyrrhus was content for the moment to execute the leaders of the revolt. He was more concerned with Rhegium. In 280 BC its small garrison of 800 Campanians and 400 Sidicini was replaced with a full-sized legion made up of half-citizens from northern Campania, but Pyrrhus' victories at Heraclea and Ausculum, and the example of the Mamertini just across the Straits at Messana, emboldened the *legio Campana* to mutiny and seize the city. As Rome started to recover lost ground in 278 BC, the Campanians feared the consequences of their actions, and seem to have acted in the interests of Rome, although it may be that they were actually working to consolidate their position in Bruttium. They certainly captured Caulonia from its Epirote garrison.

Whether acting independently or following orders from Rome, the Campanian Legion represented a considerable threat to Pyrrhus' precarious hold on the toe of Italy, but the king's assault on Rhegium was repulsed. The Campanians had received 10,000 reinforcements from the Mamertines, probably transported to Italy in Carthaginian vessels. The Mamertines, and presumably also the Campanians, harassed Pyrrhus' army as it retreated back to Locri. When Pyrrhus' army became strung out over rough ground, the Mamertines launched a determined attack on the rearguard and inflicted heavy casualties.

Two of the war elephants had been killed by the time Pyrrhus made his way from the head of the army:

> Riding up in person from the van, Pyrrhus sought to ward off the enemy, and took great risks in contending with men who were trained to fight and were inspired with high courage. When he was wounded in the head by a sword and withdrew a little from the fighting, the enemy were all the more elated. One of the Mamertines ran forward, far in advance of the rest, a man who was huge in body and resplendent in armour. In a bold voice he challenged Pyrrhus to come out, if he were still alive. This angered Pyrrhus, and wheeling round despite his guards, pushed his way through them, full of wrath, smeared with blood, and with a countenance terrible to look upon. Before the barbarian could strike, Pyrrhus dealt him such a blow on the head with his sword that, what with the might of his arm and the excellent temper of the blade, it cleaved right down through the body, so that at one instant its sundered parts fell to either side. This checked the barbarians from further attacks. They were amazed and confounded at Pyrrhus and thought him some superior being.[77]

That Pyrrhus cut the Mamertine in half sounds like a gross exaggeration, but the late Roman officer Ammianus Marcellinus reports that in a cavalry battle outside Amida in AD 359 he saw 'in front of me a soldier with his head cut in two, and split into equal halves by a powerful sword stroke, was so pressed on all sides [by other soldiers] that he stood erect like a stump.'

The Mamertines made no more attacks but Pyrrhus returned to treacherous Locri in foul humour. He was persuaded by three of his *philoi* to break into the treasury of the temple of Persephone (Proserpina), the vengeful queen of the Underworld, and seize its untouched treasures, that is the accumulated offerings made to the goddess and income from the temple lands. The robbing of the temple complex may have developed a wider sack of the city. The plunder was loaded onto Pyrrhus' ships, but when they set sail for Tarentum, a storm blew up and forced them back to Locri; the warships escorting the treasure ships were lost. This was clear evidence of the goddess' fury at desecration of her temple. The treasures were restored, but the goddess was not placated and Pyrrhus wrote in his *Memoirs* that this impious act lost him the war against Rome.

The Vengeful Goddess

The wrath of Persephone was only one factor in Pyrrhus' undoing in Italy. In 278 BC Fabricius Luscinus was awarded a triumph over Samnites, Tarentines, Lucanians and Bruttians (celebrated 13 December). We know little about the course of his campaign (Aemilius Papus may also have campaigned against the Tarentines) but Luscinus convinced Heraclea to abandon Tarentum and Pyrrhus and to become an ally of Rome. The Samnites did score a victory in 277 BC. Retreating before the armies of Cornelius Rufinus and Iunius Bubulcus (son of the Ploughman), the Samnites drew the consuls into the forested Cranita Mountains (location unknown). The Romans were defeated in the rough terrain and lost many men. The debacle caused the consuls to fall out, and they divided their forces. Bubulcus ravaged part of Samnium, and then fought the Lucani and Bruttii, earning a triumph. Rufinus laid siege to Croton, but suffered a defeat when its strong Epirote and Lucanian garrison made a sudden sortie. The consul had to devise a ruse to take the city:

> He sent two captives as pretended deserters into Croton – one immediately, who declared that Rufinus had despaired of capturing the place and was about to depart for Locri, which was being be- trayed to him, and the other later, corroborating this statement with the report that the consul was already on his way. For, in order that the story might gain credence, he actually packed up the baggage, and affected to be in haste. Nicomachus, accordingly, believed the story, inasmuch as scouts made the same report, and leaving Croton, he set out hastily for Locri by a shorter road. And when he had now arrived in Locri, Rufinus turned back to Croton, and escaping observation because he was not expected and because of a mist that then prevailed, he captured the city. Nicomachus, when he learned of this, went back to Tarentum, and encountering Rufinus on the way, lost many men. And the Locrians came over to the Roman side.[78]

Croton's territory was undoubtedly ravaged during the campaign, and Rufinus probably allowed his men to sack the city. Livy remarks that the city never really recovered from the devastation of the Pyrrhic War, and the same was true of Caulonia. In 276 BC Fabius the Glutton (Gurges) was consul for the second time. Having learned from his failures in 292 and 291 BC, he fought successfully against the Samnites, Lucani and Bruttii. The details of his campaign are lost, but it was successful enough to earn him a triumph (not celebrated until 17 February 275 BC) and caused the Samnites to make a desperate appeal to Pyrrhus, who was still at Syracuse, to return to Italy.

Despite the casualties inflicted by the Mamertines, Pyrrhus finally arrived back at Tarentum with 20,000 infantry and 3,000 cavalry, almost three times as many troops as he had taken to Sicily. Some were presumably mercenaries recruited in Sicily; Bruttii and Lucani may have joined him when he was based at Locri; and the main garrison of Epirotes left with Milo at Tarentum could have contributed to the campaign against the *legio Campana*. In spring 275 BC he added the best of the Tarentine levy to the army, and marched into Lucania. Here he split his army in two. The smaller part was to remain in Lucania and draw off the forces of the consul Lucius Cornelius Lentulus, while Pyrrhus took the larger part into Samnium, where he hoped to defeat his colleague, Curius Dentatus, at strategic Malventum and win back the Samnites. Few Samnites joined the king as he advanced towards Malventum through the country of the Hirpini. They were angry with him for abandoning them in 278 BC and for taking so long to respond to their appeal, but Dentatus had also experienced difficulties in finding troops. The heavy defeats at Arretium, Heraclea, Ausculum and Cranita had resulted in *assidui* having to serve more regularly than they were used to. This, and a recurrence of plague, led to resistance to the levy in 275 BC. Dentatus made an example of one unfortunate citizen who failed to respond to the summons; the man was arrested, condemned to slavery and his property was seized by the State. This encouraged other *assidui* to take their places in the legions.

Dentatus established his camp in the hilly country surrounding Malventum because he considered the rough terrain would prevent the king from using his phalanx effectively, but the consul did not emerge from his camp when Pyrrhus arrived. The priests attached to the army announced that the omens were bad and this prevented him from deploying the Roman army. He was also hopeful that Lentulus would yet appear with his legions.

When Dentatus failed to emerge, Pyrrhus decided to occupy the high ground behind the Roman camp that night and to launch a surprise attack on it. Pyrrhus selected his fiercest war elephants and best soldiers for this mission, which he himself led. Dionysius of Halicarnassus reports that the soldiers carried the *thureos*, that is, the Greek word for a *scutum*, and so suggests Pyrrhus chose Sabellian warriors for this enterprise, as they would be more suitable than Epirote phalangites. He presumably employed local Samnite guides, but:

> It was bound to happen, as might have been expected, that soldiers burdened with helmets, breastplates and shields (*thurei*) and advancing against hill positions by long trails that were not even used by men but were mere goat paths through woods and crags, would keep no order and, even before the enemy came in sight, would be weakened in body by thirst and fatigue.[79]

> Pyrrhus took a long circuitous route through heavily forested country, his torches burned out, and his soldiers lost their way and straggled. This caused such delay that at daybreak he was in full view of the enemy as he advanced on them from the heights.[80]

Dentatus was elated. The omens had finally come good. He led part of his army up the slope and Pyrrhus' disarrayed and exhausted men were overwhelmed. Two of the war elephants were killed; eight more were surrendered by their Indian mahouts. The Romans pursued the broken troops, driving them into gullies and glens where they were slaughtered, but Pyrrhus escaped down the slope, and rejoined his main army.

Dentatus followed, and quickly arranged the legions and allies into a battle line on the more level ground in front of the camp to meet the advance of Pyrrhus' army. A fragment of Dionysius' account of the battle reports that the consul had equipped the legionary *principes* 'with cavalry spears grasped by the middle with both hands.' These 'cavalry spears' were presumably sarissas, captured or copied from the Epirotes and probably intended as a defence against the war elephants. The fighting was evenly balanced until Pyrrhus concentrated his remaining war elephants against one part of the Roman line. This section of the line buckled and broke and the Lucanian Cows pursued the Romans to the camp. Dentatus had left a strong guard of veterans at the camp, perhaps concerned that Pyrrhus still had men in the hills. The veterans charged down from the ramparts and hurled their *pila* at the elephants. Such was the force of the barrage that it halted the elephants. Other Roman and allied troops came to support the veterans, hurling javelins and burning torches at the elephants. The maddened creatures turned about and stampeded through the ranks of Pyrrhus' army and the Romans followed. The Eagle knew this was the work of Persephone:

> It was for this reason that Pyrrhus was defeated by the Romans also in a battle to the finish. For it was no mean or untrained army that he had, but the mightiest of those then in existence among the Greeks and one that had fought a great many wars; nor was it a small body of men that was then arrayed under him, but even three times as large as his adversary's, nor was its general any chance leader, but rather the man whom all admit to have been the greatest of all the generals who flourish at that same period; nor was it any inequality in the position he occupied, nor the sudden arrival of reinforcements for the other side, nor any other mischance or unexpected excuse for failure that ruined the cause of Pyrrhus, but rather the wrath of the goddess [Persephone] whose sanctity had been violated, a wrath of which not even Pyrrhus himself was unaware, as Proxenus the historian relates and as Pyrrhus himself records in his own memoirs.[81]

Pyrrhus made his escape with a few horsemen. His losses are not known; the casualty figures reported in two late Roman sources (23,000 and 33,000) are impossibly large, but the flight of his defeated army was so total that no effort was made to retreat to camp. This was inspected with great interest by Dentatus and his legates and features were subsequently incorporated into Roman camps.

Dentatus did not pursue Pyrrhus. The Triumphal Fasti record that in February 274 BC he celebrated a triumph over Pyrrhus and the Samnites, suggesting that after Malventum he remained in southern Samnium to carry out the usual work of a consul; devastating the land and capturing hill forts. Cornelius Lentulus was also rewarded with a triumph, for victories over the Lucani and Samnites. It is not known if he ever encountered the detachment from Pyrrhus' army. He took the *cognomen* Caudinus, indicating that his operations in Samnium were directed against the Caudini and their capital. As a relative of the Cornelius Lentulus who had urged acceptance of Gavius Pontius' disgraceful terms at the Caudine Forks, the consul was keen to restore his family's reputation. It was probably at Caudium that Servius Cornelius Merenda, one of Lentulus' legates, displayed the bravery that won him a gold crown, weighing 5 pounds.[82]

Malventum was Pyrrhus' last battle with Rome. He gave up the Italian war as a lost cause and made ready to return to Epirus, but he had no wish to evacuate Tarentum; its wealth, navy and location made it a very valuable outpost. When Pyrrhus sailed for Epirus he had only 8,000 infantry and 500 cavalry, a mere third of the force he brought over five years before, but he left a very strong garrison at Tarentum, and loyal Milo remained in the city as governor. The king may also have installed troops in Metapontum; its wealth and grain surpluses could be exploited to his advantage. In 274 BC Pyrrhus defeated Antigonus Gonatas and regained the throne of Macedonia, but his popularity plummeted when his Gallic mercenaries plundered the tombs of the Macedonian kings at Aegae. In 272 BC he fought Gonatas for control of the Peloponnese, but Pyrrhus' son Ptolemy was killed at Sparta and the Eagle lost his life at Argos. While fighting his way through the streets, the king was struck just below the rim of his helmet by a roof tile thrown by an old woman. He was knocked unconscious and, as he lay on the ground, one of Gonatas' soldiers decapitated him. It was said that the goddess Demeter, the mother of Persephone, possessed the old woman and guided her hand.

The Conquest Complete

Curius Dentatus paraded through Rome in triumph in February 274 BC. The crowds were delighted at the sight of the once-dreaded Lucanian Cows:

> These huge beasts with towers on their backs, which they had feared so much, now followed the horses which had conquered them, and with heads bowed were not wholly unconscious that they were prisoners.[83]

Dentatus was re-elected consul for 274 BC. It was fitting that the man who, in 290 and 284 BC, had catalysed the process of conquest, began the final reduction of the Sabellians. He campaigned against the Lucani and earned an *ovatio* (ovation), a lesser form of triumph. Gaius Claudius Canina, consul in 273 BC, built on Dentatus' victory and captured Posidonia. The city was re-established as the Latin colony of Paestum. Canina ('the Dog' or 'Snarler') fought the Samnites and Bruttii as well, but Carvilius Maximus and Papirius Cursor achieved the final defeat of the Sabellians. Consuls for the second time in 272 BC (they were colleagues in 293 BC), Maximus engineered the surrender of the Samnites, while Cursor received the submissions of the Lucani and Bruttii. Unfortunately, no details of their successful campaigns are preserved. There was probably little hard fighting; according to Dionysius of Halicarnassus, the Bruttii 'submitted willingly', indicating they had little resistance left in them. The same was probably true of the Lucani. However, when the consuls had disposed of the Sabellians they turned their attentions to Tarentum. Maximus probably devastated the terrain of the city and possibly attacked Metapontum as well. Cursor laid siege to Tarentum, aided by the Carthaginians, whose fleet blockaded the harbour to prevent reinforcements or supplies reaching Milo. The Epirote goverenor was at the end of his tether. The Tarentines had risen up against him, and he may have learned of the death of his beloved king. He was eager to surrender the city to Cursor, who allowed the Epirotes to depart safely with much of the loot they had exacted from the Tarentines and Italiote Greeks. Tarentum and Metapontum were treated lightly; they were enrolled as allies of Rome, expected to supply ships to the Roman navy. A legion was based in Tarentum to guarantee its loyalty, and a smaller garrison was installed in Metapontum. All of the Italiote Greek cities, except Rhegium, were now allied to Rome. The Campanian legionaries of Rhegium regained their boldness following the departure of Pyrrhus and while the Romans were embroiled with the Samnites and Lucani; they attacked Croton, massacred its Roman garrison and sacked the city. The end of the Sabellian wars and the capture of Tarentum allowed Rome to finally deal with the *legio Campana*. In 270 BC the consuls, Gaius Genucius Clepsina ('the Wine Cup') and Gnaeus Cornelius Blasio, laid siege to the city, but the town only fell with the assistance of Hieron, now king of Syracuse and an ally of Rome, who supplied additional troops and a fleet to maintain a sea blockade.[84] The Campanians who survived the fall of the city were hauled back to Rome where they were scourged and decapitated. It interesting to note that the Campanians were defended by the plebeian tribune, Marcus Fulvius Flaccus, who claimed it was illegal to mete out such harsh punishment to Roman citizens.

In 270 or 269 BC a Samnite called Lollius escaped from captivity in Rome. He was from the Caraceni tribe and was certainly of noble rank. When he was a captive in Rome, his tribesmen were prevented from taking up arms against Rome, but his return to the north of Samnium triggered a substantial rebellion. It required both consular armies to capture his hill fortress in 269 BC. This was the last gasp of Samnite defiance. Between 272 and 263 BC Samnium was reorganized into *ager Romanus*, Latin or allied territory. In 268 BC Malventum and a great chunk of Hirpinan territory was formed into the Latin colony of Beneventum; it was so named because Malventum sounded inauspicious to the Romans (Latin *malus* = bad, wicked). The colony served to cut off the Hirpini from the rest of Samnium; they were organized as an allied people and they gradually lost their Samnite identity. The territory of the Caudini (and the integrity of the tribe) was broken up into numerous small states centred on towns. Some were annexed to the *ager Romanus* and their inhabitants given citizenship without the vote, while others formed small allied states. Most of the Caraceni's country was annexed to the *ager Romanus*; a portion may have been awarded to the loyal Frentani, conspicuous for their service at Heraclea and Ausculum. Aesernia was established as a Latin colony in 263 BC, and the rest of the Pentrian country organized as an allied territory called Samnium. Boxed in by the Latin colonies at Aesernia, Beneventum and Luceria, by the swathes of *ager Romanus* centred on Aufidena and Allifae, and by the territories of the Frentani and northern Apulians, this Samnium was only a fraction of the size of the lands dominated by the Samnite League at the start of the long confrontation with Rome.

Apart from the land seized around Posidonia-Paestum, Lucania was organized as allied territory. The capture of Rhegium was the final move in the conquest of Bruttium. Like the Lucanians, the Bruttii received lenient treatment because they had submitted. They were enrolled as allies and permitted to retain their league; the maintenance of this organization made it easier for the Romans to levy troops from them. The Romans took over the eastern part of Bruttium called Sila and exploited its vast timber resources:

> Sila is full of timber suitable for the building of houses and ships and every other kind of construction. For much fir grows there, towering to the sky, much black poplar, much pitch pine, beech, stone pine, wide-spreading oak, ash trees enriched by the streams flowing through their midst, and every other kind of tree with densely-intertwined branches that keep the mountain in shadow throughout the whole day. Of this timber, that which grows nearest the sea and rivers is felled at the root and taken down in full lengths to the nearest harbours, sufficient in quantity to serve all Italy for ship-building and the construction of houses. That which grows inland from the sea and remote from rivers is cut up in sections for the

making of oars, poles and all kinds of domestic implements and equipment, and is carried out on men's shoulders. But the largest and most resinous part of the timber is made into pitch, furnishing the most fragrant and sweetest pitch known to us, the kind called Bruttian, from the farming out of which the Roman people receive large revenues every year.[85]

The final campaigns in Rome's conquest of central and northern peninsular Italy have been described already. All that remained was Calabria. In 267 BC the Romans used the involvement of the Sallentines with Pyrrhus, and their apparent raids into Apulia, as an excuse to invade their territory and seize the important harbour of Brundisium:

> Their excuse was that the people had received Pyrrhus and were overrunning their allied territory, but in reality they wished to get possession of Brundisium; for the place had a fine harbour, and for the traffic with Illyricum and Greece there was an approach and landing-place of such a character that vessels would sometimes come to land and put out to sea wafted by the same wind. They captured it, and sent colonists both to this point [delayed by the First Punic War until 244 BC] and to others as well.[86]

During the battle for Brundisium, the consul Marcus Atilius Regulus called on the aid of the goddess Pales and vowed her a temple. That the consul felt the need for divine assistance suggests the difficulty of the conflict, but it remains a mystery why he chose to call on the obscure patron goddess of shepherds. In 266 BC Decimus Iunius Pera ('the Satchel') and Numerius Fabius Pictor ('the Painter') conquered the Sassinates, the most northerly of the Umbrians. The consuls returned to Rome to celebrate triumphs on 26 September and 5 October. Despite the lateness of the campaigning season, Pera and Pictor then marched south to finish off the Sallentini and other troublesome Messapians, who were defeated and divided into small allied states. On 1 and 5 February 265 BC they celebrated their second triumphs in Rome. This was the final campaign in the Roman conquest of peninsular Italy.

The Roman conquest of Italy was driven by the need for more land to settle and cultivate and by the desire of patrician and plebeian alike for plunder and glory. Competition between Rome's leading clans and families grew, and the senators and consuls they produced involved the city in wars of increasing scope and scale, and the conquest built up an irresistable momentum. Modern historians can get caught up in this momentum, fascinated by the endless battles and the heroic deeds, but the conquest cost the lives of hundreds of thousands (perhaps even more), either killed or enslaved, and the number of cities, towns, hill forts, villages and farmsteads destroyed in the process can only be guessed. The Romans did not halt their conquests in 265 BC – they would move on to Sicily in 264 BC – but the reduction of Calabria did mark the end of the conquest of Italy. The Romans did not yet consider the Po Valley, Liguria, the territory of the Veneti or the Alps to be part of Italy: it was a foreign and barbarian land, it was part of Gaul. It was not until the later third century that they embarked on the occupation of what is now continental Italy. In 265 BC all of Italy, as they conceived it, was controlled by the Romans, either directly or through alliances. The conquest was complete.

Notes

1. Polybius 1.1.5 and 1.2.6.
2. As late as 82 BC, an army of rebellious Samnites advanced on Rome and came close to capturing the city.
3. Dionysius of Halicarnassus, *Roman Antiquities* 6.95.2.
4. Construction of the so-called 'Servian Wall' began in 378 BC. The wall and its towers were repaired in 353 BC following a campaign against Falerii.
5. The settlement of the *ager Veientanus* was completed by 387 BC when its new occupants were organized into four voting tribes.
6. Forsythe (2005), p. 257, suggests that the 'Sardinia' notice in Diodorus is in fact a manuscript error for the colonization of Satricum.
7. Gabii was not a member of the Latin League but had an individual treaty with Rome.
8. The *cognomen* Medullinus may commemorate the role of the Furii in a victory over the Latin town of Medullania and the Sabines in 494 BC, or simply indicate that he lived/possessed property there.
9. The *cognomen* Poenus may translate as the 'Phoenician', suggesting involvement with the negotiation of the second treaty with Carthage (348 BC; Poenus was consul for the second time in 351 BC). Another possibility is that it means 'the Punisher' or 'the penalty'.
10. The meaning of the *cognomen* Peticus is uncertain, possibly to do with striving.
11. It is tempting to view the special Hernican cohorts as *sacer*, like the later Linen Legion of the Samnites.
12. The Latins complained to Rome of serious Volscian raiding in 353 BC. It is possible that the Volsci of *Latium Adiectum* were targeting the territories of Latin states following the collapse of the Antiate-Latin alliance in 377 BC, but Volscian raiders may have come from the Liris valley.
13. Volsinii was defeated in this war and 'granted' (i.e. compelled to accept) a truce of twenty years.
14. San Giovenale: Forsythe (2005), p. 257.
15. Privernum was situated in the hills rising to the east of the Pomptine plain. It is possible that the raids began while the Romans were still preoccupied with the Hernici and the Gauls at Pedum.
16. Possible accuracy of number of captives: Oakley (1997–2005), vol. II, p. 190.
17. Tibur was part of the Latin alliance against Rome around 500 BC, and before that probably fought against Lars Porsenna.
18. It remains possible that this was an independent Gallic operation concerned with taking booty and slaves.
19. On the forms of the *pilum* in the fourth century, see Small (2000). The Romans later asserted that they had adopted the *pilum* from the Samnites, boasting that they defeated the Samnites with their own weapons and tactics. However, the *pilum* was common throughout Italy. Gauls, Etruscans and Sabellians all employed forms of the javelin, and if the Romans had not developed their own 'proto-*pila*' in the course of the fifth and fourth centuries BC, they would have adopted the weapon from the Etruscans or the Gauls, i.e. enemies they fought long before the major Samnite wars of the later fourth and early third centuries BC.

20. A *laenas* was a type of woollen cloak, presumably a favourite garment of the consul.
21. Legion of *ordines*: Harris (1990), pp. 507–8. *Antesignani* ('Those who fight before the standards') a synonym for those in the first legionary battle line, are reported by Livy at Privernum in 357 BC, and *hastati* and *principes* at Saticula in 343 BC. I do not intend to discuss the question of the apparent transition of the legion from the hoplite phalanx of the late regal and early republican periods, because I do not believe that it was a true hoplite phalanx. I also reject the tradition that the Romans adopted the maniple from the Samnites in the later fourth or very early third centuries BC.
22. The Roman mint was later based in the temple, hence the modern derivation of 'money' from *Moneta*, but the original meaning of the epithet was probably 'Advisor'. Forsythe (2005), p. 254.
23. Samnite population: Afzelius (1942), p. 138, with Cornell (1989), pp. 351–3.
24. Salmon (1967), p. 200, suggests that the *cognomen* Mamercinus was adopted in recognition of the consul's success in Oscan-speaking Samnium. Mamercus ('Man of Mamers'), from which Mamercinus derives, was originally an Oscan *praenomen* (i.e. a first or personal name like Marcus or Lucius), but it was also adopted as a *praenomen* in Latium and used by Romans, including members of the Aemilii clan. Therefore it may have been an inherited *cognomen*.
25. Livy 8.8.9–13.
26. On Italian spears of this era, see Small (2000).
27. Battle fought at the Roccamonfina: Frederiksen (1984), p. 185.
28. Livy 8.14.2–11.
29. Livy has the other consul, Marcus Atilius Regulus (Latin *regulus* = 'Little King'), only conduct devastation of the Sidicini territory, but a late Roman list of consuls gives Regulus the additional *cognomen* Calenus. This suggests that he was also involved in the capture of Cales, but his part was overshadowed by the more famous Corvus, and was ultimately forgotten.
30. Livy 8.40.4–5.
31. The *cognomen* Cerretanus may signify a connection with Etruscan Caere. Some noble families sent their sons there to be educated.
32. Livy 9.31.6–16.
33. Zonaras 8.1.
34. Posidonia (Paestum) tomb: Pontrandolfo and Rouveret (1992), pp. 174–7 (figures) and 344–5 (discussion); Pontrandolfo et al. (2004), pp. 59, 66 and Fig. 68. For the painting representing the defeat of Bubulcus, see Briquel (2001), pp. 135–46.
35. Dennis (1848), p. 170.
36. Livy 9.39.5–11.
37. Livy 9.43.6–7.
38. Livy 9.44.6–16.
39. Diodorus Siculus 20.90.3–4.
40. But not Tarquinii or Caere. The latter even supplied contingents to the Roman army.
41. Frontinus, *Stratagems* 1.6.1.
42. Frontinus, *Stratagems* 1.6.2.
43. Frontinus, *Stratagems* 1.11.2.
44. Livy 10.21.9–10.
45. Frontinus, *Stratagems* 2.5.9.
46. Location of the battle: Sommella (1967), pp. 35–47. The Sanguerone is a tributary of the River Sentino.

47. Livy 10.30.4–5. I have emended the number of infantry to 330,000 following Oakley (1997–2005), vol. IV, pp. 330–2.
48. Livy 10.27.8–9.
49. Livy 8.9.6–8.
50. Livy 10.28.16–17.
51. Livy 10.29.1–2.
52. *Devotio* practised by Picentes: Holland (1956). *Devotio* understood and feared by Samnites and other Italians: Salmon (1967), p. 146.
53. Livy 10.29.3–4.
54. Altar of Victory grave: Forsythe (2005), pp. 330–3.
55. Including the so-called 'dictator years', erroneously added to the chronology by later Romans.
56. Livy 10.31.10–15.
57. The *quaestor* was concerned with the supply of the army.
58. Livy was probably correct in placing Regulus at Luceria, but noted that some earlier Roman historians disagreed about the identity of the Roman commander. Claudius Quadrigarius, writing around 80 BC, asserted that it was Postumius Megellus and he was defeated outright, but this probably stems from an earlier source hostile to the arrogant consular. The version of Fabius Pictor, the first Roman historian who composed his work at the end of the third century and was therefore much closer in time to the event, placed both consuls at Luceria and had the fighting end in stalemate (often cover for a Roman defeat), with serious losses to both sides.
59. Frontinus, *Stratagems* 1.8.4.
60. On *cognomina*, see Kajanto (1965).
61. Livy 9.16.17–18.
62. Plutarch, *Pyrrhus* 7.4–5.
63. Plutarch, *Pyrrhus* 8.1.
64. Strabo, *Geography* 5.3.5.
65. After various adventures, Demetrius attempted to carve out a new kingdom in Asia Minor, but was abandoned by his army and taken captive by Seleucus, the most successful of the Diadochi. The Besieger was held in luxurious confinement and drank himself to death (283 BC).
66. Calabria was the Roman name for the heel of Italy, but is now applied to the toe.
67. Livy 10.2.14–15.
68. Ceraunus was the disinherited son of Ptolemy I, and nicknamed 'Thunderbolt' because of his daring.
69. It is possible that one of these episodes belongs to Aemilius Papus' operations against the Tarentines in 278 BC.
70. Polyaenus, *Stratagems* 6.6.3.
71. Plutarch, *Pyrrhus* 16.7–8.
72. Plutarch, *Aemilius Paullus* 19.3.
73. Florus, *Epitome* 1.13.17–18.
74. The meaning of the *cognomen* Papus is uncertain. It may mean 'Old man' or 'White beard'.
75. The meaning of the *cognomen* Saverrio is uncertain, it possibly means 'Severe' or 'Savage'.
76. Diodorus Siculus 22.6.2.
77. Plutarch, *Pyrrhus* 24.2–4.
78. Zonaras 8.6.
79. Dionysius of Halicarnassus, *Roman Antiquities* 20.11.1.

80. Plutarch, *Pyrrhus* 25.3.
81. Dionysius of Halicarnassus, *Roman Antiquities* 20.10.1–2.
82. Latin *merenda* was an afternoon meal, and perhaps used as a *cognomen* to commemorate an event that occurred at the usual time this meal was eaten.
83. Florus, *Epitome* 1.13.28.
84. The meaning of Blasio is uncertain. It is possibly a variant of Blaesus: 'Stutterer' or 'Lisper'.
85. Dionysius of Halicarnassus, *Roman Antiquities* 20.15.1–2.
86. Zonaras 8.7.

Bibliography

Ancient Sources

The principal source, up to 292 BC, is Livy, books I–X, and must be read in conjunction with the commentaries of Ogilvie (1965) and Oakley (1997–2005). For the supplementary ancient literary sources (Dionysius of Halicarnassus, Diodorus Siculus, Plutarch, Strabo, Appian, Dio, Zonaras, Pliny the Elder, Polybius, Florus, Frontinus, Valerius Maximus, *et cetera*) and epigraphic materials, consult Broughton (1951) and Degrassi (1947, 1957–1963), and see Oakley (1997–2005) for critical discussion. For sources specifically relating to the Roman army of the early and mid-Republican periods, see Sage (2008).

Modern Works

Affreschi Romani: Dalle Raccolte dell'Antiquarium Comunale. Exhibition Catalogue (Rome: 1976).

Afzelius, A., *Die römische Eroberung Italiens (340–264 v. Chr.)*. (Copenhagen: 1942) reprinted in Afzelius, A., *Two Studies in Roman Expansion* (New York: 1975).

Alfödi, A., *Early Rome and the Latins* (Ann Arbor: 1965).

Bottini, A. (ed.), *Armi. Gli Instrumenti della Guerra in Lucania* (Bari: 1994).

Benassi, R., *La Pittura dei Campani e dei Sanniti* (Rome: 2001).

Bradley, G., *Ancient Umbria: State, Culture, and Identity in Central Italy from the Iron Age to the Augustan Era* (Oxford: 2000).

Brauer, G.C., *Taras: Its History and Coinage* (New York: 1986).

Briquel, D., 'Le tombe Andriuolo 114 de Paestum', in Briquel and Thuillier (2001), pp. 135–46.

Briquel, D. and Thuillier, J.P. (eds), *Le Censeur et les Samnites: Sur Tite-Live, livre IX* (Paris: 2001).

Broughton, T.R.S., *The Magistrates of the Roman Republic, Volume I, 509 BC–100 BC* (New York: 1951).

Brunt, P., *Italian Manpower, 225 BC–AD 14*, revised edition (Oxford: 1987).

Capini, S. and Di Nero, A. (eds), *Samnium: Archeologia del Molise* (Rome: 1991).

Carelli, F., *Numorum Italiae Veteris* (Leipzig: 1850).

Cianfarani, V., Franchi dell'Orto, L. and La Regina, A., *Culture Adriatiche Antiche di Abruzzo e di Molise* (Rome: 1978).

Cornell, T.J., 'Book VI of Ennius' Annals: A Reply'. *Classical Quarterly* 37 (1987), pp. 514–16.

Cornell, T.J., 'Rome and Latium to 390 BC', 'The Recovery of Rome' and 'The Conquest of Italy' in Walbank (1989), pp. 243–419.

Cornell, T.J., *The Beginnings of Rome: Italy and Rome from the Bronze Age to the Punic Wars (c. 1000–264 BC)*, (London and New York: 1995).

Cowan, R.H., 'The Clashing of Weapons and Silent Advances in Roman Battles', *Historia* 56 (2007), pp. 114–17.

Cowan, R.H., 'An Important Italic Helmet Rediscovered', *Archäologisches Korrespondenzblatt* 37(3) (2007), pp. 379–87.

Crawford, M.H., *Roman Republican Coinage* (Cambridge: 1974).

Curti, E., Dench, E. and Patterson, J.R., 'The Archaeology of Central and Southern Roman Italy: Recent Trends and Approaches', *Journal of Roman Studies* 86 (1996), pp. 170–89.

D'Agostino, B., 'Military Organisation and Social Structure in Archaic Etruria', in Murray, O. and Price, S. (eds), *The Greek City: From Homer to Alexander* (Oxford: 1990), pp. 59–82.

De Franciscis, A., *Stato e Società in Locri Epizefiri (L'archivio dell'Olimpieion locrese)*, (Naples: 1972).

Degrassi, A., *Inscriptiones Italiae, volume XIII, fasicule 1: Fasti Consulares et Triumphales* (Rome: 1947).

Degrassi, A., *Inscriptiones Latinae Liberae Rei Publicae*. Two volumes. (Florence: 1957–63).

Dench, E., *From Barbarians to New Men: Greek, Roman and Modern Perceptions of Peoples of the Central Apennines* (Oxford: 1995).

Dennis, G., *The Cities and Cemeteries of Etruria* (London: 1848).

Eroi e Regines: Piceni Popolo d'Europa. Exhibition catalogue (Rome: 2001).

Flower, H., 'The Significance of an Inscribed Breastplate Captured at Falerii in 241 BC', *Journal of Roman Archaeology* 11 (1998), pp. 224–32.

Forsythe, G., *A Critical History of Early Rome: From Prehistory to the First Punic War* (Berkeley and Los Angeles: 2005).

Franke, P.R., 'Pyrrhus' in Walbank (1989), pp. 456–85.

Frederiksen, M., *Campania* (London: 1984).

Fronda, M.P., 'Livy 9.20 and Early Roman Imperialism in Apulia', *Historia* 55 (2006), pp. 397–417.

Gabrielli, C., 'Lucius Postumius Megellus at Gabii: A New Fragment of Livy', *Classical Quarterly* 53 (2003), pp. 247–59.

Garoufalias, P., *Pyrrhus: King of Epirus* (London: 1979).

Griffith, G.T., *The Mercenaries of the Hellenistic World* (Cambridge: 1935).

Guzzo, P.G., 'The Encounter with the Bruttii', in Pugliese, G.P. (ed.), *The Greek World: Art and Civilization in Magna Graeca and Sicily* (New York: 1996), pp. 559–62.

Hammond, N.G.L., *Epirus: The Geography, the Ancient Remains, the History and the Topography of Epirus and Adjacent Areas* (Oxford: 1967).

Harris, W.V., *Rome in Etruria and Umbria* (Oxford: 1971).

Harris, W.V., *War and Imperialism in Republican Rome, 327–70 BC*, revised edition (Oxford: 1985).

Harris, W.V., 'Roman Warfare in the Economic and Social Context of the 4th Century B.C.', in Eder, W. (ed.), *Staat und Staatlichkeit in der frühen römischen Republik* (Stuttgart: 1990), pp. 494–510.

Holland, L.A., 'The Purpose of the Capestrano Warrior,' *American Journal of Archaeology* 60 (1956), pp. 243–7.

Höleskamp, K.-J., 'Conquest, Competition and Consensus: Roman Expansion in Italy and the Rise of the *Nobilitas*', *Historia* 42 (1993), pp. 12–39.

Kajanto, I., *The Latin Cognomina* (Helenski: 1965).

Keppie, L., *The Making of the Roman Army: From Republic to Empire* (London: 1984).

Kruta, W. (ed.), *The Celts* (Milan: 1991).

Lévèque, P., *Pyrrhos* (Paris: 1957).

Lomas, K., Rome and the Western Greeks, 350 BC–AD 200: Conquest and Acculturation in Southern Italy (London and New York: 1993).

McCall, J.B., *The Cavalry of the Roman Republic: Cavalry Combat and Elite Motivations in the Middle and Late Republic* (London and New York: 2002).

Malden, H.E., 'Pyrrhus in Italy', *Journal of Philology* 10 (1882), pp. 172–7.

Maule, Q.F. and Smith, H.R.W., *Votive Religion at Caere: Prolegomena* (Berkeley and Los Angeles: 1959).

Momigliano, A., 'The Origins of Rome', in Walbank (1989), pp. 52–112.

Naso, A., *I Piceni. Storia e Archeologia delle Marche in Epoca Preromana* (Milan: 2000).

Oakley, S.P., 'Single Combat in the Roman Republic', *Classical Quarterly* 35 (1985), pp. 392–410.

Oakley, S.P., *The Hill Forts of the Samnites* (Rome: 1995).

Oakely, S.P., *A Commentary on Livy, Books VI–X*. Four volumes (Oxford: 1997–2005).

Ogilvie, R.M., *A Commentary on Livy. Books 1–5* (Oxford: 1965).

Pontrandolfo, A. and Rouveret, A., *Le Tombe Dipinte di Paestum* (Modena: 1992).

Pontrandolfo, A., Rouveret, A. and Ciprano, M., *The Painted Tombs of Paestum* (Paestum: 2004).

Potter, D., 'The Roman Army and Navy', in Flower, H.I. (ed.), *The Cambridge Companion to the Roman Republic* (Cambridge: 2004), pp. 66–88.

Purcell, N., 'South Italy in the Fourth Century BC', in Lewis, D.M. et al. (eds), *The Cambridge Ancient History, Volume 6: The Fourth Century BC*. Second edition (Cambridge: 1994), pp. 381–403.

Putzger, F.W., *Putzgers Historischer Schul-Atlas zur Alten, Mittleren und Neuen Geschichte* (Leipzig: 1905).

Rawlings, L., 'Condottieri and Clansmen: Early Italian Raiding, Warfare and the State', in Hopwood, K. (ed.), *Organised Crime in Antiquity* (Cardiff: 1999), pp. 97–127.

Roma Medio-Repubblicana: Aspetti Culturali di Roma e del Lazio nei Secoli IV e III a.C. Exhibition catalogue (Rome: 1973).

Sage, M.M., *Warfare in Ancient Greece: A Sourcebook* (London and New York: 1996).

Sage, M.M., *The Republican Roman Army: A Sourcebook* (London and New York: 2008).

Salmon, E.T., *Samnium and the Samnites* (Cambridge: 1967).

Salmon, E.T., *Roman Colonization Under the Republic* (London: 1969).

Salmon, E.T., *The Making of Roman Italy* (London: 1982).

Sannio: Pentri e Frentani dal VI al I sec. a.C. Exhibition catalogue (Rome: 1980).

Schneider-Herrmann, G., *The Samnites of the Fourth Century BC as Depicted on Campanian Vases and Other Sources* (London: 1996).

Skutsch, O., 'Book VI of Ennius' Annals', *Classical Quarterly* 37 (1987), pp. 512–14.

Small, A., 'The Use of Javelins in Central and South Italy in the 4th Century BC', in Ridgeway, D. (ed.), *Ancient Italy in its Mediterranean Setting: Studies in Honour of Ellen Macnamara* (London: 2000), pp. 221–34.

Sommella, P., *Antichi Campi di Battaglia in Italia* (Roma: 1967).

Stavely, E.S., 'Rome and Italy in the Early Third Century', in Walbank (1989), pp. 420–55.

Szabó, M., 'Mercenary Activity', in Kruta (1991), pp. 353–6.

Stary, P., 'Foreign Elements in Etruscan Arms and Armour: 8th to 3rd Centuries BC', *Proceedings of the Prehistoric Society* 45 (1979), pp. 179–206.

Studi sull'Italia dei Sanniti. Exhibition catalogue (Milan: 2000).

Tagliamonte, G., 'I Mercenari Italici', in *Studi sull'Italia dei Sanniti*, pp. 202–7.

Tagliamonte, G., '*Et Vetera Spolia Hostium Detrahunt Templis Porticibusque ... Annotazione sul Riuso dell'Armi Dedicante nell'Italia Antica*', *Pallas* 70 (2006), pp. 265–87.

Toynbee, A.J., *Hannibal's Legacy: The Hannibalic War's Effects on Roman Life. Volume I: Rome and Her Neighbours Before Hannibal's Entry* (London: 1965).

Versnel, H.S., 'Two Types of Roman Devotio', *Mnemosyne* 29 (1976), pp. 365–410.

Vitali, D., 'The Celts in the South of Italy', in Kruta (1991), pp. 230–47.

Walbank, F.W., et al. (eds), *The Cambridge Ancient History, Volume VII, Part 2: The Rise of Rome to 220 BC*. Second edition (Cambridge: 1989).

Ward Perkins, J.B., *Landscape and History in Central Italy* (Oxford: 1964).

Index